THE
ANNOTATED
RULES OF
HOCKEY

THE ANNOTATED RULES OF HOCKEY

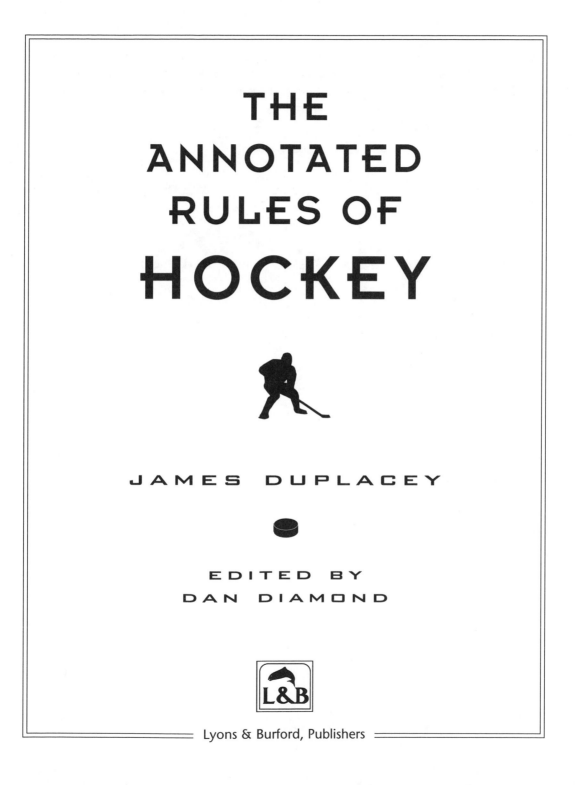

JAMES DUPLACEY

EDITED BY
DAN DIAMOND

L&B

Lyons & Burford, Publishers

Printed in the United States of America

Design and composition by Rohani Design, Edmonds, WA

10 9 8 7 6 5 4 3 2 1

Library of Congress Cataloging-in-Publication Data

Duplacey, James.
    The annotated rules of hockey / James Duplacey ; edited by Dan Diamond.
        p. cm.
    Includes index.
    ISBN 1-55821-466-6
    1. Hockey—Rules. 2. National Hockey League. I. Diamond, Dan. II. Title.
    GV847.5.D87 1996
    796.962'02'022—dc20   96-22710
                                                                          CIP

CONTENTS

INTRODUCTION

FROM THE VERY earliest days of hockey, the game's rules have codified the evolution of the sport. The origins of hockey are frequently debated, with several towns laying claim to the distinction of hosting the first game, but one thing is clear: rules for an informal folk game played on ice were first formalized in Montreal in the 1870s. Engineer JGH Creighton drafted a set of modified rugby rules that featured nine men on each side, one referee, and two goal judges. Enthusiastic participants played Creighton-rules hockey every day at Montreal's Victoria rink. Newspaper ads promoting the new game of ice hockey first appeared in late February, 1875.

Today's game with six men on each side, blue lines, changing on the fly, numerous kinds of penalties, time clocks, and video replays is the evolutionary descendant of these early Montreal games.

The Annotated Rules of Hockey traces this 120-year voyage from the Victoria Rink to today's ultra-modern ice palaces. The evolution of today's high-speed international game is discussed rule by rule, with plenty of anecdotes and illustrations. Often, there is one particular incident or unusual happening that resulted in a rule being changed. We've uncovered some of hockey's most remarkable moments in searching out the roots of many NHL rules. We have also examined some of the game's most rarely called rules and we describe the circumstances when some of the least-known clauses in the *NHL Rule Book* come into effect.

Each rule is printed in the outside margin of the page where it is discussed. The NHL's Official Rules are printed in their entirety beginning on page 171. To be an NHL-caliber referee, every rule, clause, note, and exception in the *NHL Rule Book* has to be etched in your mind, ready to be applied quickly and correctly in the midst of the world's fastest game. It isn't easy. As a reader of this book and a fan of the game, you have a double advantage over even the NHL's best officials: you have ample time to consider which rules apply in every situation and, through what's on the pages that follow, you know the "why" and "how come" behind every rule.

CHAPTER ONE

THE RINK

THE RINK

ACCORDING TO THE *Oxford English Dictionary,* second edition, volume 13, the term "rink" was first used in 399 A.D. to refer to a fighting man or warrior. Fourteen centuries later, in 1787, the term was used to refer to "a stretch of ice measured off and marked for curling." By 1867 a rink was "a sheet of ice used for skating, especially one artificially prepared and roofed." From the earliest days of the game, ice hockey has been played on a surface known as a rink. The word is of French origin, meaning "round."

DIMENSIONS OF RINK

In the earliest rule book for the game, a Spalding publication of 1898, the dimensions of the rink were given as 112 feet by 58 feet. In the 1916 *Spalding Sports Guide,* the rule had been amended to state that the rink must be at least 112 by 58 feet and no larger than 250 by 116 feet. The National Hockey League did not include specific rink dimensions in its rule book until the 1929–30 season. That year, the NHL passed legislation requiring all rinks to have an ice surface that mea-

RULE 1

The game of "Ice Hockey" shall be played on an ice surface known as the "RINK".

RULE 2

(a) The official size of the rink shall be two hundred feet (200') long and eighty-five feet (85') wide. The corners shall be rounded in the arc of a circle with a radius of twenty-eight feet (28').

The rink shall be surrounded by a wooden or fibreglass wall or fence known as the "boards"

The ice surface at Maple Leaf Gardens, the oldest hockey rink in the NHL, in all its splendor. With the closure of the Montreal Forum and the Boston Garden, the Leafs' home is now the NHL's oldest arena.

which shall extend not less than forty inches (40") and not more than forty-eight inches (48") above the level of the ice surface. The ideal height of the boards above the ice surface shall be forty-two inches (42"). Except for the official markings provided for in these rules, the entire playing surface and the boards shall be white in color except the kick plate at the bottom of the board which shall be light yellow in colour.

Any variations from any of the foregoing dimensions shall require official authorization by the League.

sured 200 by 85 feet—the dimensions used to this day. Through the years, the Boston Bruins (191 by 88), Chicago Black Hawks (188 by 85), and, later, Buffalo Sabres (193 by 84) played on ice surfaces smaller than the required proportions. Since both Boston's and Chicago's arenas were already built or under construction by the 1929 season, their teams were allowed to play on smaller rinks. When the Buffalo Sabres entered the League, they moved into the War Memorial Auditorium, built in 1940. They received permission from the NHL to play on a smaller surface provided they increased seating capacity from 10,000 to 15,000.

There have been numerous revisions in the rules concerning rink size, dimensions, and equipment over the years. For instance, rules regulating the height of the boards at not more than 4 feet and no less than 3 feet, 4 inches were estab-

When the newly-formed New York Americans entered the NHL in 1925, they practiced on this ice surface in Niagara Falls that was as wide as it was long.

lished in 1940–41. Although there's no evidence that it was needed, a rule requiring all doors on the ice surface to swing in toward the bench was initiated by common sense in 1947–48.

To help the referees and goal judges determine if a goal had been scored, a rule was passed in 1947–48 that required each NHL team to highlight the area defined by the goal line and the base of the goal with white paint. This proved very popular with both fans and officials and led to one of the most important visual improvements to the game in 1949–50, when the entire ice surface was painted white for the benefit of television. Although national TV coverage of the game in Canada would not occur until 1952–53, games had been shown in limited markets in the United States since 1947. The Chicago Black Hawks were the first NHL team to broadcast their home games to a local TV market, on station WBKB, starting in the 1946–47 season.

Although the *NHL Rule Book* stipulates that the ice surface and the boards must be white in color, the NHL has

allowed on-board and on-ice advertising since the 1989–90 season. While on-ice markings had previously been allowed for special sponsorships and charities, advertisements for commercial products are recent innovations.

On March 1, 1978, only days after purchasing the Canadian Football League's Hamilton Tiger Cats franchise, Toronto Maple Leaf owner Harold Ballard ran into hot water when he put the Ti-Cats logo on the ice of Maple Leaf Gardens. Ballard, a renowned Toronto (football) Argonaut hater and baiter, hoped this display would rankle the brass in Argoland. Ballard was ordered to remove the offending logo, but not before he had received an abundance of free publicity for himself and his football team.

The kick plate at the bottom of the boards is painted light blue or yellow for the benefit of television. This contrasting band of color serves to define the boundary of the ice surface for the TV viewer. Early in the color-TV era, an experiment was staged in Madison Square Garden that saw a broad band at the bottom of the boards painted fire-engine red. This red band proved to be too dark, however, making the puck difficult to follow. The light blue or yellow kick plate was reinstated.

 RULE 3

(a) Eleven feet (11′) from each end of the rink and in the center of a red line two inches (2″) wide drawn completely across the width of the ice and continued vertically up the side of the boards, regulation goal posts and nets shall be set in such manner as to remain stationary during the progress of a game. The goal posts shall be kept in position by means of flexible pegs affixed in the ice or floor. The flexible pegs shall be eight inches (8″) in length.

Where the length of the playing surface exceeds two hundred feet (200′), the goal line and goal posts may be placed not more than fifteen feet (15′) from the end of the rink.

GOAL POSTS AND NETS

In the earliest days of the game, the distance between the end boards and the goal line was set at 5 feet. By 1909 that distance soon grew to "at least 10, no more than 15" feet from the end boards. The space behind the goal was at that time used mainly as an area for the defense to stop and regroup before leading an attack up the ice. The location of the goal line was eventually standardized at 10 feet from the end boards.

In the 1970s and 1980s teams began firing the puck into the corners and sending in forechecking specialists to pressure the defense relentlessly for possession. This often led to spirited, but boring, battles or scrums behind the net and resulted in numerous stoppages in play. However, the NHL didn't feel it necessary to increase the area behind the net until the 1980s, when many players, especially Edmonton Oiler Wayne Gretzky, began to use that area as a strategic offensive weapon.

The behind-the-net area quickly became known as "Gretzky's office." By situating himself in back of the net, Gretzky could survey the entire ice surface, as well as confuse the defenders as to which way he would pass or which side of the net he would attack. Fans loved this purposeful offensive ploy, and many of the League's smartest and quickest players adopted the strategy. In 1990–91 the NHL moved the goal line 1 foot farther out from the end boards, eliminating 2 feet of space in the neutral zone but giving the players more room to maneuver in the defensive zone.

Hockey nets have measured 6 feet by 4 feet since the first hockey rules were put to paper. While virtually everything about the game has been modified to some degree over the years, the size of the net has remained stable. So imagine Montreal Canadien goalie Jacques Plante's surprise when he discovered that the nets in Chicago were not of legal size. Plante made his discovery during his warm-up prior to a game against the Chicago Black Hawks on January 26, 1962. As he was backing into his crease, Plante noticed that the crossbar of the net was not touching his back at the usual spot. He brought this to the attention of the referee and the net was found to be 3 feet, 10 inches high instead of the required 4 feet.

The NHL sent out a directive to have the nets in every arena checked. In Boston, referee Vern Buffey and Bruin general manager Lynn Patrick were dispatched to measure the nets at the Garden. The net at the end the Bruins defended in the first and third periods was found to be the proper height and width at the crossbar, but was ¾ inch too narrow at the bottom, where the posts fitted onto pegs embedded in the ice. This net had apparently been undersized for many years. All the other nets used in the six NHL arenas (Boston Garden, Chicago Stadium, the Olympia in Detroit, the Forum in Montreal, Madison Square Garden in New York, and Maple Leaf Gardens in Toronto) measured up to the 6-foot-by-4-foot standard.

When hockey was first played in the 1870s, the goal area was marked by two posts stuck in the ice. The first netting was added to the posts by—believe it or not—hockey-playing fishermen in Halifax, Nova Scotia, in 1899. It received such acclaim that a reporter from the *Toronto Globe and Mail* traveled down east to see the spectacle for himself.

Percy LeSueur, a Hall of Fame goaltender for the Ottawa Senators, developed the first "modern" net with a crossbar and boxlike shape, 17 inches deep at the top and 22 inches deep at

(b) The goal posts shall be of approved design and material, extending vertically four feet (4') above the surface of the ice and set six feet (6') apart measured from the inside of the posts. A cross bar of the same material as the goal posts shall extend from the top of one post to the top of the other.

GOAL NETS FOR HOCKEY.

One great drawback to the game of hockey, wherever played, has been the constant wrangles over the scoring of goals. The puck travels at such a tremendous velocity that it is usually simply a matter of impossibility to tell whether or not it has passed between the goal-posts in its flight from the players' sticks to the end of the rink. Umpires are but human, and no matter how attentively they may be watching the game, they cannot always give the correct decision. It is well known that few matches are played in which a number of disputes do not arise. Something must be done to obviate this difficulty, and the Senior Canadian Amateur Hockey League, at its annual meeting a week ago, decided to give a new kind of goal-net a thorough trial, and if it proves acceptable to the sub-committee appointed, viz., Messrs. Drinkwater, Trihey and James, it will be adopted by the League, and used in all scheduled matches. The public trial will be held at the Arena rink Christmas week, when the Shamrocks and Victorias will play a match, using this system of net.

The Net to be Used at the Arena Christmas Week.

The accompanying cut gives a front and side view of a goal-net modelled on the lines of the one in use in the Canadian Lacrosse Association. The playing rules of the C.A.H.L. provide that the goal-posts shall be placed at least ten feet from the end of the ice, and the adoption of this system will not necessitate any alteration. The goal-posts are four feet high and six feet apart, so that the above illustration will give an excellent idea of the appearance of the net on the ice. The off-side play spoken of in the description of the Quebec method will not prevail under this system, but carom shots from the sides of the rink, where the puck goes through the poles from the rear, will be effectually stopped. This is the only drawback, if such it can be termed. Otherwise the net seems as perfect as can be devised. The lacrosse men of the West have found the net to work most satisfactorily, not a single dispute having been reported since their adoption.

The trial Christmas week will be watched with the greatest interest, not only by the hockeyists themselves, but by all patrons of Canada's great winter sport.

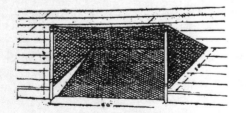

Net Proposed by Quebec Hockey Club.

Above is pictured the goal-net which the Quebec Hockey Club has been advocating. It is to be situated flush with the end of the ice, and offers no obstruction to the players. There is a drop even with the poles, so that the puck, once having entered, cannot slide out again. Some objection has been raised to this scheme, the contention being that some provision ought to be made to give the defending side a chance to clear the goal. The goal-keeper being at the extreme end of the ice, when he stops a shot and throws the puck out, every other player on the same side is off-side, and the players have to wait until the puck is touched by one of the opposite side. This would give the attacking players an opportunity for another shot, which it hardly deserved. It is also claimed that the adoption of this idea will do away with a lot of good work around the poles, and that a lot of brilliant attack will be missed.

In the early 1900s, hockey pioneer Art Ross took a design by goaltender Percy LeSueur and refined it. This design became known as the Art Ross net. Seen here in an early advertisement, it was used in the NHL for more than sixty years. (Hockey Hall of Fame)

Two views of a net introduced in Montreal in 1899. Four years earlier, Queen's University hockey team was introduced to the ice polo cage in Pittsburgh, Pa. *PAC*

ART ROSS & CO

High Class Sporting Goods.

PEEL ST.,
MONTREAL

the bottom. The net used in the NHL for decades was designed by Art Ross, longtime general manager and coach of the Boston Bruins. The "Art Ross net" was similar to today's version in shape. It had a double semicircle-like enclosure at the top, with a frame and netting that trapped the puck from all angles. The Art Ross net was the accepted model used in all NHL arenas until the 1984–85 season.

Although the Art Ross net had many advantages over other models, it did present a couple of problems. The base of the net was shaped like the number "3," with an extended, sharply shaped point in the middle. This center section served three purposes: It gave the net a firm foundation to rest on; the outside of its curved base kept pucks off the back of the net; and its inner lip helped deflect pucks entering the goal upward into the netting, aiding the referees and goal judges by preventing the puck from bouncing out of the goal.

The extended center bar would prove costly to the Hartford Whalers' All Star defenseman Mark Howe. Although it rested firmly on the ice when the net was in its normal position, it jutted dangerously upward if the net tipped backward. In a game against the New York Islanders on December 27, 1980, Howe was checked into his own net by John Tonelli, lifting the cage off its moorings. Howe fell onto the base of the frame and the point punctured his rectum, missing his spine by an inch. Although Howe recovered to play again that season, he came within an inch of a career-ending and life-threatening injury.

Another complaint about the Art Ross net, ironic in light of the Howe incident, was that the goal and frame were held too firmly in place by iron pegs embedded in the concrete below the ice surface. The only way to dislodge the net was to lift it off these pegs. This certainly cut down on play stoppages, but it was also a hazard. Many knee injuries were sustained by players sliding into an unforgiving—and immovable—goalpost.

In 1984 Ayr, Ontario, native Dennis Meggs and partner Terry Riley invented the Megg-Net, a goal frame held in place by magnets instead of pegs. The goal frame was rounded at the back, with the center point eliminated. A sturdy waterproof cover on the base of the net was designed to provide protection from skates, and also allow the puck to slide off and stay in play. The Megg-Net was tried for the first time by the Toronto Maple Leafs in a pregame warm-up on December 3, 1984. The net was given a much more strenuous workout during the 1984 Canada Cup tournament, and was adopted by the NHL for the 1984–85 season. The innovation was met with praise in its early years, but there was also concern that the magnets lost some of their power as the season went on, making it too easy to dislodge the net from its moorings.

The Megg-Net and the semi-circular goal crease were two innovations introduced by the NHL in the 1980s. (Diane Sobolewski)

In the 1992–93 playoffs the NHL was faced with constant interruptions in play by the dislodging of the nets, both purposeful and accidental. In the 1993–94 season the Megg-Net was replaced by the Marsh peg, a bendable plastic pin that keeps the net in place but also allows it to move on heavy contact.

GOAL CREASE

The goal crease is the netminder's domain. It was provided to protect him from intruding forwards and defensemen. The

RULE 4

(a) In front of each goal, a "GOAL CREASE" area shall be marked by a red line two inches (2″) in width.

(b) The goal crease shall be laid

concept of the goal crease originated in 1920, when the *Spalding Hockey Guide* suggested that a semicircle be painted on the ice in front of the net. However, the NHL didn't even introduce the idea of protecting the goaltender from incoming forwards until the 1931–32 season, when a penalty was assigned to any player who interfered with the goaltender. But because the goalie didn't have an assigned safe area, there were numerous arguments as to exactly what constituted "goaltender interference."

Prior to the 1933–34 season, NHL managing director Frank Patrick announced that a semicircle 53 inches in diameter would be painted on the ice surface in front of the goal. However, for whatever reason, that crease idea was never used. Instead, teams were asked to paint L-shaped markings on the ice to define a protected area near the goal that no nongoalie was allowed to enter. Toronto Maple Leaf general manager Conn Smythe refused to paint the crease markings on the ice at Maple Leaf Gardens, however, resulting in a protest lodged by the Ottawa Senators after a 4–1 loss to the Leafs on November 18, 1933. The Senator officials complained that two of the Leafs' goals were scored by Toronto players within a foot of the Ottawa goalie. Furthermore, although any player in the crease was to be penalized, there were no markings on the ice, so the Leaf players escaped punishment. Frank Patrick upheld the Toronto victory, but assured all NHL clubs that the Leafs would have the proper markings on the ice before their next home game.

The following season a rectangular goal crease measuring 8 feet by 5 feet was painted on the ice in front of all NHL nets. Prior to the start of the 1939–40 season, the crease was reduced to 7 feet by 3 feet. In a column printed in the *Toronto Daily Star* on January 13, 1949, New York Ranger coach Frank Boucher suggested that the crease be increased in size. Most NHL goalies jumped on the Boucher bandwagon, and NHL officials listened. Prior to the 1951–52 campaign, a new 8-foot-by-4-foot crease was unveiled. This goaltenders' comfort zone remained unchanged until 1986–87, when it was expanded by the addition of a semicircle painted around the rectangle. In 1991–92 the rectangular crease markings were removed from the inside of the semicircle. The area defined

out as follows: A semi-circle six feet (6') in radius and two inches (2") in width shall be drawn using the center of the goal line as the center point. In addition, an 'L'-shaped marking of five inches (5") in length (both lines) at each front corner will be painted on the ice.
(d) The complete goal area, which includes all the space outlined by the crease line and the goal line, shall be painted light blue color. The area inside the goal frame to the goal line shall be painted a gloss white color.

1917–18: Center ice face-off dot is the only marking on ice.

1918–19: Blue lines added 80 feet from end boards.

1926–27: Blue lines moved in 10 feet from end boards.

1929–30: Face-off spot added 10 feet in front of each goal.

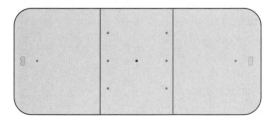

1931–32: Three face-off spots added outside of each blue line.

1933–34: L-shaped boundaries added to define goaltender's safe area. (8′ x 5′)

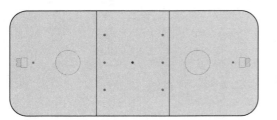

1934–35: Penalty shot circles added. Center of circle is 38 feet from goal line. Goal crease added. (8′ x 5′)

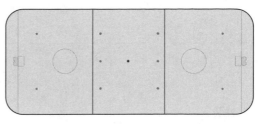

1937–38: Face-off spot in front of each goal removed. Two face-off spots added in each defensive zone. Goal line now runs across width of ice.

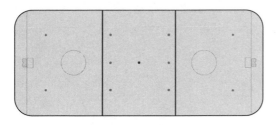

1938–39: Width of blue lines increased to 12″.

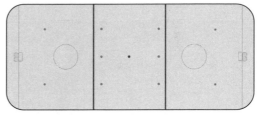

1939–40: Crease now 7′ x 3′.

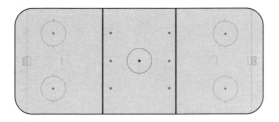

1941–42: Ten-foot face-off circles added at center ice and in each corner. Penalty shot circle replaced with penalty shot line.

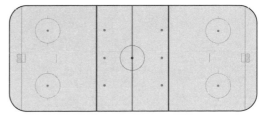

1943–44: Center ice red line added.

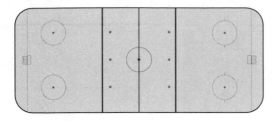

1945–46: Penalty shot line deleted.

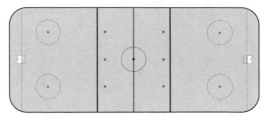

1947–48: Goal area painted white.

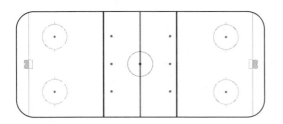

1949–50: Entire ice surface painted white.

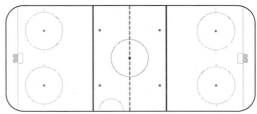

1951–52: Crease now 8′ x 4′. Face-off circles now 15 feet in diameter. Hash marks added to circles in defensive zones. Center face-off spot in neutral zone eliminated. Referee's crease added. Center red line now checkered.

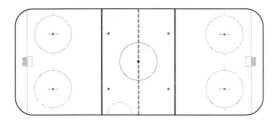

1961–62: "Crosshairs" added to face-off spots in defensive zones.

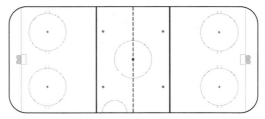

1982–83: Double hash marks and modified face-off dots on face-off circles in defensive zones.

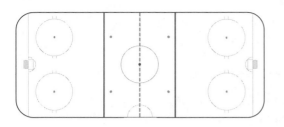

1984–85: Goal frame modified.

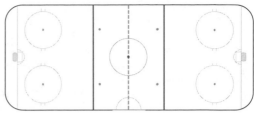

1986–87: Round crease added. Players' benches now on same side of the ice.

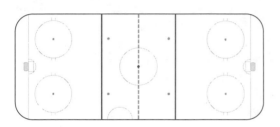

1990–91: Goal line moved one foot further out from back boards.

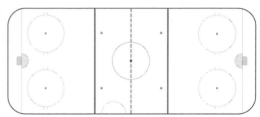

1991–92: Square crease eliminated. Goal area and crease now tinted blue. Goal line moved one foot closer to blue line.

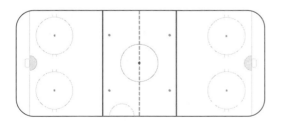

1995–96: Goal area tinted white. Crease remains blue.

1996–97: (**Not shown.**) L-shaped positioning marks added to defensive zone face-off spots. (Experimental rule change to be evaluated after the pre-season.)

by the semicircular crease is now painted light blue while the space inside the net remains white.

PLAYERS' BENCHES

RULE 9

(a) Each rink shall be provided with seats or benches for the use of players of both teams and the accommodations provided including benches and doors shall be uniform for both teams. . . .

(NOTE) Where physically possible, each players' bench shall have two doors opening in the neutral zone and all doors opening to the playing surface shall be constructed so that they swing inward.

(b) No one but players in uniform, the Manager, Coach and Trainer shall be permitted to occupy the benches so provided.

Over the years the NHL made numerous alterations to the rules concerning the players' benches. In 1947–48 the NHL decided that the benches should be separated by a "substantial" distance. In 1950–51 it was determined that all doors should open into the neutral zone. In 1955–56 it was stipulated that benches and doors should be uniform for both teams.

Although both benches were supposed to be the same, with doors opening into the neutral zone, this was not always the case. Some rinks created an unfair advantage for the home team by placing one door inches closer to the defensive zone on the home bench than on the visitors'. This gave the home team an edge when changing on the fly. In Chicago Stadium, the Black Hawks' home bench had two doors, whereas the visiting team's bench had only one, creating all kinds of confusion for the visitors when they attempted to change players.

Until the 1965–66 season the players' benches were on opposite sides of the ice. In June 1965, when the NHL ruled that each arena was to have separate penalty boxes in the center ice zone, it also ruled that the players' benches had to be on one side of the ice and the penalty boxes on the other.

In the modern era of the NHL, the rule governing team personnel permitted on or behind the players' bench has been strictly enforced. Although the rule does allow the general manager to be in the bench area, this is rarely seen today unless the coach holds the dual title of coach and general manager.

In the early, six-team era of the NHL, a more relaxed approach to the bench and its occupants was taken. It was commonplace to see Toronto Maple Leaf general manager Conn Smythe come out of the stands and stand behind the bench, usually to berate the referee or an opposing coach or manager. One of hockey's greatest feuds was between Toronto's Conn Smythe and Boston Bruin coach and general manager Art Ross. The bitter dispute, which was orchestrated for publicity as much as anything, came to a head in 1939. Smythe put an advertisement in the *Boston Globe* on

December 19, stating that the Bruins played "sleep-inducing" hockey and that if Boston fans wanted to see the classiest team in the League, they should make their way to Boston Garden to watch the Leafs that evening. Smythe appeared behind the Leafs' bench wearing a top hat and tails and badgered the Bruins most of the evening. Of course the joint was jumping for the game, and the Bruins took a small measure of revenge for Smythe's slight by slipping past the Leafs with a 3–2 over-time victory.

It was not uncommon for a coach's son to sit on the bench with the players, acting as an unofficial mascot. Dick Irvin Jr. recalls sitting on the bench when the Montreal Canadiens defeated the Detroit Red Wings 9–1 on December 28, 1944. Conn Smythe's sons Hughie and Stafford were frequent visitors to the Leafs' bench, as was coach Hap Day's son.

PENALTY BENCH

Until the 1963–64 season, penalized players sat beside each other in the same penalty box. On some occasions, a League official would be appointed to sit between the combatants, but in most instances the two players who had battled it out on the ice were left to supervise their own behavior in the penalty box.

RULE 10

(a) Each rink must be provided with benches or seats to be known as the "PENALTY BENCH". These benches or seats must be capable of accommodating a total of ten persons including the Penalty Timekeepers. Separate penalty benches shall be provided for each team and they shall be situated on opposite sides of the Timekeeper's area, directly across the ice from the players' benches. . . .

Hockey Hall of Fame

In the years before there were separate penalty benches, opposing players sat beside each other in the sin-bin. At times—such as this confrontation between Frank Mahovlich, Jean Beliveau (#4), and Ab McDonald (#15) on February 12, 1959—the local constabulary was forced to act as peacemaker.

Madison Square Garden in New York didn't even have a penalty box. Penalized players sat in an aisle behind the Rangers' bench. Some chairs were set out in the aisle and, depending on how many players were occupying the "box," an appropriate number of New York's finest would surround the guilty parties to ensure that Garden fans seated nearby didn't interfere with justice.

This on-ice collision between Montreal Canadiens' sniper Maurice Richard and NY Ranger defenseman Bob Dill led to the infamous "pickling of Bob Dill" incident during the 1944–45 season.

Dan Diamond and Associates

Luckily, every other arena did have a penalty-box area. There was the odd skirmish in the sin bin, including the infamous "pickling" of Bob Dill by Maurice Richard on December 17, 1944. In that match, Dill, a sophomore defenseman with the Rangers, challenged Richard to a one-on-one fistic exchange. One solid right hand later, Dill was out cold on the ice and Richard was being escorted to the penalty box. Moments later, Richard was joined in the box by an obviously dazed and confused Dill, who attacked the Rocket again. Richard soundly whipped the Ranger rear guard and sent him to the infirmary with a sizable cut above his eye. A rule requiring separate penalty boxes wasn't passed until more than twenty years later.

The turning point came during a game between the Montreal Canadiens and the Toronto Maple Leafs on October 30, 1963. Leaf Bob Pulford and Hab Terry Harper were sent off for fighting and continued their confrontation in the penalty box, leading to a lengthy delay in the proceedings. Each player blamed the other for igniting their set-to, but Pulford gave this explanation: "In the penalty box he said something that would make any man fight." It seems that Harper had questioned Pulford's sexual preference and suggested that the Maple Leaf forward "didn't have the guts to fight him."

One week later, on November 8, Maple Leaf Gardens became the first rink to install separate penalty-box doors for each team. The Montreal Forum added a touch of humor when it unveiled its separated facilities, also in November. One penalty box was labeled: LES CANADIENS—GOOD GUYS; the other was designated: VISITEURS—BAD GUYS. These labels didn't last long.

Although the Gardens and Forum both erected separate boxes during the 1963–64 campaign, it wasn't until the 1965–66 season that the League passed a rule requiring each rink to have separate penalty-box entrances.

SIGNAL AND TIMING DEVICES

During the Board of Governors meetings following the 1929–30 season, League executives were shown a four-faced electric clock, the same model that would eventually become the standardized clock required in each NHL arena.

It took a few years for technology to catch up with demand, but by the 1933–34 season all NHL hockey rinks were required to have a visible time clock. In earlier seasons, time was kept with a stopwatch at the official scorer's bench. Even after large arena clocks were required, the official time was still recorded in this way. The time posted on the arena clock was unofficial.

Although a visible time clock was mandatory, the Boston Bruins still hadn't installed one in Boston Garden when Lester Patrick and the New York Rangers arrived in Beantown to play the Bruins early in the 1934–35 season. The relationship between the Bruins' Art Ross and the

◗ RULE 11

(b) Each rink shall be provided with some form of electrical clock for the purpose of keeping the spectators, players and game officials accurately informed as to all time elements at all stages of the game including the time remaining to be played in any period and the time remaining to be served by at least five penalized players on each team. . . .

Although primitive by today's standards, the four-sided "SportTimer" in Maple Leaf Gardens was a technical marvel in the 1930s. (Dan Diamond and Associates)

(c) Behind each goal, electrical lights shall be set up for the use of the Goal Judges. A red light will signify the scoring of a goal and a green light will signify the end of a period or a game. (Note) A Goal cannot be scored when a green light is showing.

Rangers' Lester Patrick was strained at best, and both men played it to the extreme, knowing that colorful controversy made for good press.

In their first meeting of the season in New York, Art Ross had let it be known in the press that Ranger goaltender Davey Kerr's goalie sticks were illegal, and that Ross planned to measure them that night. Patrick was furious, since he knew that Bruin goaltender Tiny Thompson had also used an illegal stick at one time. At any rate, when Patrick caught wind of Ross's plan he was able to alert Kerr, who managed to pare his sticks down to size. What really steamed Patrick was not that Ross had masterminded the scheme, but that he had pulled it off in the Rangers' own backyard.

Then Patrick got an idea. He realized that Boston still didn't have its time clock in place, and that this was how he could exact his revenge during the Rangers' next visit to "da Gahden." Since there was no time clock, visiting teams could request a time-out and ask the referee how much time was left in a penalty or in the period.

During the first period of the Rangers-Bruins tilt in Boston, the Rangers went to the referee after every faceoff to inquire about the time remaining in the period. The first period took over an hour and a half to play, and the paying public was none too pleased, showering the ice with rubbish. Ross pleaded with Patrick to desist, and they must have come to some kind of understanding, because the rest of the game was played without incident—but not before Patrick had gained some measure of retribution.

While the rule governing the goal judge's light at each end of the rink has been in the rule book since the early 1940s, there has been a change in the way the lights are operated.

In a game between the Toronto Maple Leafs and Detroit Red Wings on November 3, 1956, the Wings were leading 2–1 with 8 seconds to play. Leaf coach Howie Meeker pulled goaltender Ed Chadwick and put on an extra attacker for a key draw deep in Red Wing territory. There was a brief scramble after the faceoff but the puck came free to Leaf Dick Duff, who unleashed a wrist shot toward the Wings' cage that went in just as the siren sounded to end the game. Seeing that the blue lights indicating the expiration of time were flashing above the net, referee Frank Udvari waved off the goal, saying the puck had entered the goal after the game was over. The Leafs disagreed to a player, insisting that the red light had flashed first, then the blue lights had come on. Udvari consulted with his linesmen, but they hadn't seen the red lights flash either. With that, the game went into the books as a 2–1 Red Wing victory. (As early as the 1948–49 season, the NHL had a rule that required the expiration-of-time light to be green, although Maple Leaf Gardens was allowed to keep its blue lights since they were installed prior to the rule entering the books. After this incident, green expiration-of-time lights were installed in Toronto.)

Right after the game, the Leafs issued a protest to NHL president Clarence Campbell, stating that they had a film clip showing that the red light had indeed gone on prior to the blue, and that the Duff goal should have counted. In a League meeting on November 19, Campbell viewed the film and saw that the red light had flashed first, followed by the blue. Campbell admitted that while the goal should have been allowed, he was not going to overturn the game result. "In my opinion, the decision of the referee was an error in judgment. As such it cannot be entertained as a ground for protest." On the other hand, Campbell acknowledged that there was a problem with the goal lights signaling the end of the game. He suggested devising a method for the red light's illumination to stop the clock; the light would stay on. This idea was quickly accepted and remains in effect to this day.

POLICE PROTECTION

While it certainly hasn't been common, there have been occasions through the years when the police were called out onto the ice to break up a fight by officials needing extra pairs of arms to put an end to the fisticuffs. And though police were assigned to each arena, there was never any official requirement to have police protection until the 1945–46 season. However, it wasn't until the infamous Gordie Howe incident during the 1964–65 season that this police protection requirement was needed to protect one of the league's marquee stars.

It was quite a week for the Detroit Red Wings even before the Howe Affair. In a six-day period, January 2–7, the Wings

RULE 12

All clubs shall provide adequate police or other protection for all players and officials at all times.

The Referee shall report to the Commissioner any failure of this protection observed by him or reported to him with particulars of such failure.

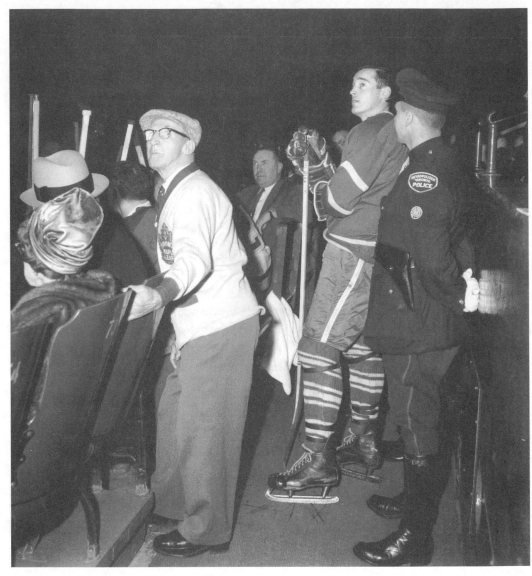

A police officer stands guard beside Frank Mahovlich to protect the Toronto Maple Leafs star from an especially rowdy group of fans.

Hockey Hall of Fame

played four games. In a match against the Toronto Maple Leafs on January 3, three Detroit players were cut by Toronto high-sticks without any penalties being called. Wing Ted Lindsay, the veteran who had come out of retirement for the 1964–65 season, was assessed a game misconduct for his verbal dressing-down of referee Vern Buffey during the match. Game misconducts carried an automatic fine and a presidential review, and Lindsay was outspoken in his criticism of Buffey and NHL president Clarence Campbell and flatly refused to pay any fine or serve any suspension. When the Red Wings arrived in Boston on January 7 for their fourth game of the week, they were surrounded by reporters. In addition to the brewing Lindsay affair, Vern Buffey was scheduled to referee the match. Although the crowd was small by Boston standards—only 7,700—fireworks were anticipated.

Late in the third period, with the Bruins leading 5–2, Wing Gordie Howe slammed Bruin rookie Bill Knibbs into the boards and was assessed a 5-minute major penalty. For one of the few times in his career Howe was roundly booed. As he sat in the penalty box, he was accosted by some unruly fans, one of whom threw a drink in his face. Buffey called for extra security, and Howe was accompanied to the dressing room by police. More officers were called to the scene and Howe was escorted back to his hotel under a police guard. The incident greatly concerned the League, especially because the circuit's marquee player was involved. Although police protection had been in the rule books for years, it was firmly enforced from that point on.

TEAMS

 RULE 13

(a) A team shall be composed of six players on the ice who shall be under contract to the Club they represent.

COMPOSITION OF TEAM

THROUGHOUT ITS HISTORY, the NHL has played six-man hockey in the regular season and League playoffs. On occasion, however, the League has played with seven players per side. In the Stanley Cup playoffs from 1918 to 1922, the champion of the NHL would take on the champion of the Pacific Coast Hockey Association (PCHA) for possession of Lord Stanley's trophy. The PCHA played seven-man hockey, utilizing a "rover" as the seventh man. (The rover was a seventh man who lined up midway between the forwards and the defense and had both offensive and defensive responsibilities. He "roved" all over the ice surface.) During the Stanley Cup challenge series, the teams would switch back and forth between East Coast and West Coast rules. Prior to the start of the 1922–23 season, the PCHA dropped the seventh player and became a six-man league like the NHL. The last professional game played with seven men per side was on March 25, 1922, when the Toronto St. Pats defeated the Vancouver Millionaires 6–0. The rover on the St. Pats' roster that evening, Cy Denneny, scored one goal in the victory. (The

PCHA and its successor, the Western Hockey League disbanded following the 1925–26 season. At that time, the NHL took possession of the Stanley Cup trophy. Beginning with the 1926–27 season, the Cup has been awarded to the play-off champion of the National Hockey League.)

Hockey was one of the first team sports to have its players wear numbers. Although some amateur teams began wearing numbers as early as 1910, it wasn't until Lester and Frank Patrick formed the Pacific Coast Hockey Association in December 1911 that professional teams began wearing numbers. When the NHL was formed in 1917, its bylaws stipulated that all players must wear numbers on the backs of their jerseys. In the late 1950s numbers were also placed on skates and on the sleeves of players' jerseys. These additional numbers aided player identification in newspaper photographs and in the new medium of black-and-white television.

(b) Each player and each goalkeeper listed in the line-up of each team shall wear an individual identifying number at least ten inches (10″) high on the back of his sweater and, in addition, each player and goalkeeper shall wear his surname in full, in block letters three inches (3″) high, across the back of his sweater at shoulder height.

Dan Diamond and Associates

The 1975 Stanley Cup final between the Buffalo Sabres and the Philadelphia Flyers was the first championship round in which both teams wore their names on the back of their jerseys.

In August 1970 the NHL passed a resolution permitting teams to put players' names on the backs of their home uniforms. Visiting teams were also permitted to add names to their uniforms, but because some clubs felt that program sales would be damaged by this, the home team's permission was required to do so. In February 1978 the NHL passed a new rule requiring that names be placed on the backs of both home and away jerseys.

Harold Ballard, the owner of the Toronto Maple Leafs, refused to comply with the new League ruling, reasoning that compliance would be expensive and would hamper program sales. NHL president John Ziegler threatened to make the rule truly expensive for the crusty owner by levying a series of fines. Ballard finally called off his protest, but not without one final dig at the NHL's first-year president. In a game in Chicago on February 26, 1978, Ballard ordered that players' names be sewn onto the back of the uniforms in letters the same color as the jersey—in this case blue on blue—making the names unreadable. Ziegler wasn't impressed by Ballard's sense of humor. From that point on, the Leafs wore readable names on the back of their uniforms, but only on the road. At home the Leafs had an airtight alibi, citing a contract with the manufacturer of their program stipulating that there would be no names on the backs of the home jerseys in 1977–78. The next year, however, the Leafs wore readable names on their uniforms like every other team in the NHL.

 RULE 14

(a) One Captain shall be appointed by each team, and he alone shall have the privilege of discussing with the Referee any questions relating to interpretation of rules which may arise during the progress of a game. He shall wear the letter "C". . . in a conspicuous position on the front of his sweater. In addition, if the permanent Captain is not on the ice, Alternate Captains

CAPTAIN OF TEAM

Ever since organized hockey began in the late 1880s, teams have appointed a captain to act as a liaison between the teams and the umpire or referee. In the early days the captain sometimes also served as a sort of playing coach. However, when the National Hockey League was formed in 1917, League rules stated that a team captain could not double as a coach, citing too many instances of an unruly captain who was doing duty as a coach bopping a referee on the nose. Beginning in 1946–47, an NHL rule stated that the team captain must wear a "C" on the front of his uniform, while assistant captains wear an "A." In North American hockey, the customary location for these cloth letters is the upper left corner of the front of the jersey. Some European teams use an armband to identify their team captain. In much of Europe, the captain wears a "K" rather than a "C."

Only six goaltenders in NHL history have been appointed team captain, five of them in the early years of the League's development. John Ross Roach of the Toronto St. Pats, Roy Worters of the New York Americans, George Hainsworth of the Montreal Canadiens, Alex Connell of the Ottawa Senators, and Charlie Gardiner of the Stanley Cup–winning Chicago Black Hawks all served as team captain. Worters, Connell, Hainsworth, and Gardiner were appointed as captains in 1932–33 in response to the NHL's newly created rule stating that a team captain had to be on the ice at all times.

In 1947–48 Bill Durnan of the Montreal Canadiens shared the captain's duties with Elmer Lach. By all accounts, Durnan was a responsible team captain—too responsible, in fact. He would repeatedly leave his crease—as was his legal right—to question the referee on certain calls. Some teams protested, saying that Durnan's actions slowed the pace of the game and gave the Canadiens unscheduled time-outs at strategic points in the game. Prior to the start of the 1948–49 season, the NHL passed a rule prohibiting goaltenders from serving as captains or assistant captains.

(not more than two) shall be accorded the privileges of the Captain. Alternate Captains shall wear the letter "A" . . . .

(d) No playing Coach or playing Manager or goalkeeper shall be permitted to act as Captain or Alternate Captain.

Dan Diamond and Associates

The last goaltender to serve as team captain was Montreal Canadien netminder Bill Durnan, seen here guarding the cage in front of teammate Butch Bouchard and Toronto Maple Leafs' tough-guy Bill Ezinicki.

RULE 15

(b) A list of names and numbers of all eligible players and goal-keepers must be handed to the Referee or Official Scorer before the game, and no change shall be permitted in the list or addition thereto shall be permitted after the commencement of the game.

i) If a goal is scored when an ineligible player is on the ice, the goal will be disallowed.

ii) The ineligible player will be removed from the game and the club shall not be able to substitute another player on its roster.

PLAYERS IN UNIFORM

There have been twenty-seven revisions to this rule since 1937–38 alone, and half that many before 1937. So it's easy to see how this rule can cause confusion.

We all know that roster changes occur frequently in the modern National Hockey League. Between constant trades, injuries, call-ups, and send-downs, even a coach can become confused as to who is currently on the roster. When the Toronto Maple Leafs claimed Bill Berg on waivers from the New York Islanders on December 3, 1992, Maple Leaf coach Pat Burns responded to his newest charge by admitting, "I wouldn't know Bill Berg if I hit him with my car."

Still, there seems to be no logical explanation for Vancouver Canuck coach–general manager Pat Quinn and assistant coach Rick Ley's identity crisis before the Canucks' game against the Edmonton Oilers on January 24, 1994. On that evening, as on any other, Ley wrote up the Canucks' lineup card. Six Canuck officials examined the lineup and pronounced it fine, including Quinn, who signed it and presented it to referee Dan Marouelli. All went according to plan, except for the fact that Ley had penciled Dixon Ward's name into the Vancouver lineup, wearing jersey #17. You see, the Canucks had traded Ward to the Los Angeles Kings for Jimmy Carson three weeks earlier. At the 8-second mark of the first period, Oiler coach Glen Sather pointed out the fact that Carson, not Ward, was wearing #17. Marouelli had no choice but to inform coach Quinn that, since Carson was not on the lineup card, he couldn't be used that evening. Despite the faux pas, the Canucks downed the Oilers 5–4 on an overtime goal by Pavel Bure.

Unfortunately, Lady Luck wasn't shining as brightly on Jacques Lemaire when he was earning his coaching stripes with the Longueuil Chevaliers in the Quebec Major Junior League. On February 23, 1983, Lemaire forgot to put the name of forward Guy Rouleau on the lineup card for Longueuil's game against Trois-Rivieres. Rouleau's omission went unnoticed during the game, which ended in a 4–4 draw. But after the game, Trois-Rivieres lodged a complaint that Lemaire had dressed an ineligible player. The protest was upheld and the Longueuil team was forced to forfeit the game.

The strategy of pulling the goaltender and putting on an extra attacker has been common in the NHL for decades. It appears that Art Ross of the Boston Bruins was the first coach to pull the goalie. During game two of the Montreal Canadiens–Boston Bruins semifinals in 1931, Ross pulled goaltender Tiny Thompson and replaced him with an extra forward in an attempt to score the tying goal. Even though the Canadiens went on to defeat the Bruins 1–0, the strategy was dubbed "an amazing maneuver" in the newspapers the next day, and it wasn't long before most NHL coaches were following Ross's example.

Before the substitute-goaltender rule was introduced, NHL teams carried only one goaltender. If, during the course of a game, a goalie was struck by the puck, the game was delayed while the netminder was taken to the arena clinic and patched up. However, on those rare occasions when the goaltender was too badly injured to continue, a substitute goaltender was needed.

In the early days of the game another player from the team would don the equipment and take the injured goalie's place between the pipes. Harry Mummery, a defenseman who had already played two full games in net when he was with the Quebec Bulldogs, was the first position player to stand in for an injured goalie during an NHL game, replacing Hamilton Tiger netminder Howie Lockhart during the 1921–22 season.

Even coaches took their turn in the barrel. In game two of the 1928 Stanley Cup finals, the New York Rangers' forty-four-year-old coach, Lester Patrick, was forced to replace injured incumbent Lorne Chabot. Patrick allowed only one goal in his 46-minute stint in the Rangers' cage, helping the Broadway Blues to a 2–1 overtime victory. Patrick wasn't the only coach called upon to replace an injured netminder. Pittsburgh Pirate center Odie Cleghorn was in net on December 18, 1925, in a 3–2 win over the New York Americans.

In the 1930s and early 1940s, at least eight position players—including Andy Brannigan, Al Shields, and Roger Jenkins—were called upon to substitute for injured netminders.

By the 1950s each home team was required to have a substitute goalie in the stands. These stand-ins, who were

(c) Each team shall be allowed one goalkeeper on the ice at one time. The goalkeeper may be removed and another player substituted. . . .

(d) Each team shall have on its bench, or on a chair immediately beside the bench, a substitute goalkeeper who shall, at all times, be fully dressed and equipped ready to play.

The substitute goalkeeper may enter the game at any time following a stoppage of play, but no warm-up shall be permitted.

(e) Except when both goalkeepers are incapacitated, no player in the playing roster in that game shall be permitted to wear the equipment of the goalkeeper.

(f) In regular League and Playoff games, if both listed goalkeepers are incapacitated, that team shall be entitled to dress and play any available goalkeeper who is eligible. . . .

known as "house goalies," would play for either team in the event of an injury. The house goalies were usually junior- or senior-league players or minor-league pros. However, the best-known understudy in the 1950s was Detroit Red Wing trainer Ross "Lefty" Wilson, who appeared in three games during the decade, allowing only a single goal in 85 minutes of work. Other trainers, such as Danny Olesvich and Julian Klymkiw, were also forced into action during these years. Although many of these on-ice pinch hitters performed admirably, it was the arrival of televised hockey that finally ended the era of the house goalie. The long delay required for a house goalie to clamber into his equipment and then warm up made for a lot of dead airtime in these years before instant replays and video highlights.

Goaltending rules were changed as a result of events that took place in the 1964 playoffs. During game two of the semi-finals, Detroit's Terry Sawchuk was injured and the Red Wings were forced to use Bob Champoux, a minor-leaguer who had never played an NHL regular-season game, much less one in the playoffs. Although Detroit defeated the Chicago Black Hawks 5–4, the fact that the Wings had been forced to use a raw rookie in an important playoff game was of concern to the fans and the media. A rule requiring each team to dress two goaltenders was introduced for the 1965 playoffs and became permanent regular-season legislation prior to the 1965–66 season.

Forwards and defensemen are no longer permitted to play goal in the NHL unless both of a team's goaltenders are

When Montreal Canadiens' goaltender Jacques Plante became ill just before a game against Toronto, the Habs were forced to use a local junior goaltender named Len Broderick in the net. Broderick and the Canadiens downed the Maple Leafs 6-2 in the only professional game of his career.

Hockey Hall of Fame

incapacitated. Since teams are now required to dress two goaltenders at all times—and have the right to use a third
"eligible" goaltender should both other netminders become
incapacitated—we may never see a forward or defender play
goal again. The last NHL position player to take a bow in net
was Boston Bruin forward Jerry Toppazzini, although he
wasn't really credited with an appearance in goal. In the dying
seconds of the Bruins' 5–2 loss to the Chicago Black Hawks
on October 16, 1960, Bruin goaltender Don Simmons was
injured, and rather than wait for a replacement to come out
of the stands, Toppazzini stood in for his fallen comrade.
"Topper" wasn't forced to show his form and the game went
into the books as a 5–2 Black Hawks victory.

A skater replaced an injured goaltender in a game that
took place in the NHL's main minor-league affiliate, the
American Hockey League. This rare replacement occurred in
a game played on February 10, 1983, between the Adiron-
dack Red Wings and the St. Catharines Saints, farm clubs of
the Detroit Red Wings and Toronto Maple Leafs, respec-
tively. The Saints were forced to go into that game with only
one goaltender because backup Bob Parent was serving a
suspension for a match penalty the night before. At the 7:01
mark of the first period, with the score tied 1–1, goalie Vince
Tremblay pulled a hamstring muscle and was forced to leave.
Centerman Norm Aubin, who would later play sixty-nine
games for the Leafs, volunteered to take Tremblay's place.
Fifteen minutes later, he made his way into the Saints' cage,
wearing Tremblay's equipment and jersey. Aubin was outstanding, keeping the Wings off the scoresheet until the third
period. However, the Red Wings soon solved his unorthodox
style and pumped five pucks past him in the third period to
win the game 6–3.

The 1965 introduction of the two-goaltender rule
brought to an end the days when amateur or semipro goalies
were pulled from the stands to replace injured or ill NHL
goalies. Yet there have been a few instances of NHL clubs being
forced to use the "any available goaltender" clause of this rule.

In February 1972 the Philadelphia Flyers were on a
West Coast swing through Vancouver and California. On
February 9 Flyer goaltender Bruce Gamble checked himself
into a hospital after experiencing chest pains. It was discov-

ered that Gamble had suffered a heart attack during a 3–2 victory over the Vancouver Canucks the previous evening. Gamble was kept in the hospital, leaving the Flyers without a backup for Doug Favell for the game against the Los Angeles Kings. The Flyers signed veteran minor-league goaltender Russ Gillow to a one-game contract. Favell played the entire game while Gillow remained on the bench. It was the closest he would come to playing in the NHL. Gamble was forced to retire and never played in the League again, and Gillow went on to play four seasons in the World Hockey Association (WHA) for Los Angeles and San Diego.

The Toronto Maple Leafs found themselves in a similar position in January 1980 when three of their four goaltenders went out of commission at the same time. Number one pivot Mike Palmateer was out with a back injury and backup Jiri Crha was hobbled by a sore ankle. Farmhand Paul Harrison became bedridden with a severe case of the flu, leaving the Leafs and rookie Vince Tremblay without a backup as the club prepared to face the defending Stanley Cup champion Montreal Canadiens on January 10.

Out of the shadows came the fifty-five-year-old goalie coach of the club, Johnny "China Wall" Bower. Bower volunteered to serve as a backup to Tremblay if needed, but he warned the Leafs that if he was forced to play during the game, he would have to bring a chair out to the net with him. Luckily, the Leafs were spared that embarrassment when Harrison was able to suit up for the game. Neither Tremblay nor Harrison was up to par and the Canadiens swamped the Leafs 6–2.

 RULE 16

(a) Prior to the start of the game, at the request of the Referee, the Manager or Coach of the visiting team is required to name the starting line-up to the Referee or Official Scorer. . . .
(b) Prior to the start of the game, the Manager or Coach of the home team, having been advised by the Official Scorer or the Referee the names of the starting line-up of the visiting

STARTING LINE-UP

There have been very few occasions when a coach has iced the wrong starting line-up. But there *has* been an instance when the right starting line-up was wrong and both teams ended up losing the same game.

The case in question involved the Ontario Hockey League's Sudbury Wolves and North Bay Centennials. After struggling out of the gate with a 6-11 record, the Wolves were desperate to turn their season around. When Sudbury coach Ken Gratton handed his starting line-up to the referee prior to a game against North Bay on November 2, 1982, he listed his starting goaltender as Tim Jeanveau. This immediately caught the attention of North Bay's veteran bench boss Bert Templeton. Jeanveau had been a back-up goalie with Sudbury in 1981–82, but he was no longer on the active Wolves roster. Templeton, sensing that Gratton had made a clerical error on the line-up sheet, decided to wait until after the opening face-off to make the miscue known to the referee so he could enjoy an early power play opportunity. However, when the Wolves took to the ice, Jeanveau was indeed in the Sudbury nets.

The Wolves went on to down the Centennials 4–2, thanks in large part to a miraculous 42-save performance by Jeanveau. Following the match, Templeton filed a notice with the league office, protesting that Sudbury had used an ineligible player. After a lengthy debate, OHL commissioner David Branch upheld the North Bay protest and removed the two points and the win from the Sudbury record. Branch refused, however, to credit North Bay with a victory, so for the first time in OHL history a game was played in which neither team won, lost, or tied.

EQUALIZATION OF TEAMS

The rule governing equalization of players was deleted from the rule book in 1967. This rule covered those circumstances in which a team—through either injury or accident—found itself with fewer than five skaters or without any substitute players.

The League found itself in need of such a rule following a pair of games between the Toronto Arenas and the Ottawa Senators. On January 13, 1918, the Arenas found themselves with only four skaters because of injuries and penalties. The Senators had voluntarily dropped a player to equalize the teams. Three days later, Ottawa had only one healthy substitute player when the same two teams played again in Toronto. Early in the game, Senator forward Rusty Crawford suffered a knee injury when he collided with Arena left-winger Corbett Denneny and was unable to continue, leaving the Senators with only five skaters and a goaltender. This meant that every Ottawa player had to stay on the ice for the entire game. On this occasion, the Arenas responded in kind by playing the rest of the game without using any subs. A fatigued Arena club defeated an equally exhausted Senator squad 5–4. Both the Arenas and Senators were praised in the press for their sports-

team, shall name the starting line-up of the home team which information shall be conveyed by the Official Scorer or the Referee to the Coach of the visiting team. (c) No change in the starting line-up of either team as given to the Referee or Official Scorer, or in the playing line-up on the ice, shall be made until the game is actually in progress. For an infraction of this rule, a bench minor penalty shall be imposed upon the offending team, provided such infraction is called to the attention of the Referee before the second face-off in the first period takes place.

RULE 17

DELETED

manship, which encouraged the NHL to add an "equalization rule" to the rule book before the 1918–19 season.

Rule 17 stipulated that the team with a full complement of skaters was obliged to reduce the number of players it sent out onto the ice to match the number of skaters iced by its short-staffed opponent. As roster size increased, however, this rule lost its relevance and was deleted.

 RULE 18

(a) Players may be changed at any time from the players' bench provided that the player or players leaving the ice shall be within five feet (5') of his players' bench and out of the play before the change is made. . . .

CHANGE OF PLAYERS

Changing players "on the fly" while play continues has been a key element of hockey strategy since the mid-1920s. Before that time it was customary for the starting lineup to play the entire game, with substitution used primarily when a player was hurt or was banished from the match.

The first coach to use more than one forward-line combination in a game was probably Lester Patrick, who used a variety of line combinations during the 1925 Stanley Cup finals between the Victoria Cougars and Montreal Canadiens. Patrick knew that the Canadiens would likely play their star-laden starting lineup for most of the game, and he felt that if he could mix up his lines—including the odd line change on the fly—he could outskate the speedy Habs.

Patrick was right. A stunned Montreal scribe reported, "The Westerners simply skated the Canadiens dizzy. . . . the blazing speed of Morenz was negated, and they just could not handle the Cougars' non-stop attack." Patrick's Cougars defeated the Canadiens three games to one to become the last non-NHL team to capture the Stanley Cup.

One of the defeated Canadiens was Odie Cleghorn, who became the first coach of the expansion Pittsburgh Pirates in 1925–26. Cleghorn adopted many of Patrick's ideas, including that of changing on the fly. He cited three reasons for making player and line changes part of the game. First, team rosters were at the time set at twelve players in uniform per team; it was important to get as many of those players into the game as possible. Second, constant changes were confusing the opposition. Third, he just didn't have enough depth of talent to play only six or seven players for an entire game. By subbing regularly, every member of the team had the opportunity to make a contribution.

Hockey Hall of Fame

Pittsburgh Pirates coach Odie Cleghorn, seen here with team owner and boxing promoter Benny Leonard, was the first NHL coach to use line combinations and quick changes as part of his offensive strategy.

Cleghorn's strategy violated existing NHL rules, which stated that players could only be changed during a stoppage or delay in play. However, prior to the 1927–28 campaign, the League passed a new rule that allowed changing on the fly as long as the player leaving the ice was on the bench before the next player went on. Eventually enough leeway was given that a player could enter the game when the player he was replacing was within 5 feet of the bench.

It's surprising how rarely an illegal-goaltender-substitution call is made. When one is, it often signals the end of a very long evening for the offending team. A recent example is a case in point. On March 15, 1995, the San Jose Sharks were losing 2–1 to the Toronto Maple Leafs when coach Kevin Constantine attempted to bring goalie Arturs Irbe to the bench for an extra attacker. It's a move that should need no rehearsal, since it occurs twenty to twenty-five times a season. But on this evening Irbe was still 30 feet from the Sharks' bench when the extra attacker reached the Leafs' zone. Linesman Randy Mitton noticed the illegal change and blew the play dead, robbing the Sharks of some needed momentum and 200 feet of real estate.

INJURED PLAYERS

Before the two-goaltender rule was introduced in 1965–66, referees allowed goalies 10 minutes to recover from their wounds, although delays of 15–20 minutes were common if it was assured that the goalie could return. In fact, there wasn't a Stanley Cup playoff series played between 1917 and 1964 in which at least one game wasn't delayed waiting for an injured goaltender to be patched up. Time-outs were also given to goaltenders who fell ill, although most netminders would rather perish than leave a game because of sickness. And some did.

Georges Vezina, the Montreal Canadiens' Hall of Fame goaltender and arguably one of hockey's greatest, never missed a game in his NHL career, despite playing with primitive equipment and without a face mask. During training camp before the 1925–26 season, however, club officials became concerned about Vezina's health. He seemed thin and weak, yet he refused to remove himself from the net. While some

(NOTE 1) When a goalkeeper leaves his goal area and proceeds to his players' bench for the purpose of substituting another player, the rear Linesman shall be responsible to see that the substitution made is not illegal by reason of the premature departure of the substitute from the bench (before the goalkeeper is within five feet (5') of the bench). . . .

RULE 19

(b) If a goalkeeper sustains an injury or becomes ill, he must be ready to resume play immediately or be replaced by a substitute goalkeeper and NO additional time shall be allowed by the Referee for the purpose of enabling the injured or ill goalkeeper to resume his position. . . .

scribes attributed Vezina's condition to the fact that he had fathered twenty-three children, it was clear he was not in the best of shape.

Les Habitants opened their 1925–26 season against Pittsburgh and battled the Pirates to a scoreless draw through 20 minutes of play. Shortly after the Canadiens returned to the dressing room, Vezina collapsed and was unable to continue. The Canadiens, well aware of Vezina's condition, had a goaltender by the name of Alphonse Lacroix waiting in the wings. Lacroix became the first goaltender other than Vezina to play for the Montreal Canadiens since Teddy Groulx on March 11, 1910.

Vezina was immediately hospitalized, and he was diagnosed with tuberculosis. On March 27, 1926, Georges Vezina passed away.

Another goaltender who played through illness was Charlie Gardiner, the Chicago Black Hawks' All Star goaltender and team captain. Gardiner played much of the 1933–34 season with severe headaches, yet he refused to leave the cage. At times during the campaign he was so racked with pain that he needed to clutch the goalposts to keep from keeling over. His condition was no secret and his courage motivated his teammates to win their first Stanley Cup. In the 1934 playoffs Gardiner recorded six victories, two shutouts, and a 1.50 goals-against average. Two months later he collapsed and died of a brain hemorrhage.

Then there is the saga of Toronto Maple Leaf Frank "Ulcers" McCool. On the outside McCool was as calm as his name suggests, but on the inside he was a tangled web of raw nerves, an affliction that had earned him his nickname. Still, during the 1944–45 season McCool was outstanding, winning the Calder Trophy as rookie of the year. He continued his fine play into the playoffs, helping the Leafs eliminate the heavily favored Montreal Canadiens in the semifinals. McCool shut out the Habs 1–0 in his first Stanley Cup playoff game, and although he was trounced 10–3 in game five, he rebounded in game six to backstop the Leafs to a 3–2, series-winning victory.

In game one of the Stanley Cup finals against the Detroit Red Wings, McCool suddenly bolted from the nets and headed for the dressing room. Referee Bill Chadwick and Leaf

CHUCK GARDINER

Dan Diamond and Associates

Chuck Gardiner, the only goaltender to captain his team to the Stanley Cup title, died only two months after leading the Chicago Black Hawks to the championship.

bench boss Hap Day waited for 10 minutes when Day finally went into the Leafs' dressing room and sat down beside his apprehensive goaltender. He quietly said to McCool, "There's no one else, Frank. We need you." McCool sighed, took a long slug of milk, and headed back out onto the ice. He proceeded to throw three straight shutouts at the Wings as the Leafs captured the Stanley Cup in seven games. McCool never played another playoff game in the NHL. He died a few years later from complications of the ulcers that had caused him to retire from hockey after the 1945–46 season.

Rule 19(f) describes the actions to be taken when a player is injured. But no rule could have prepared the referee for what occurred during game two of the Smythe Division finals between the Los Angeles Kings and Calgary Flames on April 20, 1989. Midway through the first period, King forward Bernie Nicholls felt he had been speared by Flame goaltender Mike Vernon. Nicholls skated through the Kings' crease and delivered a blow to Vernon's caged head that was, as he described it, "as hard as I've ever hit anybody."

The impact sent the netminder sprawling backward onto the ice. Flame defenseman Al MacInnis picked up the puck and surged up the ice just as the Flames' trainer, Jim "Bearcat" Murray, hopped over the boards and scurried to Vernon's side, courtesy of his specially designed cleated running shoes. Play continued while Murray tended to Vernon. MacInnis dished the puck to Hakan Loob, who slipped a pass to Joe Nieuwendyk, who in turn dropped the puck back to MacInnis.

The hard-shooting rear guard stepped over the Kings' blueline and fired a sizzler past Los Angeles goalie Kelly Hrudey to give the Flames a commanding 4–0 lead. The Kings' bench, meanwhile, was up in arms, demanding that the goal be disallowed. Since neither the linesmen nor referee Bill McCreary had noticed that Murray had jumped onto the ice, the goal was legal because the Flames had never surrendered possession of the puck. Director of Officiating John McCauley was equally confused by the event. "I don't think I've ever seen anything like it," he said after the game. "I don't think we have a call for that. The referee didn't see it. He has to live with what he does see."

(f) When a player is injured so that he cannot continue play or go to his bench, the play shall not be stopped until the injured player's team has secured possession of the puck; if the player's team is in possession of the puck at the time of injury, play shall be stopped immediately unless his team is in a scoring position.

In the formative years of the NHL the game featured hard-edged pucks, heavy woolen jerseys, one-piece sticks, tube skates, and gauntlet-style goalie gloves.

CHAPTER THREE

EQUIPMENT

STICKS

THERE WAS NO RULE governing the length of hockey sticks until the 1927–28 season, when the NHL ruled that no stick could exceed 53 inches in length. The League didn't want anyone emulating Ernie "Moose" Johnson, an All Star winger and defenseman in the PCHA who used a stick that was said to be 75 inches long.

⬤ RULE 20

(b) No stick shall exceed sixty inches (60″) in length from the heel to the end of the shaft nor more than twelve and one-half inches (12½″) from the heel to the end of the blade.

. . . The curvature of the blade of the stick shall be restricted in such a way that the distance of a perpendicular line measured from a straight line drawn from any point at the heel to the end of the blade to the point of maximum curvature shall not exceed one-half inch (½″).

Ernie "Moose" Johnson was renowned for his long reach (99 inches) and his 75-inch hockey stick. Johnson, who played on four Stanley Cup championship teams as a member of the Montreal Wanderers in the early 1900s, played pro hockey until 1931.

EQUIPMENT

The first use of a curved stick is often credited to either Andy Bathgate of the New York Rangers or Stan Mikita of the Chicago Black Hawks. However, Hall of Famer Jack Adams said that Cy Denneny, his teammate on the 1926–27 Ottawa Senators, was the first player he had ever seen use a curved blade. Denneny would dip the blade of his stick in hot water to soften it, then bend it. Adams said he tried Denneny's method but couldn't control his shots, and as far as he knew no one else tried it. While some players used a curved shaft on their sticks (and some, like Hall of Famer Harry Cameron, could curve their shots), the blade remained straight because of the emphasis on stickhandling and the importance of the backhand shot.

In the late 1950s Andy Bathgate noticed that if he twisted the blade of his stick, his slapshots would hook, dip, and rise. At about the same time Black Hawk Stan Mikita was at practice when he broke the blade of his stick, leaving it twisted at the end of the shaft. As he was leaving the ice to get a new stick, he took a slapshot that caused the puck to dip dramatically. Mikita and Chicago teammate Bobby Hull experimented and gradually learned to modify the curves on their sticks. Not only did their slapshots increase in velocity, they felt that their accuracy increased. Soon players around the League were modifying their sticks and experimenting with the size of the curve. Soon, the age of the "banana blade" was born and manufacturers designed sticks with curved sticks for players of all ages.

In the NHL the curved stick represented a problem. Despite protests to the contrary, the simple truth was that the shooter using a curved stick really had no idea where his shot was going. Many of the League's big blasters were stepping over the blueline and letting fly, leaving the goaltender to guess which way the dipping and diving puck would go. More often than not, the goalie guessed wrong. Of the top twenty scorers in 1968–69, nine were using the "banana blade." And if the goalie didn't know where the puck was going, the slapshot launched by a curved stick became a dangerous weapon. Prior to the start of the 1967–68 season, the maximum allowable curve was reduced to 1 inch. In 1970–71, it was reduced again to ½ inch, and it remains so to this day. New York Ranger goaltender Eddie Giacomin put it best: "They had to do something before someone got killed."

Any player caught using an illegal stick is subject to a minor penalty. To prevent coaches from requesting stick measurements as a way of gaining an unofficial time-out, the NHL rules committee has directed that only one request be allowed per game; if the stick proves to be legal, the team asking for the measurement is penalized for delay of game. This directive works wonderfully, adding a measure of suspense to games, since coaches usually only ask for measurements at critical moments.

One of the most famous instances of strategic stick measurement occurred during game two of the 1993 Stanley Cup finals between the Montreal Canadiens and Los Angeles Kings. Los Angeles won the first game 4–1 in Montreal and entered the final 2 minutes of game two with a slim 2–1 lead. If the Kings could hang on, the series would move back to California with the Kings two games closer to their first Stanley Cup title. At the 18:15 mark of the third period, Canadien coach Jacques Demers asked referee Kerry Fraser to measure

Dan Diamond and Associates

A penalty to Los Angeles Kings defenseman Marty McSorley (right) for using an illegal stick was the turning point in the 1993 Stanley Cup finals between the Kings and the Montreal Canadiens.

King defenseman Marty McSorley's stick. If Demers was wrong, the Habs would spend the rest of the game short-handed; if he was right, the Habs would have an all-important man advantage. Fraser measured the stick and found it to be illegal. Montreal went on the powerplay and 32 seconds later defenseman Eric Desjardins tied the game at 2–2, sending the match into overtime. Less than a minute into the extra frame, Desjardins stuffed a rebound past Los Angeles goalie Kelly Hrudey to win the game and tie the series. Montreal went on to win the series and the Stanley Cup in five games.

When he was coaching the Los Angeles Kings in the late 1980s, Mike Murphy prided himself on his knowledge of the rule book. On March 28, 1987, Murphy's Kings were entertaining the Calgary Flames. Late in the third period, with the Kings trailing the Flames 4–3, Los Angeles goaltender Al Jensen was caught out of position. Calgary forward Joe Mullen corralled a loose puck and unleashed a shot toward the vacated net. In a frantic effort to stop the shot, Jensen threw his stick at the puck, which according to Rule 81(a) called for an automatic penalty shot. Mullen skated in and scored on the shot to give the Flames a commanding 5–3 lead. Instead of skating to the official scorer's table to confirm the goal, however, referee Kerry Fraser headed to the Flames' bench and measured the blade on Mullen's stick. The stick proved illegal, nullifying the goal that Mullen had just scored. In compliance with the rule, no penalty was charged to Mullen.

Interestingly, Murphy had had to ask for the stick measurement before Mullen took his shot, which he did by sending forward Bernie Nicholls over to referee Fraser. Although the Kings lost the game, Rule 20(e) will always be known as Murphy's Law.

An event occurred during the 1994–95 season that pointed out once again that there are always exceptions to any rule. Late in the third period of a game between the Tampa Bay Lightning and Hartford Whalers on February 10, Whaler Steven Rice was penalized for hooking. On the ensuing powerplay, Lightning forward Petr Klima slipped a pass from defenseman Chris Gratton behind Whaler goaltender Sean Burke to give the Lightning a 4–3 advantage.

After the goal was scored, Whaler coach Paul Holmgren requested that referee Paul Stewart measure Klima's stick. As

(e) In the event that a player scores on a penalty shot while using an illegal stick, the goal shall be disallowed and no further penalty imposed. However, if no goal is scored, the player taking the penalty shot shall receive a minor penalty.

(f) A minor penalty plus a ten-minute misconduct penalty shall be imposed on any player who refuses to surrender his stick for measurement when requested to do so by the Referee. . . .

Stewart approached the Lightning's bench to obtain the stick, Klima broke the blade off the shaft and threw it behind the bench. Then, according to the letter of Rule 20(f), Stewart penalized Klima for unsportsmanlike conduct and added a 10-minute misconduct penalty. However, the goal was allowed to stand, and it turned out to be the winning marker in a 4–3 Lightning victory. There was considerable media backlash over the incident and an NHL spokesman stated that a revision to the rule was possible.

SKATES

In the first forty-five years of the NHL's existence, it made numerous equipment improvements to reduce injury. Of particular concern was the heel of the skate blade. Although the back of the blade was rounded, and later covered with a steel guard, its unprotected edge could still inflict serious cuts. But its greatest threat occurred when two players collided and their skates became tangled. In the frantic effort to quickly return to their feet and to the play, skate heels could inflict serious tendon tears.

On November 13, 1958, Montreal Canadien Maurice Richard and Toronto Maple Leaf defenseman Marc Réaume collided in just this way. When Richard attempted to regain his feet, the heel of his own skate severed his Achilles tendon. Richard missed forty-two games that season, and although he returned to action later in the schedule, he never fully recovered from the injury.

In 1960 skate manufacturer CCM announced that it had developed a plastic guard for use on the heels of hockey skates. The new "safety heel" was tested in various leagues and organizations and found to be most reliable. The NHL passed legislation prior to the 1964–65 season requiring every skater in the League to use the safety heel.

The "fancy-skates" rule was entered into the rule book on September 24, 1927. In the early years of the NHL the rule book banned all skates with "long reachers." In essence, these were the old-style skates that featured regular tempered-steel blades that could still be detached from the boots. Today, "fancy skates" refers to figure skates or speed skates, both of which have longer blades and are not equipped with safety heels.

RULE 21

(a) All hockey skates shall be of a design approved by the Rules Committee. All skates worn by players (but not goalkeepers) and by the Referee and Linesmen shall be equipped with an approved safety heel. . . .

(b) The use of speed skates or fancy skates or any skate so designed that it may cause injury is prohibited.

When Maurice Richard cut his Achilles' tendon in a game against Toronto in the 1957–58 season, it prompted skate manufacturers to invent a new lightweight plastic blade guard.

Hockey Hall of Fame

By the 1927–28 season the preferred skate of most players was the "tube" skate, which had a blade made of hardened steel, riveted and soldered into a tube that was attached to the sole and heel of the boot. It was invented in Norway in 1900 and introduced to Canada in 1905. The mounting of the tube to the skate boot allowed for better weight distribution, providing the skater with the means to a smoother and more efficient stride over the ice surface. By forbidding the use of fancy skates and long reachers, the *NHL Rule Book* virtually mandated the use of tube skates for forwards and defensemen.

At least one player found it difficult adapting to tube skates. Murray Murdoch was an outstanding college player with the University of Manitoba when he caught the eye of Conn Smythe, then working as the first general manager of the New York Rangers. Smythe signed Murdoch and invited him to the Rangers' first training camp, to be held in Toronto in October 1926. Murdoch had learned to skate and play hockey in Winnipeg wearing long reachers, the old steel-bladed skates that were open at both ends. At the first workout Smythe took one look at Murdoch's antiquated blades and ordered him to put on tube skates.

Smythe was an astute hockey mind, and he had signed some of the finest amateur talent in the country, including Lorne Chabot, Frank Boucher, and Ching Johnson, to play for the Rangers. However, the Rangers' owners felt they

couldn't introduce the game of hockey to the New York audi-
ence they hoped to attract with "rank amateurs." So, after
only one week of practice, Smythe was fired and Lester
Patrick brought in to run the show. Patrick, who had introduced professional hockey to the West Coast in 1911, was
also familiar with the contributions that Murdoch could
make to the new squad. However, he was puzzled by
Murdoch's poor performance in early practices and called
him into the office. Murdoch explained that he had never
worn tubes before and was having a difficult time adjusting
to them. Patrick told the rookie to go back to the old skates
if it would make him feel more comfortable. Murdoch did,
and he made the team, collecting 10 points as a freshman.

Near the end of the 1926–27 season, Conn Smythe
reappeared on the NHL scene as the general manager of the
newly formed Toronto Maple Leafs. And so it was that at a
Board of Governors meeting in September a new rule ban-
ning "reachers" was introduced. The governor who suggested
the rule be adopted? Conn Smythe.

As for Murdoch, he eventually mastered the tube skate,
and he went on to become the League's first ironman forward, playing eleven years without missing a single game.

Tube skates remained in use until the 1970s, when the
lighter, plastic blade carriers used today were introduced.

GOALKEEPER'S EQUIPMENT

As this rule reads today, it is designed to prevent any goaltender from gaining an unfair advantage from equipment that
would assist him in stopping the puck. Yet many of the tools
of the trade that are taken for granted today caused considerable stir when they were introduced.

In a game against the Detroit Red Wings during the
1947–48 season, Chicago Black Hawk netminder Emile
Francis appeared in goal wearing a baseball glove, specifically
a first baseman's mitt. Up to this time, goalies had used gloves
very similar to those of regular players, with a strip of leather
sewn between the thumb and forefinger on the catching hand.
When Wing general manager Jack Adams caught a glimpse of
Francis's new contraption, he immediately lodged a protest,
saying the new equipment gave the diminutive Black Hawk

RULE 22

(a) With the exception of skates
and stick, all the equipment worn
by the goalkeeper must be constructed solely for the purpose of
protecting the head or body, and
he must not wear any garment or
use any contrivance which would
give him undue assistance in
keeping goal.

goalie an unfair advantage. NHL president Clarence
Campbell quickly ruled that Francis had broken no rules, and
he was allowed to wear the glove as often as he pleased. And
with that, the "modern" goaltender's catching glove was born.

Although it is not, in the real sense, a piece of goaltenders'
equipment, the water bottle has become an important piece of
the netminder's arsenal. The first documented use of the now
familiar green plastic container came during the 1984–85
season, although its use probably originated in the college
ranks. When the Providence College Friars and the Boston

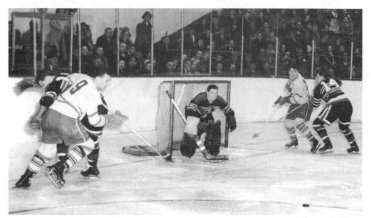

*In addition to introducing the
"trapper" catching glove to the
goaltender's arsenal, Emile
"The Cat" Francis also fash-
ioned an improved stick glove
by taping an outer layer of
sponge rubber to his blocker.*

Hockey Hall of Fame

College Eagles met during the NCAA playoffs on March 16,
1985, both Chris Terreri of the Friars and Scott Gordon of the
Eagles had water bottles on the top of their nets. Terreri certainly needed his. He made sixty-five saves as the Friars upset
the Eagles to advance to the NCAA Final Four.

In the pro ranks, it was Philadelphia Flyer goaltender Bob
Froese who first brought the bottle out with him and placed it
on top of the net, held in place by a strip of Velcro. The on-ice
officials found nothing in the rules to prevent Froese from
using the bottle and soon most of the goalies in the League
were following his example. When television audiences got
their first glimpse of the new addition to the top of the net
during the New York Islanders–Philadelphia Flyers Wales
Conference semifinal series, many presumed it was a television
camera of some sort. When Edmonton Oiler coach Glen
Sather first saw the water bottles, he remarked, "What are they
going to want up there next, a bucket of chicken?"

The first goaltender to wear leg guards in Stanley Cup competition was George "Whitey" Merritt, the goaltender for the Winnipeg Victoria team that captured the Stanley Cup on February 14, 1896. Merritt appeared in net wearing cricket pads, and for the next three decades goalies wore pads that closely resembled those worn by cricketers.

The first patented goal pads were designed by Andrew Cleland of Toronto in February 1898, but it doesn't appear that too many netminders took Mr. Cleland up on his idea. A more popular variety of "shin pad for goal keepers" was designed in 1911 by Bruce Ridpath, an outstanding right winger in the Ontario Professional League. Soon many professional and amateur goaltenders were wearing pads that closely resembled Ridpath's.

In the early 1920s Hamilton harness and leather worker Emil "Pop" Kenesky was watching a Catholic League hockey match when he noticed that a number of goals were being scored by pucks deflecting off the rounded, cricket-style pads of the goalies. Kenesky started experimenting with his own design, widening the pads by adding stuffing. During the 1923–24 season Hamilton Tiger owner Percy Thompson asked Kenesky to repair netminder Jake Forbes's pads. In his first game wearing the new leg guards, the Tigers halted an eight-game losing streak.

After that victory, Thompson asked Kenesky to design a new set of pads for Forbes. Noting there were no rules in place governing the size of goalie equipment, Kenesky made his new pads 12 inches wide so they extended out from the leg instead of curving around it. Kenesky's new pads were an instant success, and soon almost every goaltender was wearing the new protection. In 1925–26 the NHL passed legislation okaying the Kenesky-brand pad, with a width limitation of 12 inches. The legal width was reduced to 10 inches in 1927–28, and remained so until the 1989–90 season, when the 12-inch rule was restored.

The Kenesky pads were made of horsehide and tough cotton sheeting, stuffed with bombax malabaricm or kapok from Java. Although they were the finest on the market,

(b) The leg guards worn by goalkeepers shall not exceed twelve inches (12″) in extreme width when on the leg of the player. . . .

Hockey Hall of Fame

When Percy LeSueur tended goal for Ottawa in the early 1900s, he wore cricket-style pads, primitive gloves and no upper body protection. He also used the same goal stick for five straight seasons.

Kenesky pads were by no means perfect. As a game progressed, they became waterlogged and heavy. They also became softer as they got wetter.

A common sight in the 1930s and 1940s was the goalie repeatedly banging his goal stick against his leg guards, supposedly to shake residual water and snow off the pads. In fact, goaltenders were doing this to reshape the fronts of the pads to make them slightly wider.

The first team manager to notice this was Red Dutton of the Brooklyn Americans. In the third period of a game between Dutton's Americans and the Chicago Black Hawks during the 1941–42 season, Dutton called referee Bill Chadwick over to the bench and insisted that he measure Black Hawk goalie Sam LoPresti's pads. Chadwick grabbed a tape measure and discovered that LoPresti's pads were 10¼ inches wide, ¼ inch wider than allowed in the rule book.

Black Hawk manager Paul Thompson was beside himself. He insisted that Chadwick also measure the pads of Amerk goalie Earl Robertson. Much to Thompson's delight—and Dutton's embarrassment—Robertson's pads were found to be 10½ inches wide. Chadwick was at a loss. There was no penalty provided in the rule book for wearing illegal goalie pads, so Chadwick allowed the game to continue. The following season a rule was introduced providing a minor penalty for wearing illegal pads, although the measurement was to take place at the intermission, not during the game. The NHL will introduce new legislation for the 1996–97 season calling for a one-game suspension to any goaltender found wearing illegal equipment.

 RULE 23

(a) All protective equipment, except gloves, headgear and goalkeepers' leg guards must be worn under the uniform. For violation of this rule, after warning by the Referee, a minor penalty shall be imposed.

(b) All players of both teams shall wear a helmet of design, material and construction approved by the Rules Committee at all times

PROTECTIVE EQUIPMENT

Until this rule was introduced prior to the 1945–46 season, players on some teams, including the New York Rangers, wore their elbow pads on the outsides of their uniforms, mainly because the sleeves of their jerseys were not big enough to fit over the bulky pads. Direct contact with these rock-hard elbow pads could cause injury, and they often came loose in scrambles and fights. Some goalies wore long belly pads, similar to a baseball catcher's chest protector, that extended below the waist of the jersey and hung over the groin area. In 1945, for reasons of safety and to give NHL players a uniform appearance, all exposed equipment except helmets and special injury-protecting headgear was banned.

It has never been firmly established who wore the first helmet in the history of the NHL. There is some evidence to suggest that Boston defenseman George Owen, who played football at Harvard before joining the Bruins in 1928, wore a leather football helmet in his rookie season. During the 1933–34 season, Toronto Maple Leaf forward Irvine "Ace" Bailey was upended from behind by Bruin defenseman Eddie

Dan Diamond and Associates

while participating in a game, either on the playing surface or the players' or penalty benches.

Players may elect for exemption from the operation of this sub-section (b) by execution of an approved Request and Release form and filing it with the League Office.

Outside elbow pads, like the ones worn by Toronto's Red Heron and New York Rangers goaltender Davey Kerr, were the norm in the NHL until the 1945–46 season.

Shore and crashed heavily to the ice, suffering a serious head injury that required three delicate brain operations. Although Bailey recovered, he never played hockey again. After the incident, several Bruin players wore helmets, fearing retaliation from other players in the League. Shore himself wore a helmet on and off for the rest of his career, but mainly to protect, not prevent, an injury. Over the next three decades only a handful of players wore helmets full time. When the NHL expanded from six to twelve teams prior to the 1967–68 season, helmet use was still relatively rare.

In September 1967 Minnesota general manager Wren Blair convinced former All American forward Bill Masterton to come out of retirement and join the newly formed North Stars. Blair had worked for the Amateur Hockey Association of the United States in the early 1960s and scouted Masterton when he was attending the University of Denver. After Masterton graduated, he was signed by the Montreal Canadiens and assigned to the Ottawa/Hull Canadiens of the

Hockey Hall of Fame

After suffering a broken jaw early in the 1959–60 season, Toronto's Ron Stewart wore a helmet and padded chin protector for the next six weeks.

Eastern Professional League. After one season, he was sent up the ladder to the Cleveland Barons of the AHL, finishing sixth in League scoring in 1962–63 with 82 points. However, when the Canadiens didn't open a roster spot for Masterton after his breakthrough season with Cleveland, he decided to return to university to complete his master's degree. Although he put his hopes for a professional career on hold while he concentrated on his studies, Masterton continued to play hockey. He led the St. Paul Steers to the U.S. Hockey League championship in 1966 and was a member of the U.S. National Team in 1967.

Prior to the start of the 1967–68 season, Blair purchased Masterton's rights from the Canadiens and promised him a chance to play in the NHL. Masterton agreed to Blair's terms and actually scored the first goal in the history of the Minnesota franchise. On January 13, 1968, the North Stars were entertaining the Oakland Seals when Masterton led a rush into the Seals' zone early in the first period. Just as he was passing off the puck, he was hit by Oakland defensemen Ron Harris and Larry Cahan. Masterton was lifted into the air by the force of the check and fell backward awkwardly, striking his head on the ice. It was obvious from the onset that the injury was serious, and referee Wally Harris immediately called for a stretcher to remove Masterton from the ice. He was transported to the hospital, where he was examined by a group of doctors who determined that his injuries were so severe they could not operate. On January 15, thirty hours after being injured, Bill Masterton became the first on-ice fatality in the history of the NHL.

Only two weeks before his fatal injury, Masterton had been hit in a game against Boston and developed severe headaches. Ironically, Masterton had worn a helmet in college, but, like 99 percent of the players in his era, he doffed the lid after turning pro.

The effect of Masterton's death on some NHL players was almost instantaneous. All Star defenseman Pierre Pilote of the Chicago Black Hawks donned a helmet immediately, and the entire Black Hawk Scooter Line of Stan Mikita, Ken Wharram, and Doug Mohns began wearing helmets less than a week after the Masterton incident.

Still, they were in the minority. A stick-swinging incident during a 1969 exhibition game in which Boston Bruin Ted Green was seriously hurt opened up the debate again. Yet at a Board of Governors meeting on January 20, 1970, the NHL voted down a proposal by the Bruins calling for the mandatory use of helmets. NHL president Clarence Campbell remarked that making every player wear a helmet would be like "adding five pounds to a jockey." With that the subject was closed, and by 1975 an average of only five players per team was using head protection.

During the 1970s helmet use became mandatory in the college and junior ranks. The best of these players graduated to the NHL. Helmet-wearing European players appeared in the League during this decade as well. Recognizing that its new players were all coming from leagues that required helmets, the NHL passed legislation that made the wearing of a helmet mandatory for any player signing an NHL contract after June 1, 1979. For any player who was a member of the NHL prior to that date, the use of a helmet was voluntary. By the 1995–96 season Craig MacTavish of the St. Louis Blues was the only bareheaded player still active in the NHL.

An exemption to the rule was passed in 1992–93 that allowed players to sign a waiver and go without a helmet if they liked. The NHL stated that all players should enjoy the same rights regardless of when their contracts had been signed. This change was criticized by some members of the media, who accused the League of merely attempting to improve its mar-

ketability by making the players more recognizable. To date, journeyman defenseman Greg Smyth of the Calgary Flames has been the only player to go without a helmet, and his experiment ended after only one game. St. Louis's Brett Hull played in the 1993 All Star Game without a helmet, but the annual midterm classic is basically a noncontact affair.

Carl Brewer, a defenseman with the Toronto Maple Leafs, played throughout the 1960–61 season with the palms cut out of his gloves. The innovation allowed Brewer, one of the NHL's toughest customers, to play the "clutch and grab" game to perfection. By using the palmless gloves, Brewer could slow down opponents by grabbing their jerseys with his bare hands or securing a solid enough grasp to remove players crowding the goal crease. In fact, the holes in Brewer's gloves were so large that he could slip out a fist, a disturbing thought to anyone entangled with him in an on-ice confrontation. This clever ploy often went unnoticed by the referees because from their perspective it appeared that Brewer's gloves were open, not clutching onto the other player. After numerous complaints, the League ruled that all gloves must have intact palms.

(c) A glove from which all or part of the palm has been removed or cut to permit the use of the bare hand shall be considered illegal equipment and if any player wears such a glove in play, a minor penalty shall be imposed on him. . . .

Hockey Hall of Fame

Toronto Maple Leaf defenseman Carl Brewer, seen here slipping the puck past Chicago goaltender Glenn Hall, was one of the first players to be caught wearing palmless gloves.

 RULE 24

(a) The use of pads or protectors made of metal, or of any other material likely to cause injury to a player, is prohibited.

DANGEROUS EQUIPMENT

The NHL passed this rule regarding dangerous equipment prior to the start of the 1958–59 season. While there was no evidence that any player had been injured by a metal pad or piece of protection, there was concern that some old equipment was not properly padded and could cause serious injury. One of the most famous dangerous-equipment protests came from the Montreal Canadiens, who complained that the elbow pads being worn by the Detroit Red Wings in the 1958 playoffs were little less than brass knuckles. That summer, the League passed legislation calling for proper padding on elbow pads.

In the 1958 All Star Game, played prior to the season, Montreal Canadien Bernie Geoffrion was hurt after being caught by an elbow of Detroit Red Wing defenseman Red Kelly. Canadien coach Toe Blake sent assistant trainer Red Aubut into the All Star dressing room to inspect the equipment; Aubut found that many of the players were using the old, and therefore illegal, equipment. After complaining to the League, the Canadiens were told by NHL president Clarence Campbell that referee-in-chief Carl Voss would be traveling to each NHL city to inspect all equipment. On the first weekend of the season, Boston Bruins Bronco Horvath and Doug Mohns both suffered broken jaws in a game against the Toronto Maple Leafs. Boston management cried foul, accusing the Toronto players of using illegal elbow pads that caused the injuries. President Campbell had to admit that Voss had been to every NHL city except Toronto, so he couldn't be sure that the Leafs were guilty. Campbell also admitted that there was no penalty in the books for using illegal equipment, even though the rule prohibiting its use was.

Finding that perfect piece of protective equipment that would enable an injured player to compete without causing further damage to himself or inflicting injury on others was a difficult task in the years before molded plastics were readily available. It was especially difficult to find a device that protected a broken jaw, since the bulky metal masks most trainers devised were both dangerous and restrictive. Some players wore a football-type helmet with a face guard, but that didn't give adequate protection to the jaw. Club owners frowned on players who couldn't or wouldn't play through their injuries.

When Montreal's Dollard St. Laurent broke his jaw after a collision with Detroit's Red Kelly on January 5, 1956, he missed twenty-four games. Two years later, on March 15, 1958, St. Laurent fractured his cheekbone and was sidelined again. This time he attempted to return for the playoffs wearing a wire-and-metal mask. The League ruled, however, that

(b) A mask or protector of a design approved by the Rules Committee may be worn by a player who has sustained a facial injury. . . .

his mask was too dangerous to other players, and requested that he sit out until he could play without it. He was finally able to return to the lineup on April 1, but was largely ineffective. The following season he was dispatched to the Chicago Black Hawks.

RULE 25

(a) The puck shall be made of vulcanized rubber, or other approved material, one inch (1") thick and three inches (3") in diameter and shall weigh between five and one-half ounces (5½ oz.) and six ounces (6 oz.). All pucks used in competition must be approved by the Rules Committee.

PUCK

The first documented use of a flat disk to play hockey came on March 3, 1875, in Montreal. The first recorded use of the word "puck" came in the *Montreal Gazette* on February 7, 1876. While the origin of the object known as a puck is well documented, the origin of the word "puck" is unknown. Some scholars believe that since the earliest players of organized hockey were university students, the flat disk was named after Puck, the mischievous Shakespearean character in *A Midsummer Night's Dream* who appears and disappears seemingly at will.

The puck has remained virtually unchanged in the NHL's seventy-eight-year history, although a beveled-edge puck was used for the first three months of the 1931–32 season. After numerous complaints about the performance of the new puck (it bounced oddly, wouldn't lie flat on the ice, etc.), the NHL decided to revert to the unbeveled disk effective February 2, 1932. Hockey innovator Art Ross, who had been a brilliant player from the early days of the game and went on to build the Boston Bruins NHL franchise as coach and team manager, devised and refined a puck design that behaved with consistency on the ice and was easy to manufacture. Prior to the 1940–41 season the Ross puck, adorned with an orange label bearing his name, became the official puck of the NHL. In 1955 the League began putting the crest of the home team on the puck as well.

Now, you wouldn't think that the rule concerning the size and thickness of the puck would ever be challenged. Yet in the game's infancy, when pucks weren't as well made as they are today, this rule saved one referee from controversy and a major headache.

Fred Waghorn, one of hockey's first on-ice officials and a true hockey pioneer, was refereeing a match in Belleville in 1900 when one of the Belleville forwards struck a shot that

glanced off the goalpost. At this time, the puck was manu-
factured by gluing together two separate rubber pieces. On
this evening, when the puck glanced off the post, the disk
split in two, with half of the puck caroming into the corner
and the other half rebounding into the net. The Belleville players surrounded Waghorn, demanding a goal, but the crafty
referee pulled out the *NHL Rule Book* and pointed to the
paragraph stating that the puck "must be one inch thick and
three inches in diameter." Since the puck that had entered
the goal was not one inch thick, it was not a legal puck, and
therefore no goal had occurred.

While there have been documented instances of games
being suspended in the early days of outdoor rink hockey
(losing pucks in a hole in the ice or in deep snow around the
boards, that sort of thing), only one NHL game has been
threatened by a lack of pucks.

On February 27, 1926, the Toronto St. Pats and the
Montreal Maroons were battling at Toronto's Mutual Street
Arena. In the third period with the Maroons leading 4–3, St.
Pat Hap Day threw a pass to Norm Shay, who fired the puck
at Maroon goalie Clint Benedict. The puck appeared to enter
the net and bounce quickly out, but referee Bobby Hewitson
refused to allow the goal. Tempers flared, resulting in a don-
nybrook involving players, fans, officials, and the police. When
peace was finally restored, Hewitson sent Bert Corbeau of the
St. Pats and Babe Siebert of the Maroons to the sidelines with
match penalties. However, when he attempted to restart the
game, Hewitson couldn't find the puck. It turned out that
Toronto's Babe Dye had taken the disk and was refusing to give
it back to the referee until he allowed the disputed goal.
Hewitson threatened to forfeit the match to Montreal unless
Dye gave up the prized puck. Dye finally relented and the
game proceeded without incident, with the Maroons holding
on for a 4–3 victory.

A recent NHL game was played in which one, and only
one, puck was needed. On November 10, 1979, the Los
Angeles Kings and Minnesota North Stars played an entire
game without the puck leaving the ice surface, allowing that
singular disk to be used through the entire game. That rare
chunk of vulcanized rubber is now on display at the Hockey

(b) The home team shall be responsible for providing an adequate supply of official pucks which shall be kept in a frozen condition. This supply of pucks shall be kept at the penalty bench under the control of one of the regular Off-ice Officials or a special attendant.

Hall of Fame in Toronto. On the other side of the coin, Ace Bailey, a Hall of Fame forward with Toronto who worked for years as an off-ice official at Maple Leaf Gardens, remembered that on April 13, 1967, the Black Hawks and Maple Leafs went through twenty-two pucks in one game, a record for any game in which Bailey played or served as an off-ice official.

For the first forty-five years of play in the NHL, it was the home team's trainer who handed the new disk to the referee if the puck had left the ice surface during the game. The trainer was also responsible for making sure that an adequate supply of pucks was frozen for use in each game. (Pucks have always been frozen to reduce their bounce on the ice surface.) In a close game or pressure situation, it wasn't uncommon to see a home team send a puck into the crowd and then have its trainer search in vain for a minute or two until he found the "right" puck. In the closing minutes of a close game, more often than not that "right" puck would come out of the coach's pocket, where it had been warming up. Of course, a warm puck thrown onto a cold surface bounces uncontrollably, giving the home side a distinct advantage if it's trying to hold on to a narrow lead. In 1964–65 the NHL ruled that all pucks must enter play from the neutral area of the scorer's table. Today the League freezes about twenty-four pucks before each game and provides the off-ice officials with a bucket (usually holding a dozen frozen pucks) before each period. Even a puck held by the linesman for a long period of time can warm up and bounce unduly when it is put back into play. To avoid this, the linesman places the puck on the ice during team or TV time-outs.

For the first time in decades, a new puck was introduced to the game during the 1995–96 season. The "FoxTrax," a customized puck with a built-in tracking device that allowed television viewers to follow its path more easily, was unveiled by Fox Sports and the NHL during the 1996 All-Star Game in Boston. While the disc looked and reacted like any normal puck on the ice, it shone with a blue or white translucent glow on the TV screen and displayed a red stripe, or tail, when it was shot at high speeds. The "FoxTrax" was used in one specially produced Fox Network broadcast each week from March 31 through the end of the playoffs.

CHAPTER FOUR

PENALTIES

PENALTIES

PENALTIES HAVE BEEN a part of hockey since the game first had formal rules. In the first rules of hockey—published in the *Montreal Gazette* on February 27, 1877, in an article entitled "Hockey on Ice"—tripping, kicking, and charging were not allowed, although no punishment was prescribed. However, in the "New rules for the regulation of the game" printed in the *Montreal Gazette* on January 8, 1886, it was stated that "no player should raise his stick above the shoulder; charging from behind, tripping, collaring, kicking or shoving shall not be allowed, and any player, after being twice warned by the referee, it shall become his duty to rule the player off the ice for the match."

Of course, if there are no infractions, penalties don't have to be called. There have been sixty-four penalty-free games in the history of the NHL, but none since the 1979–80 season. The last penalty-free match was a 2–2 tie between the Montreal Canadiens and the Buffalo Sabres on February 17, 1980. All 4 goals were scored in the third period. In the mid-

🏒 RULE 26

Penalties shall be actual playing time and shall be divided in the following classes:
(1) Minor penalties
(2) Bench minor penalties
(3) Major penalties
(4) Misconduct penalties
(5) Match penalties
(6) Penalty shot

1970s, when hard hitting was in vogue in the League, there were two penalty-free games in the same week. On March 13, 1976, neither the Rangers nor the Canucks committed any fouls as New York downed Vancouver 7–3 despite being outshot 42–27. Two weeks later, on March 30, the California Seals fought back from a 2–0 deficit with a pair of late-third-period goals to gain a tie with the Kansas City Scouts. A near-sellout crowd of over sixteen thousand fans in Kansas City's Kemper Arena watched the two teams combine for 59 shots, 4 goals, and no penalties.

The record for playing the most penalty-free games in a single season belongs to the Detroit Red Wings, who were involved in five such matches during the 1936–37 season. The Wings won four of these games and went on to win the Stanley Cup.

During the 1943–44 season the Toronto Maple Leafs and the Chicago Black Hawks played the only scoreless penalty-free game in NHL history. On the evening of February 20, 1944, Chicago Stadium was filled to the rafters to welcome home 6'2", 200-pound defenseman Big Joe Cooper, a fan favorite who was back in the lineup for the first time since returning from the armed forces. In a swiftly played, clean match, the Leafs and Hawks battled to a 0–0 draw in 1 hour and 55 minutes.

RULE 27

(a) For a "MINOR PENALTY", any player, other than a goalkeeper, shall be ruled off the ice for two minutes during which time no substitute shall be permitted.

MINOR PENALTIES

Prior to 1904, the only penalty for rough play or flagrant disobedience of the rules was banishment from the game—and even that was only enforced after two warnings by the referee. The first recorded mention of penalty time came in 1904, when transgressors were subjected to penalties of 2, 3, or 5 minutes at the discretion of the referee. Penalty rules changed in 1914, when players were charged both time and money for committing offenses. All penalties were 5 minutes in duration, plus a fine, but substitutions were allowed.

By 1916–17 minor penalties were reduced to 3 minutes, but since subs were still allowed, penalties had little or no effect unless a star was the guilty party. When the NHL began operation in 1917–18, the 3-minute minor was still in place, but now no subs were allowed so the offending team was forced to play shorthanded for the entire 3 minutes. The 2-minute minor—the accepted sentence to this day—was introduced in 1921–22. In 1923–24 penalty times were set at 2 minutes, 5 minutes, and 10 minutes, depending on the offense.

Rule 27(c), also known as the "Montreal Canadiens" rule, was introduced before the 1956–57 season. Prior to this, a player who was given a minor penalty would serve his entire 2-minute sentence regardless of how many goals his team surrendered while he was in the box. No team took better advantage of the new rule than the Canadiens. Under the guidance of first-year coach Hector "Toe" Blake, the Canadiens developed a devastating powerplay unit, with Doug Harvey and Tom Johnson anchoring the point and Jean Beliveau, Maurice Richard, and Bert Olmstead comprising the forward unit.

The Canadiens opened the 1955–56 season strongly, losing only three of their first twelve games. On November 5, 1955, Montreal was hosting Boston when Bruin rear guard Hal Laycoe was whistled for holding early in the second period. During the ensuing 2-minute powerplay, Montreal's Jean Beliveau erupted for three goals in just 44 seconds, leading the Habs to a 4–2 victory over the Bruins. Almost immediately, general managers from the other five NHL clubs began lobbying for a revision of the rules. Montreal's powerplay clicked for 25 goals in the first twenty-two games of the season, enabling the Canadiens to finish the season with League-leading totals in victories (forty-five) and goals (222). At the thirty-ninth annual meeting of the NHL's Board of Governors on June 6, 1956, a rule change enabling a player serving a minor penalty to return to the ice when a goal is scored by the opposing team was adopted. The rule was carried by a 5–1 margin, with the Montreal Canadiens being the lone team not to vote in favor of the new legislation.

From 1917 to 1985, if two players were penalized at the same time, both would go to the box and the teams would play "four-on-four" for the next 2 minutes. However, prior to the 1985–86 season, the NHL adopted a new rule that allowed for substitutions on coincident minors. This new law became known as the "Edmonton Oilers" rule because the Oilers had been notorious for their high scoring during four-on-four

(c) If while a team is "short-handed" by one or more minor or bench minor penalties, the opposing team scores a goal, the first of such penalties shall automatically terminate. . . .

(d) When ONE minor penalty is assessed to ONE player of EACH team at the same stoppage in play, these penalties will be served without substitution provided there are no other penalties in effect and visible on the penalty clocks. . . .

situations. With their team speed, finesse players, and Wayne Gretzky, the Oilers could capitalize on extra open ice and were scoring on one in every five four-on-four situations. And there was another aspect to that success. Some NHL general managers felt that the four-on-four had become part of the Oilers' playbook, that they were purposely drawing opponents into taking coincident penalties. In the 1985 Stanley Cup finals between the Oilers and the Philadelphia Flyers, there were twenty four-on-four situations. Edmonton scored four times to maintain their one-in-five average.

Edmonton general manager Glen Sather was outraged at the 1985 rule change, which was passed by an 18–3 vote. He was quoted as saying, "Typical, if you can't beat the Oilers on the ice, beat 'em in the boardroom." This displeasure was shared by many fans, who enjoyed the high-tempo, open-ice play created by the four-on-four rule. It took the passage of time and the trade of Wayne Gretzky to the Los Angeles Kings for the NHL to agree. In 1992–93 the old rule was brought back into effect, with the provision that four-on-four hockey would be played if "there are no other penalties in effect and visible on the penalty clocks."

 RULE 28

(a) For the first "MAJOR PENALTY" in any one game, the offender, except the goalkeeper, shall be ruled off the ice for five minutes during which time no substitute shall be permitted.

An automatic fine of one hundred dollars ($100) shall also be added when a major penalty is imposed for any foul causing injury to the face or head of an opponent by means of a stick.

(b) For the third major penalty in the same game to the same player, or for a major for butt-ending, checking from behind, clipping, cross-checking, high-sticking, slashing or spearing, he shall be ruled off the ice for

MAJOR PENALTIES

When the NHL was formed in 1917, almost every infraction of the rules was regarded as a major penalty. Tripping, holding, charging, interference, hooking, even a call known as "loafing offside" were major penalties in the first ten to fifteen years of the NHL's existence. For the first infraction, a player was sent off the ice for 5 minutes. For the second major foul in the same game, the player was penalized for 10 minutes. If the player committed a third major foul in the same game, he would be "ruled off for the remainder of the match."

Over the years most of these fouls became relegated to "minor" penalty status. By 1927 tripping an opponent was a minor, although upending someone who was trying to score was a major, as was holding in the same circumstance.

During the 1931–32 season two interesting twists on the major-penalty rule got a comical workout in Toronto, where coach Dick Irvin thought he had found a way to work the rule to his advantage.

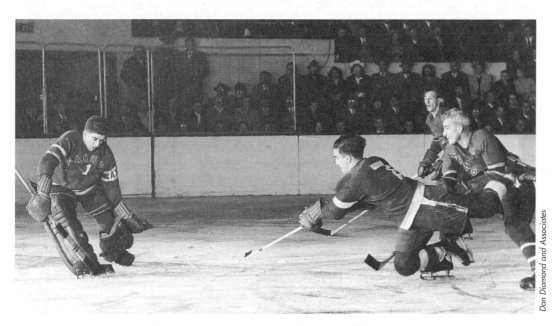

Although New York Ranger defender Neil Colville (right) tripped up Detroit's Ted Lindsay on this play, "Terrible" Ted still managed to slip the puck past Ranger netminder Chuck Rayner.

Two aspects of the major-penalty rule played a part in this drama. First, any player who received three majors in one season would be suspended for one game. When that player returned to action, his slate would be wiped clean.

Second, in an attempt to ward off bench-clearing altercations, the League decided that a major penalty would be assessed to any player who went onto the ice while his team was at full strength.

On February 18, 1932, the Toronto Maple Leafs were battling the New York Rangers at Maple Leaf Gardens. Two of the Leafs' main charges, Charlie Conacher and Red Horner, were nursing nagging injuries and, although they took part in the pregame warm-up, they saw little action. It appeared that neither player would be available for the Leafs' next match on the 20th against the Montreal Maroons.

Late in the game, with Toronto holding a 5–3 lead, coach Dick Irvin had a brainstorm. Since both Conacher and Horner already had two majors on their slates, Irvin decided to put both of them on the ice late in the game. Both men would then be the balance of the game, but a substitute shall be permitted to replace the player so suspended after five minutes have elapsed. (Major penalty plus game misconduct with automatic fine of two hundred dollars ($200).) (NOTE) In accordance with Rule 58(c) a goalkeeper shall not be assessed a game misconduct penalty when he is being assessed a major penalty for high-sticking.

penalized for going onto the ice while their team was at full strength and suspended for one game that they were sure to miss anyway because of their injuries. Even better, they would return with clean penalty records. Sure enough, with only seconds left on the clock Irvin sent both Conacher and Horner out onto the ice, giving referee Mike Rodden little choice but to penalize both men.

The ruse could have worked perfectly except for the fact that both players were badly hurt and the Toronto newspapers reported on Irvin's deception in all its detail. NHL president Frank Calder called Irvin on the carpet and instructed the Toronto bench boss to prove that both Conacher and Horner were ready and able to play. That, unfortunately, was one thing that Irvin had trouble accomplishing. Conacher had cracked a bone in his wrist and would miss four games, while Horner would be gone from the lineup for six. Calder ruled that "it does not follow that the inevitable suspension must apply to the next game in which the Leafs are scheduled to play. The rule states that the suspension shall be enforced for one game and therefore is not specific as to when said suspension shall take place." When Horner and Conacher were cleared to play by the Maple Leaf doctors, they were each forced to sit out a game to "pay their penalty." Both men were healthy and available for the playoffs, however, and helped the Maple Leafs win the first Stanley Cup title in franchise history.

Misconduct: Place both hands on hips.

RULE 29

(a) In the event of "MISCON-DUCT" penalties to any players except the goalkeeper, the players shall be ruled off the ice for a period of ten minutes each. A substitute player is permitted to immediately replace a player serving a misconduct penalty. A player whose misconduct penalty has expired shall remain in the penalty box until the next stoppage of play. . . .

MISCONDUCT PENALTIES

Misconduct wasn't defined in the rule book until the 1937–38 season. It came about as part of a larger effort by the NHL to curtail verbal and physical abuse of officials by both players and management.

The situation that may have made clear the need for the misconduct occurred during game two of the Toronto Maple Leafs–Boston Bruins quarter-final series on March 26, 1936. In that game, referee Odie Cleghorn nailed Bruin Eddie Shore with a 10-minute penalty for misconduct even though no such penalty was on the books at the time. Although it was Leaf Frank "King" Clancy's skill with the verbal needle that had incited Shore's undisciplined actions, Shore got the blame, Clancy got the credit, and the Leafs got the win.

Hockey Hall of Fame

The Leafs and Bruins were playing the back half of a two-game, total-goal series with Boston ahead 3 goals to none. The Bruins carried a 1–0 lead into the second period of game two when Eddie Shore was penalized for tripping. While he stewed in the penalty box, Charlie Conacher and Red Horner each scored to bring the Leafs to within 2 goals of the Bruins in the series. Later in the period, Conacher slammed forward Red Beattie to the ice, but no penalty was called. Conacher then tripped up Shore, but once again Cleghorn kept the whistle in his pocket.

Moments later Shore and Clancy were lined up alongside each other in the faceoff circle, and Clancy leaned over to the hard-rock Boston defenseman and said, "That Cleghorn's blind, Eddie, he's robbing you sure as hell. Look how he blew that call on Beattie." Shore glared back at Clancy, then did a slow burn at Cleghorn. Suddenly Shore bolted from the face-off circle and started yelling at Cleghorn, saying that Horner had been in the crease when he scored the Leafs' second goal. Even Clancy didn't know where that had come from—but he wasn't about to interrupt Shore's putting his skate in his mouth. Cleghorn ignored Shore, but when the Bruin rear guard wouldn't return to the faceoff area, the rattled referee thumbed him to the box for 2 minutes. Shore then retrieved the puck and duffed it off the referee's hindquarters. For Cleghorn, that was the bottom line. He wheeled around and sent Shore to the box for 10 minutes. While Shore was resting

King Clancy (left) and his gift of gab played an important role in helping put Eddie Shore in the penalty box and allowing the Toronto Maple Leafs to defeat the Boston Bruins in the 1936 quarterfinals.

in the sin bin, the Leafs scored 4 more goals to win the game and take the series 8 goals to 6.

One year later the 10-minute misconduct officially became part of the *NHL Rule Book*.

🏒 RULE 30

A "MATCH" penalty involves the suspension of a player for the balance of the game and the offender shall be ordered to the dressing room immediately. A substitute player is permitted to replace the penalized player after five minutes playing time has elapsed when the penalty is imposed under Rule 44—Attempt to Injure or Rule 49—Deliberate Injury of Opponents. . . .

MATCH PENALTIES

The match penalty is as old as the game itself. As mentioned earlier, the first form of penalty was of the "match" variety, meaning expulsion from the game. Since the formation of the NHL in 1917–18, the match penalty has been reserved for those players who deliberately attempt to injure an opponent through stick use, kicking, head-butting, or other flagrant fouls.

In 1922–23 a player committing a match foul was sent to the penalty box without substitution for 20 minutes. When the 20-minute sentence had been served, that player was ruled off the ice for the remainder of the match, but a substitute was allowed to take his place.

This New York Rangers–Montreal Canadiens battle on March 24, 1935 resulted in a match penalty being assessed to Montreal's Nels Crutchfield.

This rule led to an interesting turn of events in the 1935 playoff series between the New York Rangers and Montreal Canadiens. Near the end of the second period of game one on March 24, 1935, Canadien center Nels Crutchfield collided with Ranger Bill Cook, who was severely cut by Crutchfield's high-stick. Both benches emptied and soon the ice surface was full of players, police, managers, trainers, coaches, owners, and rink attendants. When peace was finally restored, Crutchfield was given a match and a minor penalty and sent to the penalty box for 22 minutes. With the other penalties taken into consideration, the Canadiens still had to play a man short for over 13 minutes.

When the third period began, Cook reappeared on the ice wearing a helmet and a turbanlike bandage. He had also changed his jersey, borrowing teammate Bill MacKenzie's number-11 sweater because his own was torn and covered with blood. At the 12:31 mark of the third period, with the Canadiens still shorthanded, Cook scored the game-winning goal to give the Rangers a 2–1 victory over the Canadiens.

However, repeated offenses also resulted in a type of "match" foul. If a player committed a foul, be it of the minor or the major variety, his first penalty was 2 minutes or 5 minutes. If the player committed the same foul again in the same game, he was penalized for 10 minutes. A third foul would result in expulsion from the match.

By the 1950s match-penalty rules were altered slightly. Players were immediately ruled off the ice for the remainder of the game, and although the player was still charged with 20 minutes of penalty time, his team was able to use a substitute. Because match penalties were usually handed out in conjunction with other fouls, the offending team often still had to play shorthanded for some length of time.

Any player charged with a match penalty is not permitted to play in subsequent games until his case is reviewed by the president of the League. This created problems for the Montreal Canadiens in March 1955, when Maurice Richard was faced with a season-ending suspension.

On the weekend of March 12–13, 1955, the Montreal Canadiens and Boston Bruins met in a pivotal home-and-home series that was crucial to both franchises. The Canadiens were involved in a tight race with the Detroit Red Wings for first place in the standings and home-ice advantage in the play-offs. Maurice "Rocket" Richard, who had never won the Art Ross Trophy, was in a neck-and-neck battle with teammate Bernie Geoffrion for the scoring crown. The Bruins, meanwhile, were attempting to climb from fourth to third place in the League's standings.

Montreal squeezed out a 2–1 victory on home ice in the series opener. In game two, the Canadiens were trailing 4–1 with 7 minutes remaining in the third period when referee Frank Udvari signaled a penalty to Bruin Warren Godfrey, giving the Habs a late-game powerplay opportunity. Midway through the man advantage, coach Dick Irvin pulled Jacques Plante and put out a sixth attacker. As the Canadiens stormed into the Bruins' zone, Boston defenseman Hal Laycoe clipped Maurice Richard with his stick. Udvari saw the infraction and raised his arm to signal another penalty, but allowed the play to proceed because the Habs still had possession of the puck. Meanwhile, Richard noticed he was bleeding. It was common knowledge that nothing ignited the Rocket's notoriously short temper more than the sight of his own blood. Richard immediately went after Laycoe and slashed him across the shoulders with his stick. The linesmen jumped in, grabbed Richard's stick, and tried to separate the combatants. The Rocket broke free, grabbed another stick, and attacked Laycoe again. Once again the linesmen intervened.

At this point, the facts and the fiction seem to intermingle. What is known is that somehow Richard broke free, found another stick, and hit Laycoe a third time. When linesman Cliff Thompson clutched Richard from behind a third time, the Rocket fired a couple of hard right jabs into the official's face. Finally, after 5 minutes of chaos, Richard was brought under control and sent to the Garden clinic for repairs. Referee Udvari issued a match penalty to Richard and signaled a major penalty to Laycoe. When Laycoe refused to go to the penalty box, Udvari upped the ante with an additional 10-minute misconduct.

There are those who believe that a Montreal player— Doug Harvey usually gets the credit, or the blame, depending on your perspective—helped Richard break free from the linesmen and may even have given him the stick he used for the final assault on Laycoe. There is a precedent supporting that opinion. Earlier in the season, Richard had been involved in a similar confrontation with Bob Bailey of the Maple Leafs. On that occasion, Richard's stick had been taken from him and no one on the ice would give him another. Angry that none of his teammates would help him, Richard had slapped referee George Hayes with his empty glove. If Harvey intervened, perhaps it was to keep Richard from again attacking the on-ice officials.

Richard had escaped penalty in the Bob Bailey incident, but his outburst in Boston did not go unnoticed. NHL president Clarence Campbell suspended the Canadien star for the last three games of the regular season and for the entire playoffs. The Canadiens ended up losing two of their final three regular-season contests, including the infamous forfeit game (see Rule 77) and a 6–0 decision to Detroit. They finished 2 points behind the Red Wings. Bernie Geoffrion picked up 3 points in the Canadiens' lone win, a 4–2 triumph over the New York Rangers, to clinch the scoring title that Richard would never win.

PENALTY SHOT

The original wording of the rule adopted by the NHL owners on September 22, 1934, reads as follows: "When a player is tripped and thus prevented from having a clear shot on goal, having no other player to pass than the offending player, a penalty shot shall be awarded to the non-offending side. This original rule, which remained in effect from 1934–35 through 1937–38, required that the player taking the shot do so from within a 10-foot circle located 38 feet from the goal. The player was not allowed to make any contact with the puck once it left the circle, while the goaltender could not advance more than 1 foot from his goal line while the shot was being taken.

When the penalty-shot rule was first introduced prior to the 1934–35 season, the player responsible for the penalty-shot offense also had to serve a penalty, regardless of whether a goal had been scored or not. While this seemed to constitute double punishment, the rule remained in effect

RULE 31

(a) Any infraction of the rules which calls for a "PENALTY SHOT" shall be taken as follows:

The Referee shall ask to announce over the public address system the name of the player designated by him or selected by the team entitled to take the shot (as appropriate) and shall then place the puck on the center face-off spot and the player taking the shot will, on the instruction of the Referee, play the puck from there and shall attempt to score on the goalkeeper. . . .

until the 1941–42 season and led to some interesting incidents. During game one of the 1938 semifinal series between the Chicago Black Hawks and New York Americans, the Amerks were leading 2–1 midway through the third period when Lorne Carr was hauled down by Black Hawk defenseman Paul Thompson. Referee Mickey Ion signaled for a penalty shot, but Carr was blanked by Black Hawk goaltender Mike Karakas. However, Paul Thompson was still required to serve a 2-minute minor. While Thompson stewed in the sin bin, New York American star Sweeney Schriner scored the insurance goal in a 3–1 win.

There have been many changes in the penalty-shot rule over the last sixty years. The criteria were expanded in 1937–38 to provide for a penalty shot when any defensive player other than the goaltender fell on the puck within 10 feet of the goal.

In 1941–42 penalty shots were divided into two categories: minor and major. Minor shots were awarded for infractions committed by a goaltender (holding the puck with his hands or arms for more than 3 seconds; deliberately throwing a puck toward the opponent's goal or into the stands; deliberately shooting a puck into the stands), while major shots were awarded for infractions by skaters (falling on a puck in the goal crease or tripping an opponent who is on a breakaway). The rules governing a minor-penalty shot required the player to skate in from center ice and release the shot before reaching a line located 28 feet from the goal. A major-penalty shot allowed a player to start at his opponent's blueline, skate in, and release his shot at any point in front of the goal crease.

Beginning in 1945–46, the rules governing all penalty shots allowed players to skate in from the far blueline and take their shots from any point before the goal crease. Center ice then became the starting point for penalty shots in 1962–63.

In 1961–62 penalty shots were, for the first time, taken by the player against whom the foul had been committed. In the event of a penalty shot being called when no particular player had been fouled, the penalty shot was to be taken by any player on the ice when the foul was committed.

Because the rules governing penalty shots were frequently revised between 1934 and 1945, game strategy sometimes

ALL-TIME PENALTY SHOT SUMMARY
(Regular Season)

Season	Shots	Goals	%	Season	Shots	Goals	%
1934–35	29	4	13.8	1965–66	0	0	0.0
1935–36	5	4	80.0	1966–67	7	4	57.1
1936–37	1	1	100.0	1967–68	8	2	25.0
1937–38	8	1	12.5	1968–69	4	1	25.0
1938–39	3	1	33.3	1969–70	3	0	0.0
1939–40	2	2	100.0	1970–71	5	2	40.0
1940–41	2	1	50.0	1971–72	9	3	33.3
1941–42	7	7	100.0	1972–73	8	2	25.0
1942–43	3	2	66.6	1973–74	13	5	38.5
1943–44	3	1	33.3	1974–75	14	6	42.9
1944–45	4	3	75.0	1975–76	11	1	9.1
1945–46	3	2	66.6	1976–77	13	5	38.5
1946–47	0	0	0.0	1977–78	14	2	14.3
1947–48	1	0	0.0	1978–79	10	2	20.0
1948–49	2	1	50.0	1979–80	14	5	35.7
1949–50	2	2	100.0	1980–81	12	3	25.0
1950–51	1	0	0.0	1981–82	9	5	55.6
1951–52	1	1	100.0	1982–83	15	6	40.0
1952–53	2	2	100.0	1983–84	18	10	55.6
1953–54	0	0	0.0	1984–85	19	9	47.4
1954–55	1	0	0.0	1985–86	15	6	40.0
1955–56	0	0	0.0	1986–87	25	13	52.0
1956–57	1	1	100.0	1987–88	21	9	42.9
1957–58	0	0	0.0	1988–89	26	7	27.0
1958–59	0	0	0.0	1989–90	16	9	37.5
1959–60	1	0	0.0	1990–91	20	9	45.0
1960–61	0	0	0.0	1991–92	29	12	41.4
1961–62	10	4	40.0	1992–93	30	14	46.7
1962–63	4	1	25.0	1993–94	27	11	40.7
1963–64	9	4	44.4	1994–95	17	3	17.6
1964–65	3	2	66.6	1995–96	27	5	18.5

became a war of wills among the coaches, captains, and referees as to who had a better knowledge of the rule book.

Since the penalty shot was adopted by the National Hockey League in 1934, there have been a total of 207 goals

Damian Rhodes of the Toronto Maple Leafs stopped this penalty shot attempt by Edmonton Oiler forward Scott Pearson on November 20, 1993.

Hockey Hall of Fame

scored on 523 shots, for a 39.6 percent success rate for shooters. The officials took great liberties in the penalty shot's first season, awarding 29 shots in just 216 regular-season games.

During a game between the Boston Bruins and the Toronto Maple Leafs on February 19, 1944, Jackie Hamilton was awarded a penalty shot after being pulled down by Boston's Dit Clapper. Referee Norm Lamport tried to ignore the Bruins' howls of protest but appeared to be confused. He placed the puck at center ice and ordered the penalty shot to begin. Hamilton picked up the puck, skated in toward goaltender Bert Gardiner, and scored. Clapper, who was the Bruins' captain at the time, protested the goal, pointing out that on a penalty shot the puck was to be placed at the opposite blueline, not at center ice. Lamport stood corrected, and he had no choice but to eat crow. He approached the Leafs' bench and informed coach Hap Day of his error. He then placed the puck on the blueline and had Hamilton come out again. Hamilton calmly retrieved the puck, skated in, and scored, becoming the only player to score twice on the same penalty shot.

In another instance a referee's confusion over the penalty-shot rule may have cost a player a shot at the NHL scoring title. During a game between the Boston Bruins and Chicago Black Hawks on November 8, 1959, Bruin Bronco Horvath got behind the Black Hawk defense and had a clear breakaway on goaltender Glenn Hall. When Hawk defenseman Al Arbour threw his stick in an attempt to knock the puck off Horvath's stick, referee Dalton McArthur signaled a penalty shot, which was the proper call.

Now, by today's rules, the player who had been fouled takes the penalty shot, but in 1958 the fouled team could appoint anyone to take the shot. However, since this was only the tenth penalty shot that had been called in the past ten years, McArthur naturally became confused. Instead of permitting the Bruins to choose their own penalty shooter, he allowed the Black Hawks to make the selection. Naturally, the Boston bench was incensed. Boston general manager Lynn Patrick came down from the press box waving an *NHL Rule Book* and offered to pay his own coach's fine if he would go on the ice and point out McArthur's folly. Meanwhile, the Hawks appointed seldom-used Larry Leach to take the shot, and he was stopped easily by Glenn Hall. Horvath, who was in the midst of an NHL-record twenty-two-game scoring streak, ended up missing the scoring title by a single point.

GOALKEEPER'S PENALTIES

In the first fifteen years of the NHL's existence it was very rare for a goaltender to be penalized. However, when the goalie did commit an infraction he was required to serve the penalty himself, forcing his team to play without a goaltender. Usually a defenseman stepped into the net, using only the goal stick for protection. On December 2, 1931, the Chicago Black Hawks defeated the Montreal Canadiens 2–1 on a last-second goal by Tommy Cook. Cook scored the game-winner on Canadien defenseman Albert "Battleship" Leduc, who was protecting the crease for penalized goaltender George Hainsworth.

In 1932–33 a rule was introduced allowing the offending team to appoint a position player to take the goalie's place. Any goals allowed by the player were charged to the penalized goaltender's record. This new rule was given a full

RULE 32

(a) A goalkeeper shall not be sent to the penalty bench for an offense which incurs a minor penalty, but instead, the minor penalty shall be served by another member of his team who was on the ice when the offense was committed. . . .

workout on March 15, 1933, during a game between the Toronto Maple Leafs and Boston Bruins. Four minutes into the game, Leaf goalie Lorne Chabot tripped up Cooney Weiland and was sent to the penalty box. Red Horner took Chabot's place in net and quickly gave up a goal. Alex Levinsky then tried his luck in net but had none, as the Bruins scored on their first shot. Leaf coach Dick Irvin then put King Clancy in the "hempen hut," but the Bruins quickly scored their third goal. Leaf general manager Conn Smythe was so upset at the penalty call and its results that he attacked referee Bill Stewart and had to be removed from the Leafs' bench by the local constabulary.

Of all the position players to play in goal, it was Hall of Fame forward Charlie Conacher who had the most success. The Big Bomber stood in for a penalized goalie on three different occasions, playing a total of 9 minutes without allowing a goal. Conacher's first appearance in goal came during the final week of the 1932–33 season in a game between the Detroit Falcons and Toronto Maple Leafs. In that game, Maple Leaf goaltender Lorne Chabot was penalized 2 minutes for high-sticking Falcon forward Ebbie Goodfellow. Conacher held the Falcons scoreless, but Detroit still downed Toronto 1–0. It was the final home-ice victory in the history of the Falcon franchise. The team was sold in the off-season and renamed the Red Wings before the start of the 1933–34 campaign. Conacher was used again during the 1934–35 and 1937–38 seasons.

By 1937–38 a goaltender receiving a major penalty was allowed to remain in goal with a substitute serving his penalty. If a goalie received a minor penalty, he still had to serve his sentence, but position players were allowed to use his gloves and sticks in net. In 1941–42 the penalty rules concerning goalies were changed again. For a minor infraction, a "minor"-penalty shot was awarded to the opposing team, which allowed a player to skate to within 28 feet of the goal and take a shot.

(b) A goalkeeper shall not be sent to the penalty bench for an offense which incurs a major penalty, but instead, the major penalty shall be served by another member of his team who was on the ice when the offense was committed. . . .

Prior to Rule 32(b), if a goaltender received a major penalty, the opposing team was awarded a penalty shot. In the first ten years of the rule's existence it had been called into effect only a handful of times, usually without controversy. That changed after incidents in 1948 and 1949.

The first occurred during the 1948 Stanley Cup finals between the Detroit Red Wings and Toronto Maple Leafs. As the teams were leaving the ice at the conclusion of game two, mild-mannered Red Wing winger Jim Conacher elbowed Maple Leaf Joe Klukay. This brought the teams back onto the ice and a small skirmish ensued. Just as the waters were beginning to calm, goaltenders Harry Lumley and Turk Broda skated toward each other and began fighting. Both goalies earned misconduct penalties, but it was clear that had the incident occurred during regulation time, both netminders would have deserved major penalties for fighting. The referee would have had an interesting situation on his hands had he awarded each team a penalty shot.

The final straw came the following season during a game between the Montreal Canadiens and Detroit Red Wings on January 16, 1949. Late in the game, Canadien Ken Reardon bumped Wing goaltender Harry Lumley, an infraction that referee Jim Primeau immediately signaled as interference against the goaltender. When Primeau turned to report the penalty, Lumley reacted to Reardon's bump by dropping his gloves and landing several punches on Reardon's head, all unseen by the referee. Primeau gave Reardon the only penalty on the play, which created chaos on the Montreal bench. The Habs refused to continue the game until Primeau either penalized Lumley or gave the Habs a penalty shot. Primeau, who hadn't seen Lumley's tirade, refused. Murph Chamberlain uttered a few expletives and was given a misconduct. Ken Mosdell banged the referee's hand with his stick and received a misconduct as well.

When the Habs still refused to play, Primeau issued a delay-of-game penalty. With that, the Canadiens reluctantly skated to the faceoff circle and the game continued without incident. Still, the League realized it had a problem on its hands when referee Primeau reported he had been handicapped by the goaltender's major-penalty rule.

At the NHL's annual Board of Governors meeting on June 1, 1949, subsection (b) was added to Rule 32, allowing for penalty-box substitution in the event that a goaltender was assessed a major penalty.

It was a case of too many roving goalies that forced the NHL to amend Rule 32 by adding subsection (i). Although in

(i) If a goalkeeper participates in the play in any manner when he is beyond the center red line, a minor penalty shall be imposed upon him.

the NHL's first decades most goaltenders stayed close to home, there were exceptions, such as New York Ranger netminder "Bonnie Prince" Charlie Rayner. Rayner would often join in the play by skating up to the opposing team's blueline during a delayed penalty. Rayner's most famous journey occurred during a New York Rangers–Montreal Canadiens match on February 1, 1947. With the Rangers trailing the Flying Frenchmen 2–1 late in the game, Rayner made several mad dashes into the Habs' zone in an attempt to score the equalizer. After the rule changes of 1948, Rayner never realized his dream of scoring an NHL goal, but he did gain some measure of satisfaction. In the spring of 1951 Rayner and his Ranger teammates were on a barnstorming tour of the Maritime provinces. In a game against the Maritime Senior League All Stars on March 31, 1951, Rayner picked up a rebound, wheeled his way through the All Star defense, and neatly deposited a backhander past the Maritime netminder.

Hockey Hall of Fame

Jacques Plante was one of the first goaltenders to leave his crease to either smother a loose puck or clear it out of his own zone.

During the 1950s and early 1960s, goalies became increasingly involved in play behind their own goal lines. Montreal Canadien Jacques Plante repeatedly left his crease to stop the puck behind the net for his defensemen, pass it up ice to his forwards, or freeze it for a stoppage in play. Numerous goalies, including Chicago Black Hawk Glenn Hall and Boston Bruin Don Head, emulated the earlier exploits of Chuck Rayner by playing the point on a delayed penalty.

This new breed of roaming goalies created many anxious moments for league officials. Netminders were becoming involved in more fights, and more games were being delayed while galloping goalies recovered after taking solid bodychecks from opposing defensemen. Prior to the start of the 1962–63 season, the NHL passed new legislation restricting goalies from skating past their own bluelines.

DELAYED PENALTIES

The concept of the delayed penalty was first utilized by the Pacific Coast Hockey Association during the 1918–19 season to ensure that there would never be fewer than four players on the ice at any given time. Although the National Hockey League adopted the idea of a delayed penalty in 1925–26, it wasn't until the 1943–44 season that a separate delayed-penalty rule was included in the *NHL Rule Book*.

The penalty timekeeper has never had an easy job dealing with delayed penalties. Imagine how difficult this would have been before the era of digital clocks, video replay, and audio communication with upstairs observers. Usually, everything fell into place. But in the case of George Ogg, confusion almost led to disaster for the Toronto Maple Leafs. Ogg became rattled during the 1964 playoffs and it nearly cost the Leafs a chance at a third consecutive Stanley Cup title.

Trouble was in the air even before the Montreal Canadiens and Toronto Maple Leafs met in game one of the 1964 semifinals. Toronto club owner Stafford Smythe predicted that referee Frank Udvari would penalize a Leaf in the first minute of each period, providing plenty of action in the penalty box.

The game indeed began with a slew of penalties. In the first 2 minutes of the game, four Maple Leafs found their way to the penalty box—including the gentlemanly Dave Keon. The problems arose from the NHL's delayed-penalty system. No more than two minor penalties can be served at once, so the third and fourth penalties don't begin to tick down until the first two have expired.

Delayed Penalty: Referee extends arm and points to penalized player.

RULE 33

(a) If a third player of any team shall be penalized while two players of the same team are serving penalties, the penalty time of the third player shall not commence until the penalty time of one of the two players already penalized has elapsed. Nevertheless, the third player penalized must at once proceed to the penalty bench but may be replaced by a substitute until such time as the penalty time of the penalized player shall commence.

(b) When any team shall have three players serving penalties at the same time and because of the delayed penalty rule, a substitute for the third offender is on the ice, none of the three penalized players on the penalty bench may return to the ice until play has stopped. When play has been stopped, the player whose full penalty has expired may return to the play. . . .

Maple Leaf Dave Keon and Canadien Jean-Guy Talbot were both penalized at the 2:29 mark of the first period and, according to the rules, both had to return to the ice at the same time once their penalties had been served. Bob Baun and Bob Pulford were already in the box when Keon entered. Baun's penalty was slated to expire first at the 4:20 mark, so it was at this point that Keon's 2 minutes would begin to be served. Pulford was scheduled to return to the ice at the 5:06 mark. Pulford tried to leave the box at the appointed time, but he was told not to. This was the first indication that Ogg was confused. Pulford did eventually get out of the box at the next stoppage in play. At the 6:20 mark, Talbot of the Canadiens left the box, having served 2 minutes that began when Keon's penalty started to count down, but Ogg thought Keon was supposed to stay until the 6:51 mark. This gave the Canadiens an undeserved extra man, which they used to their full advantage. Talbot left the box, picked up a loose puck, and fed a pass to Bernie Geoffrion, who snapped a shot past Johnny Bower to give the Canadiens a lead they would never surrender. They won the game 2–0 and took a 1–0 lead in the best-of-seven set.

Despite protests by the Leafs, Udvari let the goal stand. An official investigation was conducted by Clarence Campbell after the game and, although he admitted that Ogg had been in error, he let the goal and game results stand. Nothing went right for the Leafs—including Smythe's prediction. Udvari

A prolonged stay in the penalty box by Dave Keon (#14), seen here battling the Montreal Canadiens during the 1964 semi-finals, almost cost the Toronto Maple Leafs a shot at their third consecutive Stanley Cup title.

Hockey Hall of Fame

penalized the Leafs in the first minute of the second (Baun at 0:35) and third (Stanley at 1:00) periods, but was 6 seconds off in the opening frame. The Leafs escaped judgment until Frank Mahovlich was nabbed for tripping at the 66-second mark.

CALLING OF PENALTIES

Penalties have been called in hockey since the game was first governed by rules. Play was stopped and the guilty player either warned, fined, or sent off to the penalty box, depending on the era.

In the 1940s referee Bill Chadwick began using hand gestures to signal the penalties he was calling on the ice. He would give a chopping gesture to his leg to indicate tripping; grasp an imaginary stick and raise his hands in the air to denote high-sticking; or hold his wrist in front of his body to convey a holding call. Chadwick explained that he devised these gestures to give himself something to do with his hands, but he also wanted to communicate the calls he was making to fans. Chadwick's signals were initially dismissed as unnecessarily showy, but it soon became clear that fans enjoyed these gestures and took from them a better understanding of the game.

RULE 34

(a) Should an infraction of the rules which would call for a minor, major, misconduct, game misconduct or match penalty be committed by a player of the side in possession of the puck, the Referee shall immediately blow his whistle and penalize the offending player. . . .

(b) Should an infraction of the rules which would call for a minor, major, misconduct, game misconduct or match penalty be committed by a player of the team not in possession of the puck, the Referee will blow his whistle and impose the penalty on the offending player upon completion of the play by the team in possession of the puck. . . .

Hockey Hall of Fame

Bill Chadwick, the first referee to use hand gestures to signal penalties, nails Montreal Canadien forward Murph Chamberlain for a tripping offense.

The NHL introduced hand signals leaguewide in two phases. Prior to the start of the 1947–48 season it specified four official hand signals, none of which pertained to penalties. Icing (arms folded on chest), slow whistle (arm in the air), intentional offside (arm straight out in front of body), and washout (sweeping motion with arms in front of chest) were the first official signals used by NHL officials.

Eventually the signals first used by Chadwick and improved upon by other officials became part of the NHL's official on-ice code. Today they are as much a part of the game as goals, assists, and great saves.

CHAPTER FIVE

OFFICIALS

APPOINTMENT OF OFFICIALS

WHEN ART FARRELL wrote his rule book in 1898, the only officials required for a game were a referee and two goal umpires. By 1927–28 the rules stated that, in addition to the referee and goal judges (umpires), a penalty recorder and scorer, a timekeeper, and an assistant referee must be in attendance for a game to be played. Today the NHL game is played with a referee and two linesmen on-ice and an official scorer, game timekeeper, penalty timekeeper, two goal judges, and a video goal judge off-ice.

It is the responsibility of the home team to provide off-ice officials in the regular season. Out-of-town off-ice officials are used for playoff games. The home team also provided the linesmen until the 1945–46 season, when a full slate of neutral on-ice officials was required.

In the 1930s, when the home team appointed the officials, it wasn't uncommon for changes to be made at the request of the opposing coach or general manager. In fact, between games three and four of the 1938 Stanley Cup finals, Toronto Maple Leaf manager Conn Smythe demanded the replacement of an

RULE 35

(a) The Commissioner shall appoint a Referee, two Linesmen, Game Timekeeper, Penalty Time-keeper, Official Scorer and two Goal Judges for each game.

THE ANNOTATED RULES OF HOCKEY

78

entire officiating crew—from referee to timekeeper. (See Rule 39, Penalty Timekeeper for details.)

REFEREE

When Clarence Campbell began his career as a referee, he used a bell, not a whistle, to signal stops in play. Campbell found that steel whistles stuck to his lips in cold arenas and that opponents were less inclined to attack a referee wielding a heavy brass or steel bell. (Hockey Hall of Fame)

🏒 **RULE 36**

(a) The REFEREE shall have general supervision of the game and shall have full control of all game officials and players during the game, including stoppages; and in case of any dispute, his decision shall be final. . . .

The on-ice arbiter in hockey has always been the referee. During the sport's first quarter century, games were handled by one official. When the NHL was formed the rule book stipulated that each game would be worked by one referee "and when necessary, an assistant." The assistant would have the same duties as the referee and could call offsides and fouls undetected by the referee.

Despite this rule, for the first nine years of NHL play only one official was used in a game. Early in the 1926–27 season, though, it became clear that the job had become too demanding for one on-ice official to handle by himself. This point was made clear during a Boston Bruins–Montreal Maroons game on November 23, 1926. Midway through the contest the referee rang his bell (the whistle had yet to be introduced) and called the teams to center ice, where he demanded that the players improve their behavior or he would call off the game. Days later the NHL began experimenting with a system that employed a referee and a linesman. These two officials were assigned duties similar to those given to the referee and two linesmen used in organized hockey today.

On January 4, 1933, the League decided to go with a referee-plus-assistant-referee (called a "judge of play") system, with each official handling one side of the rink. The head referee would wear a white sweater and dark pants, while the assistant would wear a blue sweater and dark pants. In February 1935 the NHL passed a new rule that required the referees to switch sides during a game.

The two-referee system was dropped prior to the 1937–38 season when the linesman was reintroduced.

It was a common practice to hire former players to serve as referees. King Clancy, Frank Foyston, Babe Dye, Hap Day, and Odie Cleghorn were just a few of the many players who remained in the game to work as on-ice officials. However, since there were no referee schools or officials' training camps at this time, the former players were just encouraged to "call 'em like you see 'em."

In 1936 the NHL opened its first referee training camp and school with Bill Stewart in charge. Stewart, who also worked as a major league baseball umpire, retired as a referee in 1937–38 to coach the Chicago Black Hawks. Despite leading the Black Hawks to the Stanley Cup championship in his rookie season behind the bench, Stewart was fired. He returned to refereeing in 1940. Stewart's grandson Paul, who played with the WHA's and NHL's Quebec Nordiques, is the only former NHL player currently working as a referee in the League. Another former player, Kevin McGuire, is a referee in the minors.

Rule 36(k) had been in the books for many years when it was given a true workout on a snowy night in Hartford during the 1982–83 season. On January 15, 1983, a wild snowstorm blanketed New England, causing referee Ron Fournier and linesman Dan Marouelli to be late for a game between the Hartford Whalers and New Jersey Devils. When it became apparent that the two officials would not arrive on time, it was determined that linesman Ron Foyt, who had arrived, would act as referee, and that one player from each team would serve as a linesman. Whaler defenseman Mickey Volcan and Devil winger Garry Howatt, both of whom were nursing minor injuries, were picked to work the game, and they skated out in sweatshirts and sweatpants to act as linesmen. Foyt handled all the faceoffs, leaving Howatt and Volcan to whistle down offsides and icings. There were no problems or altercations in the first period, and when Marouelli and Fournier arrived before the start of the second frame, Volcan and Howatt were out of their jobs. The Whalers won the game 2–1 in front of a storm-braving crowd of 4,812 fans.

Eleven days later bad luck bedeviled referee Dave Newell in a game between New Jersey and the Los Angeles Kings when he was hit by a stray shot, breaking his wrist. With the referee unable to continue, senior linesman Jim Christison took over as referee for the remainder of the game.

During the regular season it's not required that spare officials be in attendance at NHL games. If a referee or linesman should be injured or take ill, the game continues with only two on-ice officials. And if, by chance, one of the League's spares is in attendance, he can be called in as a

(k) If, through misadventure or sickness, the Referee and Linesmen appointed are prevented from appearing, the Managers or Coaches of the two clubs shall agree on a Referee and Linesman. If they are unable to agree, they shall appoint a player from each side who shall act as Referee and Linesman; the player of the home club acting as Referee and the player of the visiting club as Linesman.

(n) If, owing to illness or accident, the Referee is unable to continue to officiate, one of the Linesmen shall perform the duties of the Referee during the balance of the game, the Linesman to be selected by the Referee. In the event that an NHL Supervisor is in attendance at a game where a spare official is present, he shall have the authority to substitute the injured Referee with the spare official.

replacement. Midway through the 1978–79 campaign, NHL history was made when Frank Udvari, a member of the Hockey Hall of Fame, came out of retirement and pulled on the striped jersey one more time.

Udvari had last blown his whistle as an NHL referee during the 1965–66 season but was still actively working for the League as a supervisor of officials. On December 30, 1979, he was in attendance at the New York Islanders–Atlanta Flames contest on Long Island when Dave Newell was severely cut with 1:30 remaining in the first period. Udvari volunteered to fill in and minutes later was on the ice, wearing a pair of skates borrowed from Islander star Bryan Trottier and his own dark suit pants. "I don't know why I decided to do it," Udvari admitted. "I was fifty-five at the time and hadn't worked a game in thirteen years. But the players made it easy for me to keep up."

Although the comeback was brief, Udvari made history by becoming the first Hockey Hall of Fame member to participate in a League game after being elected to the Hall.

The Richard Riot game of March 17, 1955, has been the only forfeited game in the NHL since the forfeit rule was introduced. This infamous game between the Detroit Red Wings and Montreal Canadiens is discussed in detail under Rule 77. When the game was suspended and eventually forfeited to the Red Wings, Detroit was leading 4–1. The game went into the record books with that result, with all goals, assists, and points counting in the statistics. Wing Red Kelly connected for a pair of goals, enabling him to lead all NHL rear guards in goal-scoring during the 1954–55 season. Earl "Dutch" Reibel also scored a pair of goals for the Red Wings, giving him the only 20-goal season of his career. Calum MacKay scored the lone goal for the Canadiens, notching what would prove to be the penultimate goal of his NHL career. Bernie Geoffrion did not register an assist on MacKay's goal, but he did collect three points in the Habs' 4–2 win over the New York Rangers two nights later, enabling him to win the scoring title by a single point over the suspended Richard.

Long before the forfeit rule was introduced, there was another game in which the scoring title was decided because of one team's refusal to play. On January 26, 1921, the

(q) In the event of failure by a club to comply with a provision of the League constitution, by-laws, resolutions, rules or regulations affecting the playing of a game, the Referee shall, if so directed by the Commissioner or his designee, refuse to permit the game to proceed until the offending club comes into compliance with such provision.

Should the offending club persist in its refusal to come into compliance, the Referee shall, with the prior approval of the Commissioner or his designee, declare the game forfeited and the non-offending club the winner. . . .

If the game is declared forfeited prior to its having commenced, the score shall be recorded as 1–0 and no player shall be credited with any personal statistics.

Ottawa Senators entered the third period with a 3–1 lead over the hometown Montreal Canadiens. At the 9:10 mark of the frame Canadien Didier Pitre deflected a shot by teammate Louis Berlinquette past Senator goalie Clint Benedict to make the score 3–2. Off the ensuing faceoff, the Senators rushed the Canadiens' net and scored an insurance goal. However, goal judge Riley Hern said the puck had never entered the net, and referee Cooper Smeaton refused to allow the goal.

Five minutes later Canadiens Odie Cleghorn and Harry Mummery rushed into the Ottawa zone. It was obvious to everyone, including official scorer Elmer Ferguson, that Mummery was at least 30 feet offside, but referee Smeaton allowed play to continue. Cleghorn shot the puck just as Mummery upended Benedict to score the tying marker. Smeaton allowed the goal and the Senators team refused to take the center-ice faceoff in protest. Smeaton dropped the puck, and Canadien Newsy Lalonde picked it up and skated untouched into the Senators' zone. As he wound up and shot, Senator netkeeper Clint Benedict stepped aside and let the puck go in. Smeaton faced the puck again and this time Lalonde passed off to Amos Arbour, who fired the puck into the unguarded cage to make the score 5–3. By this point, Senator captain Eddie Gerard had already moved most of his players to the dressing room as they refused to play the remainder of the match.

Smeaton waited a moment or two for the Ottawa players to change their minds before declaring the game over. The match went into the books as a 5–3 Montreal win, and all goals—including markers by Lalonde and Arbour—counted. Those goals allowed Lalonde to win the scoring title by 2 points over the Ottawa Senators' Cy Denneny.

LINESMAN

Linesmen were first employed in the NHL during the 1926–27 season and remained part of on-ice crews until 1933–34, when an on-ice crew had to consist of a referee and assistant referee who had similar authority to call penalties. In 1937–38 the linesman's position was reintroduced, providing each game with an official charged with calling offsides and icing, conducting faceoffs, and breaking up skirmishes. The League operated with one referee and one linesman until

If the game was in progress at the time it is declared forfeited, the score shall be recorded as zero for the loser and 1, or such greater number of goals that had been scored by it, for the winner; however, the players on both clubs shall be credited with all personal statistics earned up to the time the forfeit was declared.

RULE 37

(a) The duty of the LINESMAN is to determine any infractions of the rules concerning off-side play at the blue line or center line, or any violation of Rule 61—Icing the Puck. . . .

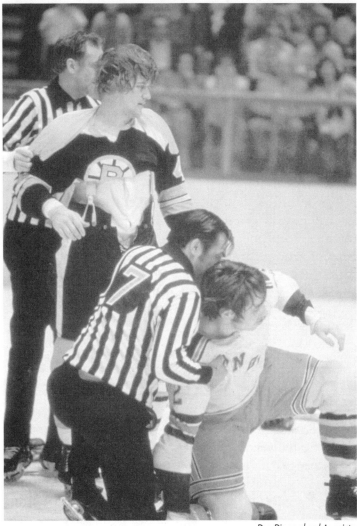

One of the less glamorous aspects of a linesman's duties is to intervene and separate players involved in scuffles, fisticuffs, and brawls. Here the linesmen separate Boston's Bobby Orr and New York Rangers defenseman Brad Park.

Dan Diamond and Associates

October 24, 1941, when the present system of one referee and two linesmen was introduced.

In 1945–46 a rule was passed requiring neutral linesmen on each rink. Prior to this rule change the home team would appoint the linesmen working its rink. Over the years linesmen have been given additional responsibility, but the control of the game and most penalty calls are still under the jurisdiction of the referee. In 1966–67 linesmen were given the right to call intent-to-injure major penalties that the referee may have missed. Linesmen have also been given the responsibility of calling stick fouls and, in 1982, were given the authority to stop play to award a goal if the referee had not seen the puck enter the net. In addition, linesmen were permitted to immediately stop play to call a major penalty; previously they could call a major, but had to wait until a play stoppage to inform the referee of the detected infraction. In 1986 the linesman calling a major penalty could also assess a minor penalty to a player on the opposite team who, through his actions, had provoked the major infraction.

GOAL JUDGE

In hockey's earliest days the goal judges or "umpires" were fans appointed just before game time. They could not always be counted on to be fair arbiters, so if a dispute arose concerning their objectivity, they were immediately replaced by other fans in attendance. The earliest goal judges stood on the ice behind the net in what certainly was a chilly and dangerous spot, because the goal area was open and devoid of any netting. If a goal was scored, the judge would raise his flag and collect the puck, and the game would continue. If the umpire failed to signal a goal being scored, he might have to deal with an assortment of "wild" shots from players on the wronged team on their next excursion down ice.

RULE 38

(a) There shall be one GOAL JUDGE at each goal. They shall not be members of either club engaged in a game, nor shall they be replaced during its progress, unless after the commencement of the game it becomes apparent that either Goal Judge, on account of partisanship or any other cause, is guilty of giving unjust decisions, when the Referee may appoint another Goal Judge to act in his stead.

(b) Goal Judges shall be stationed behind the goals during the progress of play, in properly protected areas, if possible, so that there can be no interference with their activities. They shall not change goals during the game.

Hockey Hall of Fame

In the early years of the game, goal judges stood on the ice behind the net where they were subjected to abuse from both the players and the fans.

As time went on, goal frames and goal nets were added and an area behind the end boards directly behind each net was provided for the goal judge, giving him more protection and a good view of the proceedings. The off-ice officials were provided by the home team and could be removed or replaced if one of the teams found fault with their performance. In the final game of the 1922 Stanley Cup finals between the Toronto St. Pats and the Vancouver Millionaires, goal judge Frank Warren was replaced at the request of the Vancouver team. In the first period, with Toronto up by a goal, Toronto's Harry Cameron and Vancouver's Alf Skinner were sent to the penalty box. Shortly after the faceoff, St. Pat Babe Dye took a shot from just over center that nicked Millionaire center-man Mickey MacKay's stick and seemed to sail past Millionaire goalie Hugh Lehman to give the St. Pats a 2–0 lead. The Vancouver bench insisted the puck had never entered the net, but Warren was adamant that a legal goal had been scored. The argument continued until the referee agreed to remove the goal judge. It was the first time in six years that a goal judge had to be replaced.

A similar situation occurred during game two of the Montreal Maroons–New York Rangers two-game total-goals semifinals in 1935. The game was played in Montreal with local off-ice officials. With the score tied at 1–1 after goals by Ranger Bill Cook and Maroon Cy Wentworth, Maroon forward Stew Evans scored to put the Montreal squad up by one. Or so he thought. The goal judge, Henri Quevillion, refused to allow the goal, insisting the puck had never entered the net. Evans and his teammates protested vehemently, but referee Bill Stewart upheld the goal judge's decision. It was then that the Maroons insisted Quevillion be replaced—one of the rare occasions that the home team has requested a local official be replaced. A Mr. Gauthier took Quevillion's spot on the hot seat and the game continued without further conflict. The match ended in a 3–3 tie but the Maroons won the series 5 goals to 4. Evans had reason to be upset. Quevillion's decision had robbed him of the opportunity to score his only playoff goal.

Until the 1950s goal judges were stationed behind the net but weren't situated in any sort of protective cubicle. During the 1960s the NHL required all goal judges to be

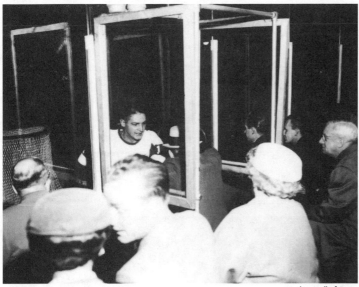

Even when goal judges were finally situated in protected areas behind the nets, they were still unable to escape the wrath of angry players such as Detroit Red Wings goaltender Terry Sawchuk.

seated in properly protected areas. Despite this regulation, Toronto's Maple Leaf Gardens still seats both goal judges on raised chairs without any additional protection.

Most goal judges are subjected to a barrage of bad language and occasional thrown garbage but a more entertaining event occurred during the decisive game of the 1938 semifinals between the Chicago Black Hawks and New York Americans. With the score tied at 1–1 in the second period, Alex Levinsky scored for Chicago to put the Hawks up 2–1. However, the goal light did not go on, causing fuss over at the Black Hawks' bench. The referee skated over to goal judge Mr. Suprenant's position behind the Chicago cage to inquire about the situation when he saw that a group of fans had grabbed Mr. Suprenant's hands and were preventing him from turning on the goal light. The tally stood, and the Hawks went on to win the game to reach the Stanley Cup finals.

PENALTY TIMEKEEPER

The penalty timekeeper has always been on the hot seat, especially in the Stanley Cup playoffs, when any wrong move could mean the difference between a team's winning and losing. We have already seen how confusion led timekeeper

RULE 39

(a) The PENALTY TIMEKEEPER shall keep, on the official forms provided, a correct record of all penalties imposed by the officials

including the names of the players penalized, the infractions penalized, the duration of each penalty and the time at which each penalty was imposed. . . .
(b) The Penalty Timekeeper shall check and ensure that the time served by all penalized players is correct. . . .

He shall upon request, give a penalized player correct information as to the unexpired time of his penalty.

George Ogg to keep Toronto Maple Leaf Dave Keon in the box too long during the 1964 semifinals (see Rule 33, Delayed Penalties). In the 1938 Stanley Cup finals, the timekeeper was responsible for not keeping a player in the penalty box long enough.

There had already been enough action off the ice during the 1938 final series between the Chicago Black Hawks and Toronto Maple Leafs to fill an encyclopedia, so it shouldn't be surprising that the action kept heating up on the ice as well. A little background is needed to fully appreciate the complexity of the situation.

Hockey Hall of Fame

Though never easy at the best of times, the penalty timekeeper's job was made far more complicated when players shared the same penalty box.

In the spring of 1938 the Black Hawks would write a fairy-tale ending to their season at the expense of the Maple Leafs. The Hawks had finished the regular season with a 14–25–9 record. The only reason they qualified for the playoffs was that the Detroit Red Wings had been even worse, winning only twelve of their forty-eight games. The Hawks caught fire in postseason play, however, defeating the Montreal Canadiens and New York Americans to reach the Stanley Cup finals.

The problems started during the afternoon of the Black Hawks' workout before game one of the finals. Chicago goaltender Mike Karakas told team officials he wouldn't be able to play. The badly bruised toe he had suffered—and played through—during game three of the Chicago–New York Americans semifinals had now been found to be a swollen and broken digit. There wasn't enough time for the Hawks to get one of their minor-league goaltenders to Toronto for the game, so Hawk general manager Bill Stewart approached Maple Leaf g.m. Conn Smythe and asked permission to use New York Ranger goaltender Davey Kerr, who lived in town. Kerr had won twenty-six games during the regular season and was one of the NHL's best goaltenders, so Smythe wasn't too keen on seeing him in Black Hawk colors stoning his Maple Leafs.

There is confusion to this day as to what happened next. According to Stewart, Smythe gave Chicago permission to use Kerr and the Black Hawks brought him to the Gardens for the game. Smythe insisted that he had given no such approval, instead suggesting that Stewart employ either Jake Forbes, who lived in town, or local minor-league goaltender Alfie Moore. Since Forbes was retired, Smythe repeated his suggestion of Moore, who had appeared in eighteen games for the New York Americans during the 1936–37 season.

Moore had spent the entire 1937–38 season with the American Hockey League's Pittsburgh Hornets but was now back in town working for a local dry cleaning firm. When he returned home from work he was told to report to the Gardens immediately. Moore, who had earlier asked Stewart for some tickets to game one for a few friends, thought that this was why he had been summoned to the arena. While folklore tells us that the dry cleaner wet his whistle with some draught beer before the match, he was in full control of his faculties when he arrived at the Gardens. Once inside the arena, Moore found himself in the middle of a hotly contested Kerr vs. Moore controversy. Stewart and Smythe were under the stands threatening to settle their disagreement with fists instead of words. Several officials and players acted as peacemakers, finally separating the combatants. Finally Stewart reluctantly agreed to use Moore, since Smythe's permission was needed before any substitute goaltender could be employed.

Moore was an unwilling participant in this debate, but this was also the Depression and he needed the money, so he

accepted the challenge. As he was heading into the dressing room, Moore yelled out at Smythe, "I'm going to win this game even if I have to eat the puck." Smythe stopped in his tracks, turned around, and hissed, "That's exactly what we're going to make you do."

Smythe's words took on some added bite when Gordie Drillon scored on the Leafs' first shot at the 1:53 mark of the opening frame. Toronto stormed back to the attack and looked to be in great shape to take an early 2–0 lead when Syl Apps broke free and rushed in on Moore. In a vain attempt to stop the charging Leaf center, he threw his stick at Apps's feet, causing Apps, the puck, and Moore's goalie stick to end up in the corner. Ordinarily, this would result in a penalty shot, but referee Mickey Ion, probably figuring that Moore needed every break he could get, merely whistled the play dead and faced the puck in the Black Hawks' zone. That settled Moore's nerves, and he stoned Toronto the rest of the way, securing a 3–1 victory for Chicago.

Moore was ruled ineligible for game two and the Hawks went with farmhand Paul Goodman, whom the Leafs solved for 5 goals in a 5–1 win. Game three was in Chicago and Stewart and the Hawks hoped to gain some measure of revenge. The swelling in Karakas's big toe had gone down and his skate was fitted with a special steel toecap, enabling him to return to the Black Hawks' crease.

Shortly after the start of the game Syl Apps fired a pass from Gordie Drillon behind Karakas to give Toronto an early 1–0 lead. Later in the period, referee Clarence Campbell whistled Leaf Red Horner for tripping. Although the Hawks pressured the Leaf defense, they couldn't put the puck past Turk Broda in the Leafs' net. Horner readied himself to return to action and, when he got the word from the penalty timekeeper, jumped into the fray and helped the Leaf defense freeze the puck, forcing a faceoff.

When the play was whistled dead Campbell was called over to the scorer's table. After a moment's consultation, he announced that Horner had left the penalty box early and sent the Leaf captain back into the box. Horner was adamant that he had been told to leave by the penalty timekeeper, but Campbell was equally insistent that Horner had departed prematurely. The Hawks returned to the powerplay and, although they were unable to score, succeeded in tiring the fragile Leaf defense corps. Carl Voss tied the game for Chicago in the second frame and Doc Romnes won it for the Black Hawks late in the game on a 30-footer that eluded Broda's grasp.

After the game, Conn Smythe demanded an explanation for the second penalty call on Horner. The penalty timekeeper, who was from Detroit, admitted that he had given Horner permission to leave the box, but was unsure whether he had made a timing error. Referee Campbell told NHL president Frank Calder that the Black Hawks' bench had called him over and asked him to check with the official scorer. When Campbell arrived at the scorer's table, he was told by the game timekeeper, who was not in control of penalty times, that Horner had left the box early. For some reason Campbell accepted this ruling and upheld Horner's penalty. Although all playoff off-ice officials were supposed to be from neutral cities, the game timekeeper was from Chicago. It appeared that he had been the official who told the Hawks' bench that Horner had left the box early. Smythe filed a protest that Calder disallowed since Horner's penalties had not led to any Hawk tallies. Smythe then insisted that Calder change both the on-ice and off-ice officials scheduled to work game four. Calder agreed to Smythe's demands, bringing in new off-ice officials and replacing referees Campbell and Dye with Johnny Mitchell and Mickey Ion.

Chicago went on to defeat Toronto 4–1 and win the Stanley Cup in four games, but there was still some disciplinary work to be done. The guilty off-ice officials were both dismissed and, although Campbell went on to become NHL president, he never refereed another game in the NHL.

OFFICIAL SCORER

The official scorer has been part of the off-ice officiating staff since the NHL was formed in 1917, recording the names and positions of players as well as scoring statistics. Assists, which are also tracked by the official scorer, were first tabulated in 1918–19, the League's second season.

The official scorer is also responsible for ensuring that the proper player gets the credit for goals and/or assists. After a goal

RULE 40

(b) The Official Scorer shall keep a record of the goals scored, the scorers, and players to whom assists have been credited and shall indicate those players on the lists who have actually taken part in the game. He shall also record the time of entry into the game of any substitute goal-keeper. . . .

(c) The Official Scorer shall award the points for goals and assists and his decision shall be final. . . .

No requests for changes in any award of points shall be considered unless they are made at or before the conclusion of actual play in the game by the team Captain.

is scored, the referee approaches the scorer's table and gives the numbers of the players he believes were involved in a scoring play. If asked by the team captain before the conclusion of the game, the official scorer can review his decision. Today, this means viewing a videotape of the goal to ensure that scoring points have been awarded accurately.

Referee Bill Chadwick (center) confers with Toronto Maple Leaf captain Ted Kennedy (#9) and defenseman Bill Barilko (right) at the official scorer's table as other players and fans look and listen in.

Hockey Hall of Fame

Since the official scorer's decision is final, the results of a tight scoring race or the authenticity of a record-breaking performance can rest on his decision.

In 1966–67 Chicago Black Hawk center Stan Mikita was having an outstanding season. He entered the final game of the schedule against the New York Rangers with 95 points, only 2 away from tying the NHL mark for most points in a season set by teammate Bobby Hull the season before. Mikita picked up an assist in the first period, but went into the final frame still 2 points away from setting a new record. At the 2:14 mark of the third period, Doug Mohns scored to give the Hawks a 7–0 lead. Mikita was on the ice but not credited with an assist. He did, however, set up Ken Hodge's goal late in the period.

At the end of the game both Mohns and Mikita approached the referee and asked that Mikita be given credit for an assist on Mohns's goal. Official scorer Lemie Crovat disagreed, saying that although Mikita had been in the flow of the play, he had not touched the puck. Mel Megaffic, another scorer in the booth with Crovat, agreed that Mikita had not been involved in the scoring play. But since the assist would give Mikita a 3-point night and a new NHL scoring record, Crovat agreed to look at the game film before making his final report. Mikita would not have long to wait for a decision. Because it was the final night of the regular season, the official game report was to be phoned into the NHL office immediately after the game, instead of being delivered.

The film proved what Crovat had known to be true. The puck had gone from Doug Mohns to Ed Van Impe to Ken Wharram to Mohns, who then scored. Mikita had never touched the puck. The decision to consult the game film did not sit well with the NHL. In 1967, an official scorer did not have the authority to review a game film to change a call. On Monday, April 3, NHL statistician Ron Andrews said, "We would not have used filmed evidence to change how the score-keeper saw the play, but the movies showed he had it right."

But what the official scorer taketh away, he sometimes also giveth. One of the most celebrated goals in the history of the Stanley Cup playoffs was scored by Bobby Baun in game six of the 1964 finals between the Toronto Maple Leafs and Detroit Red Wings. The Leafs went into that match trailing the Motowners three games to two, and faced the prospect of having to upset the Red Wings on their home ice to get back into the series. The score was knotted at 3–3 late in the third period when Maple Leaf defenseman Bobby Baun was hit on the ankle by a slapshot and crumpled to the ice. He was in such pain that he had to be removed from the ice on a stretcher and taken directly to the infirmary. Once there, it was clear to the trainer, doctor, and Baun himself that a bone was broken in his ankle. Instead of putting on the plaster, however, Baun told the Maple Leaf trainer to freeze the ankle and wrap it tight so he could get his foot back into his skate. If he could stand, he could take a shift or two if the game went into overtime. No one questioned this. It was the Stanley Cup finals. Baun had the whole summer to recover.

The score remained tied and the game went into overtime, giving Baun an extra 10 minutes to recover while the ice was being resurfaced. When the Leafs left their dressing room to return to the bench, Baun was with them. He gave coach Punch Imlach the unspoken nod, verifying he was ready, if not totally able, to play. Early in the extra session, during a faceoff deep in Detroit territory, Baun hopped over the boards and skated toward the faceoff circle. Seconds later the puck came flying around the boards back to the point. Baun one-timed a wrist shot toward the Wing net that hopped, skipped, and jumped off Wing defenseman Bill Gadsby's stick and past Wing goaltender Terry Sawchuk to give the Leafs the win.

The official scoring line in the game summary gave Bob Pulford credit for setting up this famous marker. The only problem with that scenario was that Pulford hadn't even been on the ice when Baun scored. Dave Keon, George Armstrong, Carl Brewer, Billy Harris, and Baun were the blueshirts out there, but Pulford's name is the one that shares the history with Baun. When asked about the phantom point, Pulford dead-panned, "I got it 'cause I'm so good looking."

RULE 41

(a) The Game Timekeeper shall record the time of starting and finishing of each period in the game. During the game the game timekeeper will start the clock with the drop of the puck and stop the clock upon hearing the Official's whistle or the scoring of a goal.

GAME TIMEKEEPER

The game timekeeper's job has always been difficult, especially in the early years when the clock was round-faced with a minute hand that counted off the 60 minutes and a second hand that recorded the seconds in between. Disputes over time remaining were commonplace, but none had the dramatics of the first game of the Stanley Cup finals between the Montreal Canadiens and Detroit Red Wings on April 10, 1952.

The off-ice officials that evening were from New York and included timekeeper Cappy Lane, who was in for a very long evening. His troubles started near the end of the second period, although Lane later admitted he had been confused during most of the first stanza as well. Canadien Doug Harvey was penalized at the 18:21 mark, but 39 seconds later the buzzer sounded to signal the end of the period. The on-ice officials met with their off-ice brethren and it became clear that the hands of the Montreal Forum's clock were slightly off-line. Lane announced that his stopwatch was the official clock and that Harvey's penalty should have been recorded as occurring at the 19:21 mark, not the 18:21. That settled matters for a time. An electrician examined the Forum's time clock between periods, but couldn't solve the problem in that brief intermission.

The Red Wings jumped into a 2–0 lead, but the Habs pulled to within a single marker when Tom Johnson scored midway through the third period. Lane kept his eyes peeled on the Forum's clock and his stopwatch, and all seemed to be in order. At the appropriate time, he announced, "Last minute of play in the game," at which point Canadien coach Dick Irvin pulled goalie Gerry McNeil for an extra attacker in an attempt to score the equalizer. Wing Ted Lindsay scooped up a loose puck and scored into the empty net at the 19:44 mark, giving the Wings a 3–1 lead. However, the siren didn't sound at the 20-minute mark, and the clock continued to tick for another 60 seconds.

Dick Irvin was livid behind the Montreal bench, complaining that he had pulled his goalie one minute too soon. NHL president Clarence Campbell, who was in attendance, went to the official scorer's table and decided that the Forum's clock, not Lane's stopwatch, was official. He determined that Lindsay's goal would be recorded as being scored at the 18:44 mark, not 19:44. Irvin protested the game and suggested a conspiracy between the New York off-ice officials and the Red Wings. Campbell ignored Irvin's complaints and the score stood as recorded.

The faulty timepiece almost had tragic repercussions for a husband and wife from Cartierville, Quebec. The couple were cheering for opposing sides during the game and when the confusion occurred in the third period, an argument between them ensued. The wife, an ardent Canadiens supporter, stabbed her husband in the shoulder. He later recovered, and no charges were filed.

PLAYING RULES

ABUSE OF OFFICIALS
AND OTHER MISCONDUCT

 RULE 42

(NOTE) In the enforcement of this rule, the Referee has, in many instances, the option of imposing a misconduct penalty or a bench minor penalty. In principle, the Referee is directed to impose a bench minor penalty in respect to the violations which occur on or in the immediate vicinity of the players' bench but off the playing surface and in all cases affecting non-playing personnel or players. A misconduct penalty should be imposed for violations which occur on the playing surface or in the penalty bench area and where the penalized player is readily identifiable.

THE NATIONAL HOCKEY LEAGUE didn't introduce rules pertaining to the abuse of on-ice officials until the 1938–39 season. Prior to that, penalties for abuse of a referee or linesman were at the discretion of the League president and usually amounted to a fine or, in extreme cases, a suspension. In fact, the most serious suspension ever handed out in NHL history was for abuse of an official.

The 1927 Stanley Cup finals between the Boston Bruins and Ottawa Senators seemed peaceful enough in the early going, but tempers flared during game four of the best-of-five series. Game one had to be called off after one period of overtime because of poor ice conditions in the Boston Garden. The final game of the series was marred by a third-period brawl that began when Senator Hooley Smith attacked mild-mannered Bruin forward Harry Oliver. When the referees finally restored order, both Boston's Lionel Hitchman and Ottawa's George Boucher had been tossed from the match, but Smith had somehow escaped penalty. Perhaps that is why Bruin Billy

Coutu reacted so violently after the game. Coutu, a noted hot-head, had been on his best behavior during this series, drawing only one penalty. However, seconds after the Senators had wrapped up the Stanley Cup title with a 3–1 victory, Coutu assaulted referee Jerry LaFlamme. When assistant referee Billy Bell attempted to interfere, Coutu attacked him as well. NHL president Frank Calder reacted swiftly, suspending Coutu for life. Although he was reinstated five years later, Coutu never played another NHL game.

The legislation passed in 1939 enabled the referee to penalize a player who abused a referee or linesman verbally by sending the offending player to the penalty box. For the first occurrence, the player was to be given a 10-minute miscon-duct penalty. If a second incident occurred in the same game, the player was to be given a game misconduct and could not return for the remainder of the match.

Los Angeles King coach Tom Webster should have read Rule 42(k) before stepping behind the Kings' bench. Webster was involved in two incidents, both of which pertained to this rule.

Midway through the second period of a game with the Calgary Flames on December 13, 1990, Flame defenseman Jamie Macoun decked Brad Jones of the Kings, but referee Ron Hoggarth didn't call a penalty. Seconds later, Doug Gilmour scored for Calgary to give the Flames a 2–0 lead. Webster picked up a stick and hurled it onto the ice, earning himself a $100 fine, instant ejection from the match, and a bench minor for his team. The Kings killed off the penalty, but still dropped a 4–1 decision to the Flames, stretching the team's winless streak to eight games. League officials decided not to penalize the King coach further, but they were not so lenient the next time Webster took flight.

During the second period of the Kings' 5–3 loss to the Detroit Red Wings on November 16, 1991, Tom Webster objected to a call by referee Kerry Fraser and threw a stick in Fraser's direction that deflected off the referee's skates. Fraser immediately ejected Webster and gave the Kings a bench minor. At a hearing with League vice president Brian O'Neill, Webster expressed "great regret" at the incident. However, O'Neill pointed out that the incident marked the fourth time that Webster had been ejected since becoming coach of the

Unsportsmanlike conduct Use both hands to form a "T" in front of the chest.

(k) A bench minor penalty shall be imposed against the offending team if any player, Trainer, Coach, Manager or club executive in the vicinity of the players' bench or penalty bench throws anything on the ice during the progress of the game or during stoppage of play. . . .

Kings. O'Neill suspended Webster for twelve games, the longest suspension for a coach in NHL history.

Dan Diamond and Associates

Members of the Philadelphia Flyers and the New York Rangers pair off while linesmen attempt to break up the scuffle. One of the purposes of the "unsportsmanlike" penalty is to punish players who refuse to "stop dancing and start playing."

In the 1970s, the NHL added a clause to Rule 42 providing for a minor penalty for "unsportsmanlike" conduct, a polite way of saying that belligerence on the ice would not be tolerated. If that's the case, the most "unsportsmanlike" Stanley Cup final in NHL history was the Montreal Canadiens–Calgary Flames championship series in 1989. A total of twelve unsportsmanlike-conduct penalties were called against players from the two teams. And although the series went six games, all twelve calls came in just three contests. The ill will in this series dated back to the 1986 Stanley Cup finals between these same two teams, when an NHL-record total of twenty-six misconduct penalties had been assessed.

Antidiving legislation was added to the *NHL Rule Book* before the start of the 1992–93 season. In the previous year, coaches, media, and League officials had grown increasingly concerned about the number of players who were attempting to draw penalties by "diving" or falling to the ice anytime they felt a tug on their jerseys. The extent of the problem was heightened during the 1992 playoffs when diving infractions were called in many games.

(n) A minor penalty shall be imposed on any player who is guilty of unsportsmanlike conduct including, but not limited to hair-pulling, biting, grabbing hold of face mask, etc. . . .

(o) A minor penalty shall be imposed on a player who attempts to draw a penalty by his actions ("diving").

One of the first players to be penalized under the new rule was Minnesota North Star tough guy Shane Churla, who was nabbed for diving in a preseason game. Churla, who had a good-natured bet with teammates that a European player would be the first to be whistled for a diving infraction, explained, "It had more to do with my ability to stand up than my ability to act." Washington Capital Todd Krygier was the first player to be penalized for diving in a regular-season game. In the Capitals' season opener on October 6, 1992, against the Toronto Maple Leafs, Krygier was called when he hit the deck at the 16:27 mark of the first period.

ADJUSTMENT TO CLOTHING
OR EQUIPMENT

These rules were introduced to help speed up the tempo of the game and prevent players from calling "unofficial" time-outs to gain extra breathers during powerplay or tense, late-game situations. The rule has remained virtually unchanged since it was put in the books in 1927. However, the original rule made provisions for goaltenders to call time-outs to repair equipment, such as loose straps, damaged pads, or twisted masks.

One of the wiliest uses of this rule came during the first game of the 1932 Stanley Cup finals between the New York Rangers and Toronto Maple Leafs. The Leafs entered the third period with a comfortable 5–2 lead, but the Rangers scored 2 quick goals and were all over the Leafs pressing for the equalizer when Lorne Chabot (who started his career with the Rangers) suddenly came sliding out of the net, pointing at his pads. Referee George Mallinson skated over and saw that all the straps on one of Chabot's pads were undone. The beetle-browed goalie explained that his straps had become undone during the massive pileup near the Leafs' net during the last flurry. Mallinson allowed Chabot the time to repair his equipment, giving both Chabot and the Leafs an unscheduled rest stop. Shortly after the resumption of play, Red Horner scored to cement a 6–4 victory for the Leafs.

Prior to the start of the 1974–75 season, the NHL's Board of Governors considered several adjustments to the rules that were designed to speed up the game. Not all the proposed changes were implemented, but the rule requiring

RULE 43

(a) Play shall not be stopped nor the game delayed by reasons of adjustments to clothing, equipment, skates or sticks. . . .

(c) No delay shall be permitted for the repair or adjustment of goalkeeper's equipment. If adjust-ments are required, the goalkeeper shall leave the ice and his place shall be taken by the substitute goalkeeper immediately.

Lorne Chabot
Goal, Toronto Maple Leafs

"Beetle-Browed" Lorne Chabot was an expert at using the "equipment adjustment" clause in the rule book to perfection, a ploy he also taught to young protegee Benny Grant.

that goaltenders be replaced if they go to the bench for equipment repairs was accepted.

ATTEMPT TO INJURE

Attempt to injure is one of the most serious infractions in the *NHL Rule Book*, and is punishable by penalties and suspension. Only one player has had his career ended by another player deliberately attempting to injure him, and that occurred before the current rule was put into place.

That player was Irvine "Ace" Bailey, a slick-skating right winger who was one of the best stickhandlers in the game. He was being especially efficient in a game between the Boston Bruins and Toronto Maple Leafs on December 12, 1933.

 RULE 44

(a) A match penalty shall be imposed on any player who deliberately attempts to injure an opponent and the circumstances shall be reported to the Commissioner for further action. A substitute for the penalized player shall be permitted at the end of the fifth minute.

With the Maple Leafs down two men early in the second period, Bailey had the puck on a string for almost 90 seconds, essentially killing off the penalty by himself. After a faceoff in the Leafs' zone, Bruin defenseman Eddie Shore was upended behind the Leafs' net by Leaf rear guard King Clancy, who stole the puck from the downed Bruin and charged toward the Bruins' zone.

As the Leafs moved up ice, Bailey dropped back to the blueline to cover for Clancy. Shore, still caught behind the play, snuck up on Bailey and dumped the Leaf player either by tripping him or by ramming him with his shoulder from behind. Regardless, Bailey crashed heavily to the ice, fracturing his skull. It was immediately apparent that Bailey was gravely injured and he was rushed from the rink to the nearest Boston hospital, where doctors gave him little chance to survive. Two delicate operations were performed to relieve the tension on Bailey's brain, but he remained in critical condition until late December. Bailey defied the odds to make a remarkable recovery, although he would never be permitted to play hockey again.

Hockey Hall of Fame

One of the most poignant moments in NHL history occurred when Ace Bailey (left) accepted Eddie Shore's handshake shortly after Shore's hit from behind had ended Bailey's NHL career.

A series of inquests were held concerning the incident, but despite attempts by Toronto Maple Leaf management to have Shore suspended for the remainder of the season, he was only sidelined for sixteen games.

Since the intent-to-injure rule was implemented, no other player has had his career ended by a violation, but some

Boarding: Pounding the closed fist of one hand into the open palm of the other hand.

RULE 45

(a) A minor or major penalty, at the discretion of the Referee based upon the degree of violence of the impact with the boards, shall be imposed on any player who bodychecks, cross-checks, elbows, charges or trips an opponent in such a manner that causes the opponent to be thrown violently into the boards. (NOTE) Any unnecessary contact with a player playing the puck on an obvious "icing" or "off-side" play which results in that player being knocked into the boards is "boarding" and must be penalized as such. In other instances where there is no contact with the boards, it should be treated as "charging". "Rolling" an opponent (if he is the puck carrier) along the boards where he is endeavoring to go through too small an opening is not boarding. However, if the opponent is not the puck carrier, then such action should be penalized as boarding, charging, interference or, if the arms or stick are employed, it should be called holding or hooking.

(b) When a major penalty is imposed under this rule, an automatic fine of one hundred dollars ($100) shall be imposed.

players have had their careers shortened by opponents' actions. Terry Gray of the St. Louis Blues was high-sticked by Philadelphia Flyer Earl Heiskala during a game on March 1, 1970. Heiskala was suspended for eight games for intending to injure Gray, who suffered a severe cut on his forehead. Gray didn't miss any games as a direct result of the injury, but it did give him cause him to reflect on his career. He retired from the NHL after the season to become the playing coach of the minor-pro Montreal Voyageurs, but did return to the Blues during the 1970–71 playoffs for one game. It was his last taste of action in the NHL.

The most serious attempt-to-injure penalty was assessed against Boston Bruin Dave Forbes for his hit on Minnesota North Star Henry Boucha on January 4, 1975. During Boston's 8–0 rout of Minnesota, Forbes butt-ended Boucha in the face, causing severe damage to the nerves in and around his eye. Boucha underwent three operations at the Mayo Clinic in Rochester, Minnesota, but never regained full vision. He played another fifty-seven games in the NHL before retiring midway through the 1976–77 season.

Forbes was suspended for ten games, the second-longest sentence ever handed out for an on-ice incident by president Clarence Campbell.

BOARD CHECKING AND CHECKING FROM BEHIND

Advances in hockey equipment technology and the use of helmets and face shields mean that players are better protected today than at any time in the history of the game. Despite these innovations, however, there is no way to protect a player who is driven into the boards or to the ice by a hit from behind.

Although no NHL players have suffered career-ending injuries as a result of this offense, a number of junior players have not fared as well. The most serious offense occurred in a game between the Regina Pats and Moose Jaw Warriors on March 1, 1987. Brad Hornung, a seventeen-year-old center with the Pats, crossed over the Warriors' blueline and threw a pass to a teammate. Just as he released the puck he was hit from behind by Moose Jaw's Troy Edwards, a clean-playing center who had never counted more than 47 penalty minutes in a single season. Hornung fell forward into the end boards head first. His neck snapped back and he slumped to the ice. When the trainer reached him, he saw that Hornung had swallowed his tongue and was choking. Neither the trainer nor the doctor could pry open the player's mouth, so an incision was made in Hornung's throat to free his tongue and allow him to breathe. His inability to open his mouth or move any part of his body made it clear that Hornung had suffered a severe neck and/or spine injury. The next morning it was determined that Hornung was paralyzed from the neck down and would need a respirator to breathe.

No penalty was called on the play, because at the time Edwards's hit was considered a legal play in the Western Hockey League, just as it was in the NHL. In the 1986–87 *NHL Rule Book,* only subsections (a) and (b) existed. In July 1987 the WHL passed legislation that made any hit from behind a serious offense. In 1989–90 and again in 1991–92, the NHL added clauses (c), (d), and (e) to Rule 45.

BROKEN STICK

When the game of hockey was first played, hockey sticks were made from one very solid piece of wood. These old pieces of lumber were heavy and durable to say the least. As a result, there were very few broken sticks in the "good old days." Ottawa's Percy LeSueur used the same goal stick from 1904 to 1909 and Fred "Cyclone" Taylor of the Vancouver Millionaires played with the same hockey stick for four years without breaking it.

At no time has a player ever been allowed to play with a broken stick; the damaged "cudgel" must be dropped and a new stick acquired. In fact, until the 1940s a player wasn't even allowed on the ice without a stick; he had to go directly to the bench and get a new stick or let a teammate onto the ice. However, on October 1, 1932, the NHL decided that a stick "chipped at the top, properly protected by tape, so as to prevent injury to another player, shall not be considered a broken stick."

Until the 1936–37 season, a player was penalized if he kicked the puck after breaking his stick. The following year

(c) When a major penalty is imposed under this rule for a foul resulting in an injury to the face or head of an opponent, an automatic game misconduct shall be imposed.

(d) Any player who cross-checks, pushes or charges from behind an opponent who is unable to defend himself, shall be assessed a major and a game misconduct. This penalty applies anywhere on the playing surface.

(e) In regular season games any player who incurs a total of two game misconduct penalties for board-checking under Rule 45(c) and (d) shall be suspended automatically for the next League game of his team. For each subsequent game misconduct penalty the automatic suspension shall be increased by one game. In playoff games, any player who incurs a total of two game misconduct penalties for board-checking under Rule 45(c) and (d) shall be suspended automatically for the next playoff game of his team. For each subsequent game misconduct penalty during the playoffs the automatic suspension shall be increased by one game.

RULE 46

(a) A player without a stick may participate in the game. A player whose stick is broken may participate in the game provided he drops the broken portion. . . .

(b) A goalkeeper may continue to play with a broken stick until stoppage of play or until he has been legally provided with a stick.

the penalty infraction was dropped, but play was still stopped and a faceoff conducted when the puck had been kicked. A goaltender was allowed to play without a stick, but had to drop the broken one. Midway through the 1946–47 season, the NHL passed a rule that allowed a player to remain on the ice and play without a stick. It also allowed the goaltender to play with the broken portion of his stick.

A fan once asked sportswriter Andy O'Brien whether a goal could ever be scored with a broken stick. He answered no, but upon reflection changed his mind. Since a goalie is allowed to play with a broken stick, and since goalies have been known to find the opposing net (ten professional goalies have scored a goal), it is technically possible that a goal could be scored with a damaged stick.

Interestingly, it was a broken goalie stick that once led to a rare stick measurement. It occurred during the 1954–55 season and involved coach Dick Irvin of the Montreal Canadiens and goaltender Harry Lumley of the Toronto Maple Leafs. At this time the Leafs were notoriously weak on offense, but so strong on defense that many teams accused them of trying to play every game for a tie. It would be hard to argue this fact since the 1954–55 Leafs racked up twenty-two ties in seventy games, four of them against the Canadiens.

The Leafs' defensive attitude rankled Canadien coach Dick Irvin. His team based its offense on a swift-skating, free-flowing style, a system the Leafs attempted to derail by bumping and grinding the Habs at every opportunity.

In a game against Toronto on February 3, 1955, Irvin found a way to gain some measure of revenge. Late in the second period goaltender Harry Lumley broke his stick. At the end of the game the Montreal trainer brought the broken timber to Irvin and pointed out that the stick appeared to be wider than the NHL rules allowed. With this new piece of information Irvin came up with an idea that he hoped would throw a wrench into the Leafs' works. At the start of the second period of their next meeting, on February 9, Irvin approached referee Frank Udvari and requested that Udvari measure Lumley's goalie stick.

Udvari grabbed Lumley's stick, much to the disbelief of the Leaf fans and players. A few moments later, Udvari announced that the blade of the goal stick was ½ inch wider than NHL rules permitted, and he assessed a 2-minute penalty. Rookie Brian Cullen was Lumley's proxy in the penalty box as the Habs opened the period on the powerplay, but Irvin's scheme didn't produce the desired results. The Leafs killed off the Habs' man advantage and went on to post a 3–1 victory.

It is very rare for a player to be penalized for playing with a broken stick, but Detroit Red Wing defenseman Howie Young was nailed for just that. As was usually the case with this ultracolorful tough guy, there is a story behind the incident.

Midway through the 1960–61 season the Red Wings promoted Young—a surly and sometimes uncontrollable rookie—from their farm team in Hershey. He was undisciplined to be sure, but Young played with such wild abandon that he became an instant crowd favorite. The rest of the NHL didn't exactly welcome him with open arms, and neither did the on-ice officials—especially referee Frank Udvari, who wasn't about to let any bush-leaguer run rampant in any game he controlled.

And so it came to pass that Young was spending an inordinate amount of time cooling his heels in the penalty box in games officiated by Udvari. The situation reached a point where the Red Wings wouldn't dress Young if Udvari was scheduled to referee the game. Detroit general manager Jack Adams was not afraid to communicate his displeasure to the media. For the Wings the last straw occurred in a game against the Montreal Canadiens on February 19, 1961. Earlier in the game, Udvari had thumbed Young to the box on his first shift, a penalty that gave Montreal an early powerplay and a quick 1–0 lead.

Midway through the third period, with the Wings trailing the Habs 3–2, Young was fighting Henri Richard for possession of the puck behind the Wings' net. In the struggle to gain control of the puck Young broke his stick, then slammed Richard into the glass. Udvari whistled the play dead and carded Young for playing with a broken stick—even though the damaged lumber lay in splinters by the side of the net. It seemed clear that Young had dropped his stick as soon as it broke, but Udvari's call stood, and the Wings had to go on the defensive while Young sat in the box. The Canadiens went on to post a 4–2 win, while the Red Wings went on to post a complaint against Udvari with the NHL office. Of course, no action was taken. Udvari went on to the Hockey Hall of Fame while Young went on to set a NHL record for penalty minutes in 1962–63.

CHARGING

RULE 47

(a) A minor or major penalty shall be imposed on a player who runs or jumps into or charges an opponent.

(c) A minor or major penalty shall be imposed on a player who charges a goalkeeper while the goalkeeper is within his goal crease.

Charging: Rotating clenched fists around one another in front of chest.

In today's game, any time a goalie is touched—whether he's in the crease or outside of it—he is immediately protected by his teammates and scuffles often result. Before teams carried a strong second goaltender, it wasn't unusual to see the occasional goal-mouth charge in an attempt to knock the number one netminder out of action. Of course, no player would admit to this strategy, but it could be found in the top-secret files of most teams' playbooks. Although not expressly defined in the rule book as a charging penalty at this time, it rarely went unpunished either by the referee or by the opposing team.

Interestingly, it was a goaltender-running war between the Toronto Maple Leafs and the Detroit Red Wings that was responsible for the NHL debuts of two players who went on to have lengthy careers both on and off the ice.

In 1960–61 the Maple Leafs were enjoying their finest season since the 1950–51 campaign, and were riding a lengthy undefeated streak when they arrived in Detroit for a tilt with the Red Wings on February 12, 1961. Earlier in the year, Toronto's Frank Mahovlich had incurred the wrath of the Detroit team when he barreled into Terry Sawchuk in the Detroit crease. A photograph of the event was plastered across sports pages from coast to coast, but the Wings were in no hurry to react. Under the six-team era's system of justice, patience was a virtue. Teams played each other fourteen times over the course of the season, so there was plenty of time to repay the Leafs for what the Wings felt was a cheap shot on Sawchuk.

When the first-place Leafs arrived in Detroit on this cold winter evening, they encountered a Red Wing team struggling to hold onto fourth place and the NHL's final playoff spot. Detroit fans had a new hero in the rambunctious Howie Young, who was running and gunning everyone in sight. With the Detroit Olympia's crowd cheering him on, Young

This hit by Toronto Maple Leaf forward Frank Mahovlich on Detroit netminder Terry Sawchuk led to a "goaltender-running" war between the two teams.

was at his belligerent best against the Leafs, knocking the pins out from under every blue-and-white jersey he saw.

Moments after Norm Ullman scored to narrow the Red Wings' deficit to 3–2 in the third period, Young cashed in his club's IOU by sailing through the crease and nailing Leaf goalie Johnny Bower. As expected, the Leafs were outraged. Although Young was given a major penalty, he took Leaf Dick Duff off with him. In fact, Young was given only 5 minutes in penalties, while Duff received a 10-minute misconduct. Bower was shaken by the collision but, after a 10-minute rest, insisted that he was able to continue. The Leafs held on to win the match by a 4–2 score, but it was later disclosed that Bower had strained muscles in his leg and would be lost to the team for some time. Leaf coach Punch Imlach called Bower the bravest athlete and Young the dirtiest player he had ever seen. When asked about the situation Young suggested there had been some insincerity on the part of the Leafs. "Bower says he lost a tooth in that collision. That's a laugh. No goalie who's been playing as long as him has any teeth left to lose."

In Bower's place, the Maple Leafs called up Gerry McNamara, a twenty-six-year-old veteran with no NHL

Detroit defenseman Howie Young was a "loose cannon" who exploded all over Toronto Maple Leaf goaltender Johnny Bower during the 1960–61 campaign.

Cross-checking: A forward and backward motion with both fists clenched extending from the chest.

RULE 48

(a) A minor, double minor or major penalty, at the discretion of the Referee, shall be imposed on a player who "cross-checks" an opponent.

experience who had been playing with Sudbury of the Eastern Professional League.

McNamara, who later served as the general manager of the Toronto Maple Leafs, from 1981 to 1988, replaced Bower and played very well, which was no surprise to coach Imlach. "It's not like we were putting an empty uniform in there," stated Toronto's bald prognosticator. On February 23 the Leafs downed the Montreal Canadiens 4–2 in the Habs' own backyard, with McNamara providing much of the dramatics. However, a nagging leg injury flared up after the game, forcing Big Mac to the sidelines. It would be nine long years before McNamara got the opportunity to play in another NHL game.

With two goalies down, the Leafs reached into their bag of tricks and pulled out a twenty-two-year-old rookie named Cesare Maniago, who had been playing on the West Coast with the Western Hockey League's Spokane Comets. Maniago made his NHL debut against the Red Wings and was outstanding as the Leafs tripped up the Motowners by a 3–1 count. The next night the teams played the back end of their home-and-home series and, once again, Howie Young was the focal point.

At the 10:18 mark of the first period Maniago was clearing a loose puck near his crease when Young raced in and sent the rookie flying with a solid hit. Tim Horton, who was perhaps the strongest man in the game at the time, piled into Young, and when the dust cleared Young picked up a 2-minute minor charging plus a major for his battle with Horton. This was the final regular-season game between Detroit and Toronto, and with it went most of the antagonism between the two clubs. If the Red Wings were attempting to send a message to the Leafs, it was delivered. Although the Maple Leafs finished 24 points ahead of the Red Wings, Detroit completely outplayed Toronto in the playoffs, eliminating them in five games during the 1961 semifinals.

CROSS-CHECKING

Cross-checking has been an infraction ever since the rules for the game were first introduced. It is also one of the most dangerous stick fouls in the game, mainly because the infraction is often committed from behind. For many years, cross-checking and butt-ending were both covered under the same rule. However, an incident during the 1991 Canada Cup tournament played a key role in having the cross-checking and board checking rules re-defined. It occurred during game one of the championship final series between Canada and the United States and involved the games greatest player. With 11 minutes remaining in the second period and Canada holding a slim 2-1 lead, Team USA defenseman Gary Suter cross-checked Wayne Gretzky into the corner boards near the U.S. goal. Gretzky fell head first into the boards then slumped to the ice in obvious pain. Incredibly, no penalty was called on the play, but replays showed that Suter laid a fairy wicked two-handed cross-check across Gretzky's back. Although he was able to leave the ice under his own power, Gretzky was unable to return to action for the rest of the series because of back spasms.

Gretzky continued to suffer back pain throughout the 1991–92 season, though he missed only six games during the campaign. His condition grew worse over the off-season, forcing the Great One to miss half of the 1992–93 schedule. While Suter's hit on Gretzky was considered a legal check, the NHL also realized the hit came perilously close to ending the career of the game's marquee performer. In 1992, the League issued a new edict that assessed an automatic game misconduct penalty to any player who hits or pushes another player from behind. In the 1996 playoffs, Colorado's Claude Lemieux checked Detroit forward Kris Draper from behind, driving Draper face-first into the boards. The League suspended Lemieux for two games, making him the first player since Ed Hospodar in 1987 to miss games in the Stanley Cup finals due to a suspension.

DELIBERATE INJURY OF OPPONENTS

The deliberate injury of opponents has always been of great concern to hockey executives. Any game played with an instrument in the hands, be it a stick or a bat, is bound to have incidents in which an athlete loses control. Players who lose it have always been dealt with quickly and harshly.

One of the first players to feel the wrath of organized hockey for deliberately injuring an opponent was Cully

(NOTE 1) Cross-check shall mean a check delivered with both hands on the stick and no part of the stick on the ice.

(NOTE 2) A double minor penalty must be assessed for cross-checks delivered to the neck or head area, unless a major or match penalty (Rule 44—Attempt to Injure or Rule 49—Deliberate Injury) is assessed.

RULE 49

(a) A match penalty shall be imposed on a player who deliberately injures an opponent in any manner.

(b) In addition to the match penalty, the player shall be automatically suspended from further competition until the Commissioner has ruled on the issue.

Wilson, a fiery right winger who was constantly overcompensating for his small size. Wilson stood only 5'7" and weighed less than 150 pounds, but he delighted in taking on the biggest and the strongest players in the League. Usually that was no cause for concern, but when Wilson attacked one of the game's most gentlemanly players, action had to be taken.

Wilson started his career in Toronto in 1913, but moved to the West Coast to play for the Seattle Metropolitans in the Pacific Coast Hockey Association in 1915. During the 1918–19 season Wilson was particularly feisty, but during a game against the Victoria Aristocrats on February 26, 1919, he carried the chip on his shoulder too far. During the second period he laid a vicious cross-check on Mickey MacKay that broke the Victoria star's jaw and put him out of action for almost two full seasons. Wilson was ultimately suspended for life from the PCHA and returned to central Canada to play with the Toronto St. Pats. He led the NHL in penalty minutes in 1919–20.

The first player to be suspended for life from the NHL was also banned for excessive violence from another pro league. A culmination of offenses led NHL president Frank Calder to bar Billy Coutu for life in 1927 (see Rule 42). When Coutu was reinstated in 1932 he signed up to play in the outlaw American Hockey League, but was quickly banned from that organization as well. He never played again.

Both of these players were rough, tough, and mean, but they could also play the game. Wilson was a gifted scorer who set a Western Hockey League record by scoring 3 goals in 61 seconds against the Seattle Metropolitans on December 5, 1923. Coutu was one of the Montreal Canadiens' best defensemen, regardless of the rough stuff. Indeed, the most talented player ever to skate in the NHL also had an uncontrollable temper that caused him to be suspended for deliberate injury. That player was Montreal Canadien Maurice Richard, and both times that he erupted he may have cost his team a chance to win the Stanley Cup.

Richard's first serious clash with the NHL came during game two of the 1947 Stanley Cup finals against the Toronto Maple Leafs. The Canadiens crushed the Leafs 6–0 in the first game of the series, and pundits were predicting an easy four-

game sweep for *Les Habitants.* In fact, Bill Durnan, the Canadiens' All Star goalie, went a step further and was quoted in the newspapers as saying that the Leafs didn't belong on the same ice surface as the Canadiens. Leaf bench boss Hap Day pasted those comments to the Toronto dressing room wall and walked out, knowing that Durnan had just saved him the effort of delivering a pregame motivational speech.

Game two was a highly charged, emotional affair, and the Leafs focused much of their attention on Richard, who was known to have an extremely short fuse. At the 76-second mark of the opening period, the Rocket was thumbed off the ice by referee Bill Chadwick for interference. The Leafs pounced on the early powerplay opportunity and fired a pair of goals past Durnan while Richard stewed in the penalty box.

Six minutes into the second stanza Richard and Vic Lynn collided, with Richard's stick combing a neat swath across Lynn's skull. As an unconscious Lynn was being carted from the ice, Chadwick sent Richard to the box for 5 minutes. Once again the Leafs capitalized on the Rocket's red glare, taking a 3–0 lead on a powerplay marker by Gaye Stewart. When Richard returned to the ice he was almost wild with anger. Moments later he and Leaf tough guy Bill Ezinicki bumped near the Leafs' net and the pair quickly began pushing and shoving. Referee Chadwick stepped in between them, but Richard reached over the official's shoulder and cut Ezinicki across the face with his stick. Chadwick slapped a match misconduct on the testy Rocket, which meant that the Habs would be forced to play a man short for 20 minutes— and that Richard was out of the game and, possibly, the series, pending a hearing with NHL president Clarence Campbell.

Once again the Leafs took advantage of Richard's lack of discipline by collecting their fourth powerplay goal of the game; all were scored while Richard languished in the penalty box. With the Canadiens' main offensive weapon out of the lineup, their attack collapsed, and the Habs meekly succumbed to the Leafs by a 4–0 score.

After the game Montreal coach Dick Irvin scoffed at the suggestion that Richard would be disciplined further by the NHL office. As far as Irvin was concerned, the referee had made an error in judgment by giving Richard a match penalty.

Although Ezinicki was badly cut, he returned to action in the third period and, as Irvin pointed out to the assembled journalists, Rule 49 clearly stated that "before applying this penalty, the referee must consult the Manager or Coach and be assured that the injured player will not return to the game." Since this clearly hadn't been the case, there was no way that Campbell could ground the Rocket.

A wild Maurice Richard (#9) lets loose with the lumber during this Montreal Canadiens–Toronto Maple Leafs match in the 1946–47 season. It was Richard's inability to control his wild temper that led to his problems later on in the season.

Hockey Hall of Fame

Unfortunately for the Canadiens, president Campbell didn't see it that way, and he suspended Richard for game three of the series. He strongly advised the Rocket that any further stickwork would result in greater fines and suspensions. The Maple Leafs easily downed the Rocketless Canadiens 4–2, and went on to win the Stanley Cup in six games.

The next time Richard was suspended by Clarence Campbell occurred after he drew a match misconduct in a game against the Boston Bruins on March 13, 1955. In this game Richard attacked both Bruin defenseman Hal Laycoe and linesman Cliff Thompson. (See Rule 30 for details of this game.)

No one was surprised that Richard had boiled over or that he had been given a season-ending suspension. The only surprise was that it hadn't happened earlier. Richard had experienced similar outbursts since the 1947 incident—including a wild stick-swinging barrage against Bob Bailey of the Toronto Maple Leafs only three months before the Laycoe affair.

Fleming Mackell, a teammate of Lynn and Ezinicki in 1947 and of Laycoe in 1955, summed up the Rocket and his temper when he said, "If they had thrown the book at him when he cut Bill Ezinicki and Vic Lynn in 1947, it might have stopped him and he might have become an even greater player because of it."

DELAYING THE GAME

There have many instances of players and goalkeepers being penalized for delay of game, but none as unique as the delay-of-game penalty Randy Pierce received on November 28, 1979.

The Colorado Rockies–New York Islanders game on that evening was one of the most peculiar games ever played in the NHL. The Rockies, who had never in their history beaten the Islanders, had already blown a 4–3 lead when Islander goal-tender Billy Smith was credited with a goal after Rockie defenseman Rob Ramage scored into his own net. Despite that faux pas, the Rockies were able to retake the lead with a pow-erplay goal by Ron Delorme only one minute later. The Rockies clung to that slim advantage into the final minute, when the Islanders pulled their goaltender for an extra attacker. Colorado winger Randy Pierce scored into the empty net at the 19:37 mark to supposedly seal the victory. In his exuber-ance over scoring the insurance goal, Pierce grabbed the puck out of the net, kissed it, and threw it into the crowd. That move backfired when the referee assessed a penalty to Pierce for deliberately delaying the game. The penalty gave the Islanders a powerplay and one last chance to tie the game, but there weren't going to be any more miracles. Wilf Paiement scored another empty-netter to secure the Rockies' 7–4 victory.

While it is clearly stated in the rule book that dislodging the net late in the game is punishable by a penalty shot, two plays illustrate that invoking this rule is discretionary on the part of the referee.

During the closing minutes of a game between the New York Rangers and the Washington Capitals on November 28, 1984, Capital Scott Stevens pushed the net off its moorings in the final seconds of a 2–1 Washington win. Referee Denis Morel failed to award a penalty shot, giving a minor penalty to Stevens instead.

RULE 50

(b) A minor penalty shall be imposed on any player or goal-keeper who throws or deliber-ately bats the puck with his hand or stick outside the playing area.

Dan Diamond and Associates

Unlike Randy Pierce, New York Rangers "enforcer" Nick Fotiu didn't bother to kiss this puck before giving it the toss into the stands at Madison Square Garden.

(c) . . . If the goal post is deliber-ately displaced by a goalkeeper or player during the course of a "breakaway", a penalty shot will be awarded to the non-offend-ing team, which shot shall be taken by the player last in pos-session of the puck. . . .

Eleven years later on February 3, 1995, the Toronto Maple Leafs were pressuring the Flames deep in the Calgary zone, attempting to overcome a 3–1 deficit. With 36 seconds left on the clock and the Leafs' net empty, Flame defenseman Dan Keczmer lifted the net off its moorings to gain a stoppage in play. Referee Andy vanHellemond signaled a delay-of-game penalty against Keczmer even though the rule clearly states that a penalty shot was in order. The Flames withstood the Leafs' attack and scored into the vacated cage to gain a 4–1 victory.

It is extremely rare for a penalty shot to be called in post-season play. Since 1934, when the NHL first introduced the penalty shot rule, there have been only 30 shots taken in the playoffs. And there had never been a penalty shot called in overtime. That was all about to change in game four of the Pittsburgh Penguins–Washington Capitals quarter-final series.

With the score tied 2–2 and less than five minutes remaining in the second O/T period, the Capitals appeared ready to put an end to the suspense. With a flurry of Cap forwards buzzing in and around the Penguins' cage, Washington's Joey Juneau sent a shot toward the net that slipped through Penguins netminder Ken Wregget's pads and slowly slid towards the goal line. Pittsburgh defenseman Chris Tamer dove head-first toward the rolling disc and managed to sweep the puck out of the crease. Unfortunately for Tamer, he also knocked the net off its mooring in the process. Referee Dan Marouelli immediately signalled a delay of the game penalty for dislodging the net and sent Tamer to the penalty box to serve time for his crime.

However, after consulting with the off-ice officials, Marouelli was reminded that if the net is dislodged purposely in overtime, an *automatic* penalty shot must be called. Marouelli seemed to be unaware of that clause of the edict, but there was no reversing his decision now. He released Tamer from the penalty box and signalled for Joey Juneau to take the first overtime penalty shot in NHL history. Juneau was stopped cold by Wregget and the overtime continued for another 45 minutes before Petr Nedved finally scored to give Pittsburgh a 3–2 victory. It was the third longest playoff game in history and the longest ever in the post-war era.

(d) If by reason of insufficient time in the regular playing time or by reason of penalties already imposed, the minor penalty assessed to a player for deliberately displacing his own goal post cannot be served in its entirety within the regular playing time of the game or at any time in overtime, a penalty shot shall be awarded against the offending team.

Rule 50(e) was introduced following the Montreal Canadiens–Boston Bruins semifinals in 1979, which featured a well-fought game of coaching "one-upmanship" between Montreal's Scott Bowman and Boston's Don Cherry. In game one of the series, Canadien Jacques Lemaire scored at the 13:52 mark of the first period to give Montreal a 1–0 lead. After this score the entire Canadien team piled onto the ice to congratulate Lemaire, a ploy the Canadiens had been pulling on the opposition throughout the playoffs. Don Cherry, no stranger to the sensitive psychology of playoff hockey, decided to turn the tables on the Habs by sending the entire Bruin team onto the ice when Montreal scored to console Bruin goalie Gerry Cheevers. This caused a numbing headache for referee Dave Newell, who requested that both teams stop the game-playing and start playing the game. The coaches agreed. The next season the League passed a rule outlawing excessive celebration.

Sometimes following the letter of the law can cause embarrassment. On February 22, 1993, the Toronto Maple Leafs were in Vancouver for a match against the Canucks. It was a special evening for Leaf Glenn Anderson. Not only was it a homecoming for the twelve-year veteran, but he also had a chance to reach the 1,000-point plateau. Toronto entered the third period with a commanding 5–1 lead, but Anderson was still 2 points away from 1,000. At the 11:18 mark he assisted on a goal by John Cullen and, 12 seconds later, scored himself to give the Leafs a 7–1 advantage and reach one of the NHL's most coveted scoring milestones. Every Leaf player jumped off the bench to congratulate Anderson—only the second player to reach the 1,000-point mark while wearing a Maple Leaf uniform. Referee Denis Morel wasn't in a celebratory mood, however, and charged the Leafs with a 2-minute bench minor for delaying the game. Morel was only calling the game by the book, but—had the Leafs informed him before the game that Anderson was on the verge of reaching a milestone—he could have waived the no-celebration rule.

ELBOWING AND HEAD-BUTTING

Chris Nilan always wanted to see his name in the *NHL Official Guide & Record Book* and it was an elbowing call that

(e) A bench minor penalty shall be imposed upon any team which, after warning by the Referee to its Captain or Alternate Captain to place the correct number of players on the ice and commence play, fails to comply with the Referee's direction and thereby causes any delay by making additional substitutions, by persisting in having its players off-side, or in any other manner.

RULE 51

(a) A minor or major penalty, at the discretion of the Referee, shall be imposed on any player who uses his elbow to, in any way, foul an opponent.

Elbowing: Tapping the elbow of the "whistle hand" with the opposite hand.

started him on his way to a record-breaking performance. For anyone who has followed Nilan's career it will come as no surprise that when he finally did set a record, it was for penalties in one game.

In the early 1980s Nilan was a coveted commodity in the NHL, an intimidating physical presence who could also put the puck in the net. In the two years he led the NHL in penalty minutes, he also recorded his finest offensive production: 16 goals and 338 penalty minutes in 1983–84, and 21 goals and 358 penalty minutes in 1984–85. For five seasons in the 1980s, Nilan was the best policeman on the beat.

By the 1990–91 season Nilan's career was winding down and, like an aging gunslinger, he found himself battling young up-and-comers trying to claim his crown. Hobbled by injuries and indifferent play, he had managed to dress in only forty-one games for the Boston Bruins, the third NHL team to employ his services.

When the Bruins and Hartford Whalers took to the ice on the final evening of the 1990–91 regular-season schedule, there was an air of expectancy. These same two teams were set to meet a few days later in the playoffs, so this game was bound to be a hard-hitting, chippy affair as the two sides sized each other up in preparation for the postseason.

As expected, the game was a rough tug-of-war with a number of minor and major skirmishes resulting in a total of fifty-seven penalties and six powerplay goals. Nilan played a record-breaking part in that drama, inserting his name into the NHL record book by drawing ten penalties in the game.

As the Bruins rolled to an early 4–0 lead, Nilan was an angel, spending only 2 minutes in the box—a holding penalty at the 12:53 mark of the first period. In the second Nilan was a bit more rambunctious, earning a fighting major midway through the period and a trio of penalties—elbowing, roughing, and a misconduct—with less than 5 minutes remaining in the frame.

After serving those 14 minutes, Nilan returned to the ice and quickly found himself in close quarters with Whaler Jim McKenzie. The chain of events that followed went something like this: An elbow gave him 2; dropping the gloves earned him an instigating call; a quick tussle with McKenzie resulted in a 5-minute major; and refusing to proceed to the penalty box added an unsportsmanlike-conduct minor to his record. Through all of this the Massachusetts-born Nilan was serving up a Boston chowder of chatter to referee Kerry Fraser. This less-than-poetic line of conversation earned him a game misconduct.

At the end of the game, when all accounts were totaled, Nilan had been whistled for a record-breaking ten separate penalties, surpassing the old mark of nine held by seven other heavyweights including Philadelphia's Dave Schultz and Boston's Terry O'Reilly.

The head-butting section of this rule was added in the early 1970s, but it has usually fallen into the "intent-to-injure" category. This penalty is rarely called but when it is, it usually results in a suspension. During the 1994–95 season two players were charged with head-butting, and both received suspensions. San Jose's Andrei Nazarov sat out four games after head-butting Winnipeg's Stephane Quintal on March 4, 1995. Tampa Bay's Enrico Ciccone received a two-game suspension for a head-butting incident on April 11, 1995.

Head-butting hasn't always been classified as a match-penalty offense. During 1927's wild Stanley Cup finals between the Ottawa Senators and Boston Bruins, Senator George Boucher was a whirling dervish of trouble. He was penalized in every contest, including game four, in which he received a match penalty for an out-of-control fight that almost brought the game to an early end. In game three Boucher received a 2-minute penalty for head-butting—one of the rare times this offense was deemed a "minor" penalty.

FACE-OFFS

Badly bruised shins were the root cause of the modern hockey faceoff. Before the faceoff was instituted, play would begin in much the same way as in the game of lacrosse, with the referee placing a puck between the two centermen's sticks and shouting "Play." Often the two combatants would wildly swing their sticks, bruising the referee from shin to hip. Fred Waghorn, one of hockey's first and finest on-ice arbiters, decided eventually that enough was enough. Instead of placing the puck between the players, he dropped it between their sticks. This

(c) A match penalty shall be imposed on any player who deliberately "head-butts" or attempts to "head-butt" an opponent during an altercation and the circumstances shall be reported to the Commissioner for further action. . . .

Although he set his single-game penalty record as a member of the Boston Bruins, Chris Nilan had back-to-back seasons with more that 300 penalty minutes in Montreal.

RULE 52

(a) The puck shall be "faced-off" by the Referee or the Linesman dropping the puck on the ice between the sticks of the players "facing-off". Players facing-off will stand squarely facing their opponent's end of the rink approximately one stick length apart with the blade of their sticks on the ice. . . .

No other player shall be allowed to enter the face-off circle or come within fifteen feet of the players facing-off the puck and must stand on side on all face-offs. . . .

gave him enough time to jump out of the way before his knees were battered. The players didn't object and the new maneuver soon became the accepted method of beginning play. Since that time the faceoff has remained virtually unchanged, though there have been several refinements.

Most modifications to the basic faceoff rule deal with players infringing on the draw. In hockey's early years players could crowd around the two centermen; eventually new rules were legislated to provide room for the faceoff to proceed without interruption. No player was allowed to come within 5 feet of the faceoff area, and no interference was permitted until the puck hit the ice. When the NHL decided to paint 10-foot face-off circles on the ice in 1934–35, a definite boundary was established to keep players away from the two skaters taking the faceoff. Despite these new restrictions on player movement at the draw, there were still problems with players skating into the circle before the puck was dropped. In 1938–39 it was decided that any player who crossed into the circle twice on the same faceoff would be penalized. The referee, who had previously dropped the puck on every faceoff, passed those duties on to the linesman, so that he could better judge if a player was interfering before the puck was dropped.

During the infamous Montreal-Toronto playoff game on March 26, 1964 (see Rule 33), which set records for most penalties in a single playoff game (thirty-one) and most penalties in a single period (sixteen), referee Frank Udvari gave the Leafs one last gasp by penalizing Canadien Claude Provost at the 14:56 mark of the third period for faceoff interference. The Leafs failed to take advantage of their opportunity and went down to a 2–0 defeat at the hands of the Habs.

In ensuing years rules have been passed to make the faceoff a smoother process. The linesmen can toss a player out of the faceoff circle if that player fails to get set or tries to take an unfair advantage by swiping at the puck before it is dropped. Also, the visiting player must place his stick on the ice first or be tossed from the ring. These guidelines are strictly enforced—so much so that coaches often put two faceoff men on the ice to take key draws in case one of them gets tossed.

A major change in the faceoff rule affected the positions of the players taking the draw and coincided with the introduction of the red line in 1942–43. Prior to that season

Diane Sobolewski

Hockey Hall of Fame

As this photo from a New York Americans–Ottawa Senators match on December 1, 1926 suggests, face-offs were conducted with the players facing the side boards on an ice surface that had none of the markings seen on modern rinks.

Today, face-offs are conducted with the centermen facing the ends of the rink while the forwards line up beside each other on the edge of the face-off circle.

players taking the draw would line up facing the side boards. Many coaches employed a strategy that required the players taking the faceoff to actually ignore the puck and instead take on the other faceoff man, allowing a teammate to come in and take the puck. Under the amended rule, players taking the faceoff rotate 90 degrees so that they are facing the ends of the rink with their backs toward their own goals. The intent of this legislation was to speed up play by placing greater emphasis on cleanly winning the draw.

FALLING ON PUCK

At no time has a player been allowed to fall on the puck without being penalized. However, it was at one time legal for the goaltender to dive out of his net and freeze the puck. Until Montreal Canadien Jacques Plante entered the League,

 RULE 53

(a) A minor penalty shall be imposed on a player other than the goalkeeper who deliberately falls on or gathers the puck into his body. . . .

(b) A minor penalty shall be imposed on a goalkeeper who, when he is in his own goal crease, deliberately falls on or gathers the puck into his body or who holds or places the puck against any part of the goal in such a manner as to cause a stoppage of play unless he is actually being checked by an opponent. . . .

though, most goalies stayed in their creases. Plante changed all that. He repeatedly left his crease to stop the puck behind the net for his defensemen or pass it up the ice to his forwards.

Hockey Hall of Fame

Detroit goaltender Terry Sawchuk barely stays within the boundaries of the rule as he dives outside his crease to smother a loose puck.

If he found himself in trouble he would simply dive out of the net, fish around for the loose puck, and then freeze it until he got a stoppage in play. In fact, he would perform this trick numerous times in a match, especially if the opposing team was exerting pressure. Opposing coaches and fans complained that Plante's exploits were slowing the game from a gallop to a crawl. Finally, in 1959–60, the NHL introduced a rule that penalized any goaltender who left his crease to freeze the puck. The Montreal Canadiens were very upset with the new rule and felt that it was pointed directly at Plante. "The other teams could have done the same thing as Jacques," coach Toe Blake explained, "but I guess nobody is as quick as Plante. He can get away with things that other goalies can't."

 RULE 54

(a) A major penalty shall be imposed on any player who engages in fisticuffs. . . . A player deemed to be the instiga-

FISTICUFFS

Fisticuffs. The most discussed, criticized, debated, and sometimes even praised aspect of the game of hockey. A majority of fans love it and a majority of players accept it. The simple truth remains that no NHL player has ever had his career ended by injuries sustained in a fight. The first "fisticuffs" clause, placed in the *NHL Rule Book* in 1922–23, called for a major penalty with no substitution. Over the years the rules have changed but the basic charge has remained the same— 5 minutes for fighting. Since the 1930s substitutions have been allowed, so a team is not required to play a man short unless its player has incurred an extra penalty. The advocates of fisticuffs argue that the presence of fighting makes the game *less* violent because players can relieve their frustrations without resorting to "dirty" tactics. The detractors point out that it encourages teams to employ players of lesser talent, hiring them to do little more than intimidate.

tor of fisticuffs shall be assessed a game misconduct. . . .

(b) A minor penalty shall be imposed on a player who, having been struck, shall retaliate with a blow or attempted blow. . . .

(d) A game misconduct penalty, at the discretion of the Referee, shall be imposed on any player or goalkeeper who is the first to intervene in an altercation already in progress except when a match penalty is being imposed in the original altercation. . . .

Dan Diamond and Associates

Members of the New York Rangers and the Philadelphia Flyers engage in a conga-line tug-of-war as Flyer goalie Doug Favell and Ranger tough-guy Reg Fleming engage in a lively tussle.

(g) Any teams whose players become involved in an altercation, other than during the periods of the game, shall be fined automatically twenty-five thousand dollars ($25,000) in addition to any other appropriate penalties that may be imposed upon the participating players by supplementary discipline or otherwise. . . .

In reality, the problem has never been one of two players dropping the gloves and fighting. Problems arose instead from the uncontrolled atmosphere that often prevailed when fisticuffs began. Bench-clearing brawls, fights before periods and/or after games, players leaving the penalty box to engage in fisticuffs, goalies leaving the crease to do more than swap recipes, police being called onto the ice to break up fights—all these incidents have occurred in the NHL. But by the same token these are the incidents that have been given the most attention, and today many of them have been virtually eliminated through the use of game misconducts, match misconducts, fines, and suspensions.

Since 1937 there have been thirty-seven rule revisions dealing with fisticuffs. New laws punishing the instigator and third-man-in, as well as rules restricting the number of times a player can fight, have been established. Teams no longer enter or leave the ice surface simultaneously, resulting in fewer brawls—though not necessarily fewer fights.

A silly pregame prank that somehow became larger than the game itself initiated the restructuring of this rule. It all began during the 1987 Wales Conference finals between the Philadelphia Flyers and Montreal Canadiens. Montreal's Claude Lemieux had a pregame superstition of shooting the puck into the opponent's net just before he left the ice at the end of the warm-up period. For some reason the Flyers didn't take kindly to this misuse of their goal net. Philadelphia tough guy Ed Hospodar and backup goalie Glenn Resch decided that they would attempt to stop Lemieux from succeeding at his ritual. At the conclusion of the warm-up before game three, Hospodar intercepted Lemieux's shot and fired it back into the Montreal net. The following game Resch turned the net around just as Lemieux's shot was about to enter the vacated cage.

Before game six at the Montreal Forum, Lemieux pulled a clever diversion in his attempt to sink his ritual shot. He faked leaving the ice, convincing both, Hospodar and Resch that he had given up attempting the shot. Then he and Shayne Corson rushed back onto the ice and raced toward the Flyers' net. Lemieux threw the puck ahead to Corson, who slid it into the net. Lemieux was skating around the ice in triumph when

Hospodar suddenly jumped on him and began punching. As soon as the word spread that there was a fight on the ice, the rink was filled by players in various stages of undress, who flailed away at one another. Since the referees had yet to take to the ice, they weren't there to break up the battle, and it went on unsupervised for about 10 minutes. Finally the coaches, trainers, and officials arrived on the scene and separated the players. Hospodar was deemed to have been the instigator of the entire affair, and was suspended for the remainder of the playoffs. He never played for the Flyers again.

GOALS AND ASSISTS

The rules concerning how a goal can be scored have changed little over the years. Goals have never been allowed when the puck enters the net after being struck by a high-stick, although the definition of what constitutes a high-stick has been adjusted on several occasions. Goals aren't allowed if the puck goes in after striking an official, if it is kicked in, or if it is thrown or knocked into the net with a glove or hand.

Before the current restrictions on kicking the puck were put into place (see Rule 65), it was possible to score a goal indirectly by kicking the puck. If the puck was kicked at the net and deflected in off another player or the goaltender, the goal counted. This rule remained on the books until 1992–93.

RULE 55

(a) A goal shall be scored when the puck shall have been put between the goal posts by the stick of a player of the attacking side, from in front and below the cross bar, and entirely across a red line, the width of the diameter of the goal posts drawn on the ice from one goal post to the other with the goal frame in its proper position.

(b) A goal shall be scored if the puck is put into the goal in any way by a player of the defending

Detroit defenseman Jim Morrison (#2) grimaces as the puck flyes over his shoulder into the top corner of the net signalling another goal for the Toronto Maple Leafs.

Hockey Hall of Fame

side. The player of the attacking side who last played the puck shall be credited with the goal but no assist shall be awarded.

(i) When a player scores a goal, an "assist" shall be credited to the player or players taking part in the play immediately preceding the goal, but no more than two assists can be given on any goal. Each "assist" shall count one point in the player's record.

Wash-out: Both arms swung laterally across the body with palms down. When used by referee, it means goal disallowed.

As the rule states, when a goal is scored the last person from the scoring team to touch the puck is given credit for the goal. Sometimes establishing the puck's "chain of command" can be a difficult task. In the 1947–48 season the NHL decided to try an experiment and have all players who scored a goal raise their sticks and skate back to the bench or faceoff circle so that the fans and the referee would know who had lit the lamp. You can imagine the resulting confusion.

The gimmick was first tried on November 13, 1947, in a game between the Montreal Canadiens and Chicago Black Hawks. All went well in the beginning, with Montreal's Billy Reay scoring a pair of goals and raising his stick to the rafters as asked. Then problems set in. Canadien Toe Blake scored but forgot to raise his stick. Another goal was scored but the player was in a crowd and couldn't raise his stick. Black Hawk Roy Conacher thought he scored and performed the requested victory salute, but his goal was called back because of an offside call. Needless to say, this protocol didn't last long.

Although assists were tabulated in the Pacific Coast Hockey Association as far back as 1914, they did not become an "official" NHL statistic until the 1918–19 season. From 1930–31 to 1935–36, a maximum of three assists could be awarded for any goal. Since forward passing from zone to zone

Most goals also have assists. Here, Chicago Black Hawk center Stan Mikita (#21) is about to pull the puck past Detroit goaltender Roger Crozier after receiving a perfect pass from teammate Doug Mohns (#2).

was not allowed, the instances of three assists being awarded were rare. In 1936–37 the current system of two assists was introduced, but they would only be awarded if the pass or passes that had set up the goal were made in the attacking zone. The awarding of assists was at the discretion of the official scorer. After the red line was introduced in 1942–43, assists could be awarded for passes made anywhere on the ice surface.

The NHL now awards assists to the last two players who touched the puck before the goal was scored. This includes deflections off skates, sticks, and equipment, as well as inadvertent contact with the puck. For example, if a player fires the puck at the net and it deflects off an opposing defenseman to another player who then scores, the original shooter is still credited with an assist—even though the line of contact was interrupted.

Some leagues, including those in Europe, only award assists if the puck has been passed directly from one player to another.

HANDLING PUCK WITH HANDS

Until the 1927–28 season the NHL had no rule that penalized players for closing their hands on the puck. Many old-timers followed the example of Fred "Cyclone" Taylor of the Vancouver Millionaires, who would pick up the puck and throw it into the crowd to relieve pressure. But in 1928 deliberately shooting or tossing the puck out of bounds became a minor penalty.

The current version of the rule was first introduced before the start of the 1951–52 season. Prior to that time a player could not close his hand on the puck for more than 3 seconds. However, it was legal to pluck the puck out of the air and hand it directly to the referee to stop the play and force a faceoff. Referee-in-chief Carl Voss explained, "We had to do something to stop it as it was getting ridiculous out there. Players were just grabbing the puck and tossing it back to the referee. It made for more faceoffs and delayed the game."

It is safe to assume that Detroit Red Wing goaltender Chris Osgoode did his fair share of snow shoveling in Peace River, Alberta, the prairie community where he was born. So it's only appropriate that Osgoode would use that experience to his advantage and pull the wool over the eyes of referee Paul

RULE 57

(a) If a player, except a goalkeeper, closes his hand on the puck, the play shall be stopped and a minor penalty shall be imposed on him. . . .

(b) A goalkeeper must not deliberately . . . pile up snow or obstacles at or near his net, that in the opinion of the Referee, would tend to prevent the scoring of a goal.

Stewart and Dallas veteran Dave Gagner on April Fool's Day. In a game against the Dallas Stars on April 1, 1995, the Red Wings were clinging to a slim 3–2 lead with less than a minute to go when the Stars regrouped for one final rush into the Detroit zone. With six attackers buzzing the Red Wings' goal and the Stars on the verge of scoring, Red Wing defender Martin Lapointe knocked the net off its moorings. With only 4 seconds left on the scoreboard, referee Stewart had no choice but to call a penalty shot against the Red Wings. While Stewart was discussing the rule and its implications with Red Wing captain Steve Yzerman, Osgoode decided to do a little housecleaning. Without attracting any attention to himself, he nonchalantly gathered some of the snow that had accumulated near his goalposts and fanned it out beyond the top of his crease.

Dallas appointed Dave Gagner, their leading goal-scorer, to take the shot. Starting at center ice Gagner stickhandled toward the Detroit net, deked left, and went right. There was only one problem: The puck didn't go with him. It stayed glued to the ice, its progress impeded by an odd buildup of snow in the slot that had gone undetected by the officials.

It wasn't until days after the event that the truth of Osgoode's sophomore savvy was disclosed. While it's safe to assume that the slot area will be swept in future penalty-shot attempts, it's of no consolation to Gagner, whose botched penalty shot was shown on sports blooper programs from coast to coast.

Rule 57(c) is a little-known, and rarely called, section of the rule book that penalizes any goalie who grabs the puck and tosses it forward to a member of his own team.

One of the first goaltenders to be whistled on this rule was Boston Bruin Don Simmons, who had a habit of throwing the puck up the ice. On most occasions the referee would turn a blind eye to the proceedings, since Simmons's tosses rarely exceeded a couple of feet. But when Simmons started pitching the pill down the ice, referee Eddie Powers had no choice but to become an on-ice umpire and throw the book at the Boston goalie.

It was early in the 1959–60 season that Simmons decided to "take the mound" for the Bruins. Midway through

(c) . . . (NOTE) In the case of the puck thrown forward by the goalkeeper being taken by an opponent, the Referee shall allow the resulting play to be completed, and if goal is scored by the non-offending team, it shall be allowed and no penalty given; but if a goal is not scored, play shall be stopped and a minor penalty shall be imposed against the goalkeeper.

the first period of a Detroit Red Wings–Boston Bruins tilt on October 22, 1959, Simmons gloved a drive off the stick of Norm Ullman and threw the puck up the ice to teammate Jean Guy Gendron. Referee Powers whistled down the play and thumbed Simmons for 2 minutes. Obviously Powers had been doing his homework. When Simmons confronted him as to what law he had broken, the on-ice arbiter was quick to point out Rule 57(c).

Bruin winger Nick Mickoski was sent to the box to serve Simmons's minor while the Red Wings prepared to go on the powerplay. Less than a minute later Red Wing Val Fonteyne slipped the puck past Simmons to give Detroit a lead they would never surrender on their way to a 4–1 victory.

If Simmons learned from his mistake, he didn't show it. In the Bruins' second game of the 1960–61 season, a match against the Montreal Canadiens at the Forum, referee Frank Udvari nabbed Simmons once again for tossing the puck forward to a teammate. This time Simmons's fling didn't hurt his club, which fought the Canadiens to a 1–1 tie. Following the game Udvari said he had never called the penalty before, but since Simmons had thrown the puck 20 feet up the ice, he had no choice but to make the call.

The rule also had serious repercussions for Toronto Maple Leaf goaltender Lorne Chabot. Midway through a game against the New York Americans on February 22, 1932, Chabot wandered out of the net to glove a long, looping shot off the stick of Americans' winger Tommy Filmore. Knowing he couldn't toss the puck forward, Chabot decided to throw the disk behind the net. Unfortunately, his aim was not true and he heaved the puck into his own net, giving the sad-sack Americans a 4–4 tie with the Maple Leafs.

HIGH STICKS

Once, just after the end of the Great War when football was king of the college campus, the dean of Notre Dame University was asked if he thought the game of hockey would ever be played at the school. The monseigneur paused a moment, then answered, "Goodness no, son, I could never allow a game to be played at our institution that puts a weapon in the hands of an Irishman."

RULE 58

(a) The carrying of sticks above the normal height of the WAIST of the opponent is prohibited and a minor, double-minor or major penalty may be imposed on a player violating this rule, at the discretion of the Referee.

(b) A goal scored by an attacking player who strikes the puck with his stick which is carried above the height of the crossbar of the goal frame shall not be allowed.

A goal scored by a defending player who strikes the puck with his stick which is carried above the height of the crossbar of the goal frame shall be allowed.

(c) When a player carries or holds any part of his stick above the normal height of the WAIST of the opponent so that injury results the Referee shall:

(1) assess a double-minor penalty when it is deemed to be accidental in nature by the officials;

(2) assess a major and game-misconduct when the high stick is deemed to be careless by the officials. . . .

High-sticking: Holding both fists clenched, one above the other at the side of the head.

Football is still king at Notre Dame, of course, but now it shares some of its spotlight with hockey, which has been in South Bend since the 1930s—about the same time that the high-sticking penalty was introduced to the *NHL Rule Book*. The first mentions of high-sticking infractions and of knocking the puck down or into the net with a high-stick came prior to the 1929–30 season. Originally grouped with the rule-book section concerning throwing of the stick, restrictions on high-sticking and on carrying the stick above the shoulders have been changed numerous times over the years. One thing has remained constant: Any contact by a high-stick causing injury is a major penalty.

Any goal scored as a result of the puck being knocked into the net with a stick carried above the shoulder was disallowed until 1943–44, when it was decided that a goal would count if the puck had been directed into the net with a high-stick by a member of the defending team.

Carrying the stick above the shoulder was also prohibited at any time on the ice, but a penalty for this infraction was not put in place until the 1945–46 season.

As helmet use increased in the NHL—players having grown up in youth, junior, and college hockey programs that required helmets and face protection—players became careless about how they carried their sticks. As a result, the number of high-sticking fouls rose dramatically in the 1980s. Answering a call to make the game safer, the League decided in 1988–89 that any high-stick foul that drew blood brought with it a 5-minute major and a game misconduct, even if contact had been accidental.

But that wasn't the answer either, since there was no room for compromise, and sometimes the crime didn't fit the punishment. After two more years of refinement, the current rules were put into place, allowing the referee and linesmen to sentence the guilty party to a minor, double minor, or major plus game misconduct, depending on the severity of the foul.

Another subject of considerable debate over the years was pucks knocked out of the air and into the net with high-sticks. For years play was stopped if the puck was struck by a stick carried above the shoulder. Later this rule was amended so that a stoppage occurred when the puck was struck by a

Dan Diamond and Associates

When Pittsburgh's Randy Cunneyworth (#15) brushed his stick across the chin of New York Ranger defenseman Larry Melnyk (#30), he was quickly sent to the penalty box for high-sticking.

stick above the waist. However, it remained very difficult for referees to judge where a stick was being held when it made contact with a puck flying through the air. In addition, tall players were allowed to carry their sticks higher than short ones due to their greater height at shoulder or waist level.

The League implemented a simple and effective solution prior to the 1993–94 campaign. The NHL ruled that any puck knocked into the net by a stick carried above the height of the crossbar would not be counted. Giving the referees and the off-ice officials a stationary reference point—the height of the crossbar—has virtually eliminated controversy that has surrounded this often-difficult call.

Holding: Clasping the wrist of the "whistle hand" well in front of chest.

HOLDING AN OPPONENT

Ever since the game of hockey was first played, grabbing an opponent and holding him to impede his progress has been a

🏒 RULE 59

(a) A minor penalty shall be imposed on a player who holds

an opponent with hands or stick or in any other way.

(b) A minor penalty shall be assessed to a player who uses his hand to hold an opponent's stick.

Dan Diamond and Associates

Had this play occurred today instead of the 1973–74 season, Marcel Dionne (#5) would have been cited for holding the stick and sent to the sin-bin for a two-minute vacation.

RULE 60

(a) A minor penalty shall be imposed on a player who impedes or seeks to impede the progress of an opponent by "hooking" with his stick.

(b) A major penalty shall be imposed on any player who injures an opponent by "hooking". . . .

penalty. And ever since the game of hockey was first played, the holding infraction has been called at the discretion of the referee. Some on-ice officials tolerate the "clutch-and-grab" game as long as it's not flagrant, others do not.

During the 1991–92 season, the League was faced with a new problem. More than ever before, defensive players were grabbing their opponents' sticks in an effort to slow down a fast-skating foe or prevent him from corralling a loose puck. Although the ploy had existed in various forms for years, the maneuver seemed to be part of every defenseman's arsenal during the 1991–92 season. The holding rule at the time stated "a minor penalty shall be imposed on any player who holds an opponent with his hands or his stick or in any other way." Since there was nothing in the books that definitely covered holding the stick, the referees were powerless to prevent it.

Prior to the start of the 1992–93 campaign, the NHL introduced legislation that assessed a minor penalty "to a player who uses his hand to hold an opponent's stick." In the first sixteen games of the 1992–93 regular season, thirty holding-the-stick infractions were called. Bob Rouse of the Toronto Maple Leafs earned the dubious honor of being the first player to be caught breaking the new law, entering the penalty box at 13:15 of the first period in the Maple Leafs' home opener against the Washington Capitals on October 6. The rule had the desired effect, and holding-the-stick violations dropped off considerably. In the 1993 Stanley Cup final series between the Montreal Canadiens and Los Angeles Kings, there wasn't a single holding-the-stick penalty called.

HOOKING

Hooking is the king of all restraining fouls and remains a very effective way to slow down an opponent, especially if the hook goes undetected. If apprehended in the act, a player guilty of hooking spends 2 minutes in the penalty box. During the 1970s no team spent more time in the box than hockey's "Broad Street Bullies," the Philadelphia Flyers. The Flyers led the NHL in total penalty minutes eight times in the decade and were masters at the limits of the rules. Boasting exceptional penalty-killing, the Flyers realized that they could intimidate, take penalties, and often not pay the price on the scoreboard.

Diane Sobolewski

The Flyers' ascent from also-ran to Stanley Cup champion began when coach Fred Shero instituted a system of play based on physical dominance. In their first three seasons they trailed only Boston's "Big, Bad Bruins" in total penalty minutes. In 1971–72, Shero's first season behind the bench, the Flyers collected 1,233 penalty minutes to lead the NHL. For the next eleven seasons the Bullies were the most penalized team in the League, but they managed to reach the Stanley Cup finals four times and win a pair of championships during this stretch.

Using a lethal combination of intimidation, airtight defense, and opportunistic scoring, the Flyers became the first team in NHL history to win the Stanley Cup and lead the NHL in penalty minutes in back-to-back seasons. To accomplish this rare double-double, the Flyers' powerplay and penalty-killing units had to be in top form. This was where

An unseen opponent drapes his stick across Hartford Whaler forward Kevin Dineen's chest and pulls him to the ice in a classic display of hooking.

Hooking: A tugging motion with both arms, as if pulling something toward the stomach.

the genius of Shero shone. He molded his special team to perfection, allowing his club to control the game through physical domination, then shut down the opposition power-play when the Flyers were penalized.

In 1973–74 the Flyers played at least one man short 422 times—the St. Louis Blues were next at 313—but allowed only 49 goals for a League-leading penalty-killing percentage of 88.4. The following season the Flyers fell to second in penalty-killing, but still went unscored-upon in 392 of 466 shorthanded situations. With penalty-killing this effective, the Flyers could afford to play their no-holds-barred system. Many teams coming into the Philadelphia Spectrum would find their less physical players coming down with the "Philly Flu," a peculiar twenty-four-hour virus that seemed to miraculously disappear moments after the stricken players left the Philadelphia area.

While the Flyers of the 1970s are often regarded as the roughest-and-toughest team of their era, the Philadelphia clubs of the early 1980s actually averaged more penalties-per-game and racked up more penalty minutes. However, without the special-team discipline that characterized the 1974 and 1975 lineups, the Flyers could not return to the Stanley Cup–winner's circle. In 1980–81 the Flyers were expected to make a serious run at the championship but lost in the quarter-finals to the Calgary Flames. During the regular season the Flyers had stood fifth in penalty-killing; they dropped to seventh in the playoffs. The following season the Flyers drew an average of seven more penalties per game than the Stanley Cup–winning New York Islanders, and fell to seventeenth in the League in penalty-killing efficiency. They were ousted from the postseason parade in the preliminary round—their earliest departure since 1967–68.

RULE 61

(a) For the purpose of this rule, the center red line will divide the ice into halves. Should any player of a team, equal or superior in numerical strength to the opposing team, shoot, bat or deflect the puck from his own

ICING THE PUCK

The icing rule was passed by the NHL Board of Governors on September 24, 1937. It had become the strategy of some teams to gain an early lead, then throw the puck down the ice at every opportunity in an attempt to protect their margin. If teams could be prevented from resorting to these tactics, the pace and appeal of the game would be greatly improved.

Two early-decade incidents in particular prompted the NHL to introduce rules concerning icing. The first occurred on November 8, 1931, in a game between the New York Americans and Boston Bruins. The Americans were holding a slim 3–2 lead when they began sending the puck down the ice at every opportunity. In total, the Americans iced more than fifty times. The fans at Boston Garden became so incensed at this boring maneuver that they littered the ice with paper, rubbish, and broken bottles. The referee ordered the teams to their dressing rooms, but the crowd quieted down and the game was resumed without incident.

Boston president Charles Adams was so upset by the Americans' choice of playing style that he ordered his Bruins to play the same way when the teams met again in New York on December 3. The result was a scoreless draw that saw the Bruins ice the puck eighty-seven times, disgusting the fourteen thousand fans in attendance. The media charged that the Bruins had made a mockery of the game and its rules, but NHL president Frank Calder said that he had watched the game and had seen worse. The media didn't press him as to exactly when.

Luckily, these were isolated incidents. Regardless, the League knew it needed to eliminate this potential source of embarrassing delay. Although teams still take advantage of the "no icing" rule today, it's no longer seriously abused.

On June 15, 1951, the League declared that if a goaltender came out of his net and touched the puck, icing would be nullified. Prior to the the 1990–91 season, the League ruled that if the puck passed through or touched any part of the goal crease before crossing the goal line when the goaltender had been removed, icing would still be effect.

INTERFERENCE

The interference rule came under fire in the mid-1990s with the introduction of the "neutral zone trap," a strategy of slowing down the opposition in the center-ice area by close checking (plus the odd clutch or grab) and by not allowing them to speed into the attacking zone. Coaches, fans, and media have been quite vocal in their disapproval of this new strategy, but old-timers will tell you that everything old is new

half of the ice beyond the goal line of the opposing team, play shall be stopped and the puck faced-off at the end face-off spot of the offending team, unless on the play, the puck shall have entered the net of the opposing team, in which case the goal shall be allowed. . . .

Icing: Linesman's arm folded across the upper chest.

Wash-Out: Both arms swung laterally at shoulder level with palms down. When used by a linesman, it means no icing or no off-sides.

⬤ RULE 62

(a) A minor penalty shall be imposed on a player who interferes with or impedes the progress of an opponent who is not in possession of the puck.

Interference: Crossed arms stationary in front of chest with fists closed.

New legislation introduced for the 1995–96 season would have prevented Maple Leaf defenseman Borje Salming running this type of interference on Chicago forward Steve Larmer.

Dan Diamond and Associates

again. The trap system was a common deterrent in the 1930s as well, and prompted the same reaction then that it does today—so much so that on November 29, 1933, NHL president Frank Calder announced that "the interference rule will be enforced to the letter. No interference will be allowed on any player who does not have the puck. This should open up the game considerably."

In 1965 veteran referee Frank Udvari spoke about Rule 62 and gave his own interpretation of how the interference penalty should be called. "What fans often fail to realize is that a defending player is allowed to 'shadow' an intending pass-receiver closely and stride for stride. It often happens that they get snarled—one brings the other down. If the referee judges it was accidental, there is no penalty to be called."

INTERFERENCE BY/WITH SPECTATORS

In the days before there was protective glass along the boards or behind the benches, spectators could easily interfere with the players. It wasn't uncommon for an angry or cunning fan to grab a player's stick or sweater as he fought for possession of the puck along the dashers. Although some rinks began adding glass protection along the side boards in the early 1960s, it wasn't required by the rules until 1966–67, so for most of the League's first fifty years fans were part of the action along the boards.

There were several incidents between players and fans during these years, but for the most part the spectators resisted the temptation to reach out and touch someone. One well-known exception occurred during game two of the Montreal Canadiens–Toronto Maple Leafs semifinal series on March 23, 1944. With Montreal leading 1–0, Canadien Maurice Richard was streaming down the right side when Leaf defenseman Bob Davidson shifted toward the boards to cut off Richard's lane. A fan reached out and grabbed Davidson's stick from his hands, tossing it across the ice. That caught Davidson completely by surprise and Richard was able to fly by him and score to give the Habs a commanding 2–0 lead. Davidson complained bitterly to referee Bill Chadwick, but the referee had missed the infraction and couldn't call back the goal. He did have the stick-grabber tossed from the game, much to the displeasure of the Canadien fans in attendance in the Forum. Richard went on to score 5 goals in the same game, and the Canadiens went on to win their first Stanley Cup in thirteen years.

Of course, having no glass along the boards could cause other headaches. Referee Mickey Ion and the Boston Bruins could have told you all about it. In game one of the Boston Bruins–New York Rangers semifinals on March 21, 1939, referee Ion was following the play along the boards when he and Bruin forward Milt Schmidt were checked into the boards by Ranger forward Lynn Patrick. Both Schmidt and Ion were catapulted over the boards into the crowd. While Ion and Schmidt were untangling their skates and sticks from overcoats, fedoras, and elbows, Bruin Bobby Bauer picked up the

RULE 63

(a) In the event of a player being held or interfered with by a spectator, the Referee or Linesman shall blow the whistle and play shall be stopped unless the team of the player interfered with is in possession of the puck at this time when the play shall be allowed to be completed before blowing the whistle and the puck shall be faced-off at the spot where last played at time of stoppage.

Hockey Hall of Fame

Since many arenas did not have protective glass along the sideboards until the 1960s, spectators sitting in the rail seats had a "close up and personal" view of the action.

(b) Any player who physically interferes with the spectators shall automatically incur a gross misconduct penalty and the Referee shall report all such infractions to the Commissioner who shall have full power to impose such further penalty as he shall deem appropriate.

puck, moved across the Rangers' line, and scored. Ion, however, didn't see the goal and refused to allow it. The Bruins issued a protest that they later dropped when they won the game by a 2–1 score.

One of the most disturbing images in sport is the sight of athletes climbing into the stands and confronting fans. Fortunately, these situations have occurred only rarely in the NHL, and have always been dealt with seriously by the League.

The 1954–55 season was the most challenging of the reign of NHL president Clarence Campbell. In that season Campbell confronted two adversaries, Maurice Richard and Ted Lindsay, and used the opportunity to solidify his executive powers.

On November 13, 1954, a fan named Bernard Czeponis started heckling Detroit Red Wing Glen Skov after the Wings had just dropped a 1–0 decision to the Toronto Maple Leafs. Skov and the fan became entangled, and when Wing Ted Lindsay climbed into the stands to diffuse the matter he ended up throwing a punch at the fan. The police separated the combatants and the fan decided not to press charges, asking only for an apology. One headline in the newspapers the following day reflected the media's distaste for the situation: "Who gets the black eye, the fan or the League?" Despite this bad press, Campbell decided to let Lindsay off with a warning.

Five weeks later, Lindsay was back in the news and this time president Campbell's reaction was both swift and harsh. During a game against the Maple Leafs on January 22, 1955, a fan by the name of Irving Tenney reached out and grabbed Gordie Howe's stick and, as Howe skated away, took a swipe at the Red Wing star. Lindsay, who was following the play up the ice, attacked the fan, striking him on the shoulder with his stick. Lindsay then dropped his stick, and he and the fan traded body blows. The referee stopped the game and police were called in to break up the dispute.

At a Board of Governors meeting three days later, Campbell suspended Lindsay for 10 days. The Red Wings' reaction was one of disbelief. They filed an appeal of Lindsay's sentence and asked the League's other member clubs to support them. Campbell demanded his verdict be upheld and threatened to resign if it was not. Campbell's powerplay was successful and Lindsay was sent to the sidelines for a four-game holiday. It was the longest suspension in NHL history for player/fan interference. The action solidified Campbell's position as president, demonstrating that he was in full control.

Hockey fans have long expressed displeasure by throwing objects onto the ice. However, in the International League finals of 1932, overzealous fans cost their team a chance to win the championship. In those days the NHL sent two of its referees down to the International League to handle the finals. On April 10, 1932, Mike Rodden and Jerry Goodman were officiating the championship game between the Buffalo Bisons and Detroit Olympics. At the 18:02 mark of the third period, Detroit's Leroy Goldsworthy thought he had scored to tie the game at 2–2, but referee Goodman ruled that Detroit forward Ferrand Gillie had interfered with the Buffalo goaltender. The manager of the Detroit team at the time was Jack Adams, and he was instrumental in inciting the fans to cover the ice surface with debris. The fans obliged, throwing every sort of object onto the ice. The officials were quite content to let the storm pass until referee Rodden was nailed with a rotten egg. He picked up the puck, sent the teams to their dressing rooms, and declared the game over. With that decision, Buffalo was declared the winner by a 2–1 count and Detroit—and its fans—were the losers.

The NHL was faced faced with an intriguing problem during the 1996 playoffs. While throwing objects on the ice has never been allowed, it has at times been tolerated. For instance, when a player scores three goals in a game, it is customary for the fans to litter the ice with hats to celebrate the "hat-trick." However, that was before the fans of the Florida Panthers began celebrating each and every goal scored by their team with a barrage of plastic rats.

It all started on October 8, 1995, as the Panthers were preparing for their home opener against the Calgary Flames. While the players were putting on their game faces prior to the match, Florida forward Scott Mellanby spied a rat sneaking across the floor of the dressing room. Mellanby grabbed his stick and snapped off a wrist shot, using the genus Rattus as a puck. The furry fellow flew through the air, eventually meeting his maker after striking the wall. Mellanby then went out and scored a pair of goals in the game, prompting a local scribe to describe his performance as a "rat-trick."

(c) In the event that objects are thrown on the ice which interfere with the progress of the game, the Referee shall blow the whistle and stop the play and the puck shall be faced-off at the spot play is stopped.

From that point on, the fans began throwing plastic rats on the ice whenever a Panther scored a goal. What was nothing more than a novelty in the regular season soon became a problem in the playoffs. Thousands of rats would rain down on the ice after every Florida goal. It was estimated that $55,000 worth of the plastic rodents were being tossed each night, resulting in long delays and concern over the players' safety. After the Panthers' miracle run finally ended in the Stanley Cup final, the League announced that new rules would be introduced to curb exuberant celebrations like those practiced by the Florida faithful.

 RULE 64

A match penalty shall be imposed on any player who kicks or attempts to kick another player. . . .

KICKING A PLAYER

Like head-butting or biting, kicking a player is one of the most serious offenses in the rule book and, thankfully, there have been very few incidents in the NHL of a player losing his temper to this extent. Even in the minor leagues incidents of kicking are rare.

One of the most serious infractions of Rule 64 occurred in the Manitoba Junior Hockey League during its 1960 semifinal series between the St. Boniface Canadians and Winnipeg Rangers. In the fifth and deciding game of the set, eighteen-year-old St. Boniface goaltender Paul Sexsmith kicked Winnipeg's Don McKenzie after the Ranger forward was upended and fell into the Canadian's crease. Sexsmith was a talented athlete with a promising future, but he could not control his temper. The kicking incident was only the most recent in a series of occurrences involving the goaltender. Taking into consideration the seriousness of the affair, League officials decided to suspend Sexsmith for the entire 1960–61 season. With that, the youngster's promising career came to an end.

RULE 65

Kicking the puck shall be permitted in all zones. A goal cannot be scored by an attacking player who kicks the puck directly into the net, whether intended or not. . . .

KICKING THE PUCK

Kicking the puck directly into the net has never been allowed in the game of hockey. Until 1992–93, however, a goal was allowed if a kicked puck deflected into the net off an opposing player.

For many years using skates to move the puck was outlawed. By the time the NHL was incorporated in 1917, kicking the puck was allowed in the neutral zone. In 1927, as part of the League's "antidefense" campaign to add flow to the game, players were allowed to kick the puck away from scrums along the boards in both the defensive and neutral zones. Three years later, in 1930–31, kicking the puck was permitted on any part of the ice surface.

There was one exception. If a player had broken or lost his stick, he was not allowed to kick the puck or participate in the play in any way. He must go directly to the bench to get a new stick or be replaced by another player. Such a case occurred during game one of the 1936 Stanley Cup finals between the Detroit Red Wings and Toronto Maple Leafs. Early in the second period, with the Leafs already trailing by a 3–1 score, Leaf forward Jack Shill was penalized by referee Bill Stewart for kicking the puck after his stick had been broken. The Wings went on the powerplay and quickly scored, but the goal was disallowed by Stewart because a Red Wing player had been in the crease. Detroit held on to win by the same 3–1 count, and eventually won the Stanley Cup in four games.

LEAVING PLAYERS' OR PENALTY BENCH

For many years the rules governing leaving the bench to participate in an altercation on the ice were lenient and, as a result, bench-clearing brawls were quite common. Until 1987–88 the punishment for being first off the bench varied from a small fine to a double minor with the possibility of a three-game suspension.

Prior to the start of the 1987–88 season, the NHL introduced rules that called for game misconducts and strict suspensions for players involved in bench-clearing brawls. One of the most important additions to the rule was a subsection that gave an automatic suspension to the coach of the player who first left the bench to join in an altercation.

As a result the NHL has not had a bench-clearing brawl in some years. There are more bench-clearing brawls in basketball and baseball than there are in hockey, and the game is better for it. One of the rare times the rule has been enforced came during preseason play before the 1994–95 season. In an exhibition game between the Vancouver Canucks and Los Angeles Kings, Canuck Gino Odjick left the players' bench to

RULE 66

(a) No player may leave the players' or penalty bench at any time during an altercation or for the purpose of starting an altercation. Substitutions made prior to the altercation shall be permitted, provided the players so substituting do not enter the altercation.

(u) The Coach(es) of the team(s) whose player(s) left the players' bench(es) during an altercation may be suspended, pending a review by the Commissioner. The Coach(es) also may be fined a maximum of ten thousand dollars ($10,000).

take part in a scuffle. Although there was some confusion whether Odjick, who had just finished a shift, actually left the bench, both he and coach Rick Ley were suspended for Odjick's actions. Odjick received a ten-game ban and Ley, a five-game. Because the 1994–95 season was reduced from eighty-four to forty-eight games, both Ley's and Odjick's suspensions were prorated to reflect the reduced schedule.

 RULE 67

(a) Any player who deliberately applies physical force in any manner against an official, in any manner attempts to injure an official, deliberately makes contact with an official, physically demeans an official or deliberately applies physical force to an official solely for the purpose of getting free of such an official during or immediately following an altercation shall receive a game misconduct penalty. . . .

PHYSICAL ABUSE OF OFFICIALS

Until the 1937–38 season there were no rules covering the abuse of officials, whether verbal or physical. Fines and suspensions were handed out by the president of the League if a referee was abused during a game, but the process was contingent upon a statement from the official and a hearing with the offending player. The fact remained, however, that a player, coach, or manager could actually attack an on-ice official and not be immediately penalized.

Two separate incidents on March 23, 1937, demonstrated to the NHL that this problem needed to be addressed. Near the end of game one of a very rough Boston Bruins–Montreal Maroons quarter-final series, referee Clarence Campbell penalized Bruin captain Dit Clapper for high-sticking Maroon star Dave Trottier. Without warning, Clapper punched Campbell in the face. He was hustled off to the penalty box by his teammates before he could do further damage.

On the same night in Toronto, the Maple Leafs were entertaining the New York Rangers in game one of their Stanley Cup quarter-finals. Despite outplaying the Rangers, the Leafs were losing 3–0 when, with only seconds remaining in the match, Leaf Bob Davidson cross-checked Ranger Phil Watson. The Rangers retaliated, and soon every player on the ice was paired off with a member of the opposing team. In the middle of the action Leaf manager Conn Smythe came out onto the ice and started berating referee Ag Smith. Leaf captain Charlie Conacher managed to get his boss off the ice. As Smith attempted to break up another skirmish, Leaf defenseman Red Horner punched him in the mouth.

In both cases fines and suspensions were expected, but Clapper and Horner were let off the hook by the very men they had assaulted. Referee Campbell noted that Clapper's punch "happened in the heat of the moment," and that Clapper probably thought he was hitting a Maroon player; he recommended that the Bruin captain be let off with a fine. Virtually the same report was filed by referee Smith concerning Red Horner: Smith explained that Horner had struck him by mistake. President Calder noted that since Horner hadn't been penalized, he wouldn't be fined either.

The next season, 1937–38, the League introduced legislation covering the abuse of officials, and also gave president Calder full control over the League's referees. Any player abusing a referee would receive a 10-minute misconduct. If that same player committed another offense against an official in the same game, he would receive a game misconduct. These punishments remained on the books until the mid-1960s.

In the 1966–67 season the NHL updated Rules 42 and 67 by including a clause stating that any contact between a player and an official would result in a game misconduct and a subsequent suspension. The first players to feel the sting of this new ruling were New York Ranger forward Bernie Geoffrion and Montreal Canadien tough guy John Ferguson. Both incidents occurred on February 8, 1967. Geoffrion was suspended for three games for cross-checking linesman Walter Atanas and shooting an empty beer can in the linesman's direction. That same week Ferguson was also sent to the sidelines for three games for punching linesman Brent Casselman during a brief scuffle with a Chicago Black Hawk player.

Suspensions for physical abuse of officials are rare in today's NHL, but there are still instances when players and coaches lose their cool and take out their frustration on the striped jerseys.

In 1982 the NHL passed its most comprehensive legislation concerning the treatment of on-ice officials. As a result, the most severe suspension for abusing an on-ice official was handed out only one year later, and it showed that no rule can cover all situations. During the second period of an October 30, 1983, game between the Chicago Black Hawks and Hartford Whalers, Hawk center Tom Lysiak was tossed out of the faceoff circle by linesman Ron Foyt for the fifth time in the game. After the puck was dropped, Lysiak had tripped

Foyt as the linesman moved up ice to follow the play. Lysiak was assessed a game misconduct penalty by referee Dave Newell, who in his report after the game suggested Lysiak be charged under Rule 67(a).

Rule 67(a), introduced in 1982, called for a twenty-game suspension, and Lysiak was suspended for that length of time. Video replays showed that while Lysiak's tripping of Foyt appeared to be deliberate, it was also a fairly harmless foul. The Black Hawks filed a court injunction to have the ban lifted and it was granted, allowing Lysiak to return to the lineup. However, after another hearing, the NHL upheld the twenty-game ban, the second-longest suspension in NHL history for abuse of an official. Only Billy Coutu of the Montreal Canadiens, who was banned for life after a series of offenses, had been given a stiffer sentence.

It was noted that Lysiak was a gentlemanly player who had never accumulated more than 85 penalty minutes in a season. While the League's Board of Governors upheld Lysiak's sentence, new rules were introduced that defined three different categories of abuse of officials, with suspensions ranging from three to twenty games.

RULE 68

(a) Players shall not use obscene gestures on the ice or anywhere in the rink before, during or after the game. . . .

OBSCENE OR PROFANE LANGUAGE OR GESTURES

There are those who say that profane language is as much a part of hockey as pucks and skates. Profanity is, of course, not limited to hockey. Rather, it is part of any competitive situation where nerves get frayed and tension builds.

While it is true that expletives have been part of the game since its beginning, a well-publicized outburst by Tommy Gorman, manager of the Montreal Maroons, convinced the NHL to take its first action. On November 24, 1937, during a 2–2 tie against the rival Montreal Canadiens, Gorman was fined $100 by referee E. Daigneault for continual use of bad language. At the NHL meetings on May 8, 1937, the NHL proposed hefty fines for team officials and a 10-minute misconduct for any player who verbally abused officials.

Some leagues took the battle against obscene language one step farther. In November 1951 the Ontario Hockey Association, which included a number of teams that were sponsored by NHL clubs, was swamped by complaints from fans about obscene language. When a referee resigned because he couldn't bear the swearing and obscenities, the organization decided to take action. The League announced that, effective December 15, 1951, any player who repeatedly used foul or obscene language would be suspended for three games.

The new law seemed to have a calming effect on the players, until a game between the St. Michael's Monarchs and the Kitchener Dutchmen in March 1952. Referee Jack Hogan was having trouble controlling the game, but when he allowed a goal by Kitchener that the St. Mike's faithful felt had never entered the net, the situation got out of control. Monarch net-minder Phil Hughes seemed to be the most vocal of the players and tried to climb over the end screen to get at some fans who were giving him the needle. Another of the Monarch players, Gord Hannigan, left the penalty box to give referee Hogan a piece of his mind, but before long calm was restored and the game continued. Two days later, the OHA brass ruled that Hannigan was being suspended for "using obscene and abusive language near the referee." He was the first player to get a three-game vacation for swearing.

While these rules protected the on-ice officials, they did nothing to restrict the stream of bloody-blue-murder fans sitting near players' benches were forced to endure. Even NHL president Clarence Campbell found himself powerless to end the jawing that was a standard feature of most player benches. During a game between the Detroit Red Wings and Montreal Canadiens on January 1, 1955, Campbell approached the Red Wings' bench and requested that the players and their coach refrain from swearing. Well, let's just say Campbell's appeal was turned down rather explicitly by Wing coach Jimmy Skinner. The Detroit bench boss pointed out in no uncertain terms that since Campbell was at the game as a spectator, rather than as League president, he shouldn't presume to tell the Detroit players how to act.

The media had a field day with this one, and there were numerous predictions as to what Skinner's punishment was going to be. But Campbell agreed. He admitted he had been at the game as a fan, not as a League executive, and that he was in the wrong to give his opinion to the Red Wings' bench. Campbell insisted that the fans around him had been com-

(c) Club Executives, Managers, Coaches and Trainers shall not use obscene or profane language or gestures anywhere in the rink. For violation of this rule, a bench minor penalty shall be imposed.

plaining and asked him to act. He did request, in his official position as president, that players take into account the paying public and refrain from using foul language. The subject was hotly debated for years, until glass partitions were erected separating the fans from the benches and screening the public from the comments of the players.

Of course, not every rink placed a glass wall between the fans and the players.

In the late 1970s the Montreal Forum still had no partition behind the visitors' bench. Don Cherry remembers one evening in 1978 when he and his Boston Bruins were visiting the Forum. The Canadiens were winning and coach Cherry was in a foul mood, filling the air with a potpourri of profanity. During a stoppage of play midway through the third period, a woman sitting in an aisle seat two rows behind the bench loudly demanded that Cherry save that kind of language for another time and place. As the play continued, Cherry left the bench, approached the unhappy customer, and apologized, adding, "Now, ma'am, you can't say that you've never heard that kind of language before." "That's true, Mr. Cherry," she replied, "but I've never had to pay forty dollars to listen to it."

OFF-SIDES AND PRECEDING PUCK INTO ATTACKING ZONE

The evolution of these two rules is so closely related that it is impossible to discuss one without referring to the other.

Until the introduction of forward passing, the offside rule was simple: A player from the team in possession of the puck could not touch or play the puck if he was ahead of it, no matter where he was on the ice. On the other hand, if the puck had been touched by a member of the opposing team, it could be gathered in and taken up ice. These early offside rules created a game that had no forward passing and prized stickhandling above all other skills.

With the introduction of bluelines the offside rules became more complicated. The puck could be passed forward in the defensive zone as long as the player receiving the pass was still inside his own blueline. However, the puck could not be touched by a player on the same team as the puck carrier

RULE 69

(a) . . . A player is off-side when both skates are completely over the outer edge of the determining center line or blue line involved in the play.

Wash-Out: Both arms swung laterally at shoulder level with palms down. When used by a linesman, it means no icing or no off-sides.

anywhere else on the ice unless he was behind or beside the player passing it. The offside rule also restricted a player from entering any zone ahead of the puck carrier.

When the League decided to allow forward passing in the neutral or center-ice zone for the 1926–27 season, the offside rules were redefined to reflect the new rules, but the basic laws still stood: No one could enter the neutral or attacking zone ahead of the puck, and no player could accept a pass from one zone to another.

All these rules were designed to open up the game, which had evolved into a never-ending defensive struggle. After a 1928–29 season that saw 120 shutouts, 95 tied games, and a combined goals-per-game average of 2.80, the League decided to make passing legal in all three zones and eliminated all but one offside rule—that restricting passes from one zone to another. With the exception of this rule, there were to be no offsides, which meant players could skate into the offensive zone, set up camp beside the opposition's net, and wait for their teammates to bring the puck into the zone. And many players did just that. One coach joked that Bruin Cooney Weiland and Maroon Nels Stewart were spending more time in the attacking zone than in their own homes.

While it was true that the League wanted to increase scoring, no one expected the offensive explosion that followed. In the first sixty-six games played after the offside rules were eliminated, 456 goals were scored, for an average of 6.91 goals per game. Clearly, this was not what the League had had in mind.

RULE 71

(a) Players of the attacking team must not precede the puck into the attacking zone.

(c) If however, notwithstanding the fact that a member of the attacking team shall have preceded the puck into the attacking zone, the puck is cleanly intercepted by a member of the defending team at or near the blue line and is carried out or passed by them into the neutral zone, the "off-side" shall be ignored and play permitted to continue. (Officials will carry out this rule by means of the "slow whistle".)

Slow Whistle: Arm in which the whistle is not held extended above head. If play returns to neutral zone without stoppage of play, arm is drawn down the instant the puck crosses the line.

Toronto forward Gus Mortson breaks in over the Boston Bruins blueline with the remaining four Maple Leaf skaters trailing the play. Although the center ice red line had been introduced when this photo was taken, this style of play—carrying the puck from zone to zone—was the preferred way to advance the puck prior to 1943.

Hockey Hall of Fame

On December 16, 1930, the NHL governors huddled in Montreal and decided to bring in a new "goal-hanging" rule that stated, "No attacking players shall be allowed to precede the play when entering the opposing defensive zone."

With these restrictions on the flow of the game, it was only natural that there would be constant stoppages in play, especially after the icing rule was adopted in 1937–38. Prior to the 1943–44 season, the NHL entered the "modern era" when it added the center-ice line and allowed forward passing from one zone to another. The current offside rules were adopted at this time, and with the exception of some odd tinkering, they have remained virtually unchanged since.

One important exception is the "touch-up" rule devised by NHL director of officiating John McCauley and Washington Capital general manager David Poile. Introduced prior to the 1988–89 season, the "touch-up" rule was designed to reduce the number of offside infractions called in a game. Under the old rule, if a player from the attacking team dumped the puck into the offensive zone while one or more of his teammates was over the blueline, a delayed offside was signaled. To prevent a stoppage in play, it was the responsibility of the defensive team to clear the puck from the zone without a player from the attacking team touching it. With the new "touch-up" rule, players caught in the attacking zone could skate back to the blueline, "touch up," return to the attacking zone, and pursue the puck without a stoppage in play.

A 1989–90 rule stated that if a player from the attacking team purposely touched the puck before clearing the zone, the faceoff would be held at the other end of the ice surface.

Although this new "touch-up" rule has been a great success in eliminating stoppages and shaving game time, concern has been voiced that it has reduced the importance of stickhandling, which remains one of the game's most crowd-pleasing skills.

 RULE 70

(a) The puck may be passed by any player to a player of the same side within any one of the three zones into which the ice is divided, but it may not be

PASSES

Passing the puck increased in importance in 1943–44, when forward passing from one zone to another was introduced. Since the game's earliest days hockey had stressed stickhandling and skating as its basic skills. In the early years the puck had to be carried from zone to zone. Old-timers tend to believe that these "golden years" produced players of the utmost skill. In reality, the game was played in a station-to-station manner. Teams became so bogged down in their own zone that the only way they could get the puck out was to lift a high backhander down the ice. Those players who could carry the puck out of their own zone and skate through neutral ice to the attacking zone were the real stars of the early era. What passing existed was only side to side or backward. The puck was only advanced by skating, stickhandling, and turnovers.

Despite these restrictions, hockey was still an exciting and high-scoring game. However, after the Pacific Coast Hockey Association and the Western Canada Hockey League both folded in the late 1920s, the NHL was faced with an influx of talent. With the best players in the world now confined to one major league, scoring became more and more difficult. The NHL, which averaged 10 goals a game in its first season, was down to 4 goals a game a decade later.

The first forward passing to be allowed in the NHL occurred in 1918–19, when the League followed the lead of the PCHA and placed bluelines on the ice. With the introduction of the blueline, the ice surface was clearly divided into two defensive areas and a center-ice "neutral" zone. Forward passing was allowed in the defensive zone, as long as the player receiving the puck was still inside the blueline. In 1920–21 goaltenders were allowed to pass the puck up to their own players, again providing that the player was still inside his own blueline.

In an attempt to open up the game to more offense, the League decided to adopt the "antidefense rules" that had been in effect in the western leagues. Similar to the "no-zone defense" rule that is currently in vogue in the National Basketball Association, the antidefense rules stated that no team was allowed to have more than two players behind the blueline when the puck was not in the defensive or center-ice area. If a player dropped back into the defensive zone when two of his teammates were already there, he would be cautioned by the referee. If the same player did this a second time, he would be sent to the penalty box for a 2-minute sabbatical. Over the years other rules were introduced forbidding deliberate delay of the game by skating back into the defensive zone with the puck.

passed forward from a player in one zone to a player of the same side in another zone. . . .

But scoring totals continued to dwindle and several NHL franchises struggled at the gate, forcing the League to adopt the one rule change that "purists" warned would ruin the game forever: forward passing. In 1927–28 forward passing was allowed in the defensive and center-ice zones. Still, scoring dropped to an all-time low. The following year the League opened up the game by allowing forward passing in all three zones, although the puck still had to be carried from one zone to another. The antidefense rule was also modified. The referee's warning, issued when a team stationed three players behind its own blueline, was replaced by a 2-minute penalty.

These rule changes did the trick. Scoring increased to nearly 6 goals per game, the fans returned, and the League was able to survive the Depression years.

The antidefense rule played a role in the Montreal Canadiens' defense of their Stanley Cup title in 1931. On April 11 the Chicago Black Hawks traveled to Montreal needing just one victory to capture the Stanley Cup. The Hawks entered the third period with a 2–1 lead, but early in the frame were fingered by referee Bobby Hewitson for an antidefense violation when Johnny Gottselig was caught back in his defensive zone. On the resulting powerplay, Canadien Johnny "Black Cat" Gagnon scored his second goal of the game to tie the match at 2–2. That goal deflated the Hawks and the Habs were able to pounce for another pair of goals to win the game 4–2. Montreal went on to win the series and the Stanley Cup with a 2–0 victory in game five.

Prior to the 1943–44 season, the NHL entered what is often referred to as hockey's "modern age" by adding the center red line and allowing forward passing from zone to zone. Passing from a team's defensive zone to the far side of the center red line was forbidden and the puck still had to be carried into the offensive zone, but this innovation, more than any other, opened up the game to the great skaters and passers of the future.

RULE 72

(b) Unless the puck is in the goal crease area, a player of the attacking side may not stand in

PROTECTION OF GOALKEEPER

Stronger rules protecting the goaltender were introduced prior to the 1991–92 season. Many of the subsections of Rule 72 overlap with other rules, such as those governing charging and interference, but with more and more players "driving the net" new guidelines had to be established.

As expected, the rule was strictly enforced at the beginning of the 1991–92 season. There were twenty-one goaltender-interference calls in the first two months of the season, five of them resulting in disallowed goals. Some commentators stated that the new rule went too far and was being whistled too often, but for the new rule to work, players had to be made more conscious of the crease.

This was certainly the case in the 1993 Stanley Cup finals between the Montreal Canadiens and Los Angeles Kings. In that series, a total of five goaltender-interference penalties were called in five games. None was called in the 1992 finals and only two in seven games in 1994.

In U.S. and Canadian college hockey, the crease is protected like the key in basketball. If the referee spots an opposing player positioning himself in the crease, the play is whistled dead, and the resulting faceoff is held in the neutral zone.

PUCK OUT OF BOUNDS OR UNPLAYABLE

An interesting variation on this rule was incorporated during the "4-on-4 Challenge" series held in November 1994, during the NHL lockout. Instead of having a faceoff after the puck went out of bounds, the referee would simply throw another puck into the corner and play would resume immediately—much as the players had done when they played "shinny" hockey as kids. Though this variation was never seriously considered for use in "real" games, it was refreshing to see stars playing the game with youthful abandon.

A pivotal "puck-out-of-bounds" ruling occurred in the Maritime Major Hockey League during the 1951–52 season. At this time, the Maritime Senior League had upgraded and joined the newly created Major Series, an elite division of senior hockey that would compete for a new piece of silverware called the Alexander Cup.

During the 1950s senior hockey's place in Canada was just a small step below that of the professional leagues, and many former and future NHL stars played at the senior level

the goal crease. If the puck should enter the net while such conditions prevail the goal shall not be allowed. . . .

RULE 73

(a) When the puck goes outside the playing area at either end or either side of the rink, or strikes any obstacles above the playing surface other than the boards or glass, it shall be faced-off from where it was shot or deflected unless otherwise expressly provided in these rules.

during the decade. Former stars such as Bill Warwick, Sid Smith, Gordie Drillon, and Edgar Laprade, as well as future phenoms like Jean Beliveau, Norm Ullman, and Jacques Plante, were just a few of the name players who competed at the senior or major level.

The Maritime Major Hockey League had a rich assortment of talent, including NHL players such as Pete Langelle, Grant Warwick, Len Haley, Willie Marshall, Bud Poile, and Ray Frederick. The coaching ranks included Leo Lamoureux, John "Peanuts" O'Flaherty, and Wilf Field, all of whom had fine careers in the NHL. Three of the teams, Saint John, Glace Bay, and Halifax, had NHL affiliations. Veteran NHL officials including Red Storey refereed in the MMHL. Despite the quality of the players, the league struggled at the box office and the teams were forced to play a ninety-game season to pay all the bills.

Four of the six teams in the loops qualified for the playoffs, with the league champions advancing to the Alexander Cup finals against the Quebec Senior Hockey League champions. The Saint John Beavers, first-place finishers during the regular season, defeated the Glace Bay Minors in the semifinals and took on the Halifax Saints in the finals. The Beavers won the first two games, but the Saints carried the day in game three with a 3–2 win on home ice, setting up a pivotal fourth match on April 9, 1952, once again set for Halifax.

The Saints held tough in the first two periods and were carrying the play to the Beavers in the final frame when an unlucky bounce knocked the Saints out of the series. The Halifax Forum, like many rinks of the era, had netting above the wire screen behind the goals to protect fans and save a few pucks. The rules of the day dictated that any puck striking this netting was out of bounds; the play would be whistled dead, with a faceoff coming outside the zone if the puck had last touched an attacking player.

Early in the third period Beaver sniper Matt Mesich broke through the neutral zone, skirted the blueline, and fired a wicked wrist shot that Saint goaltender Donnie O'Hearne just managed to deflect over the goal. The puck soared over the net, bounced off the netting, hit O'Hearne in the back, and trickled into the Saints' net. No one thought much of it until the referee signaled a goal, arguing that the puck had never gone out of bounds at all. According to the on-ice arbiter, the puck had hit the wire screen just inches below the edge, then bounced back, striking O'Hearne and entering the net.

The Halifax Forum erupted, but the referee held firm to his opinion. Deflated, the Saints succumbed to the Beavers by a 6–3 score to fall behind in the series three games to one. Saint John wrapped up the Maritime championship with a 4–3 victory in game five, earning the right to face the Quebec Aces for the national championship beginning in Saint John on April 17, 1952. The Aces, coached by Punch Imlach and featuring stars such as Jean Beliveau, Joe Crozier, Murdo MacKay, and Jackie Leclair, downed the Beavers in 5 games to win the Alexander Cup.

PUCK MUST BE KEPT IN MOTION

The "puck-must-be-kept-in-motion" rule was responsible for Robbie Irons having an NHL career. Mind you, the "career" in question was only 3 minutes long, but it elevated Irons from minor-league obscurity to a place in the NHL record book.

Irons's brief on-ice stint in the NHL occurred on November 13, 1968, in a game between the St. Louis Blues and New York Rangers. Irons, who had spent two seasons with the Fort Wayne Komets of the International Hockey League, was signed in 1968 to share goaltending duties with Gary Edwards in Kansas City, home of the Blues' top farm team. In November 1968 Jacques Plante suffered a slight groin pull. Since the Kansas City Blues had a week off, the Blues decided to call up Irons as backup to veteran Glenn Hall. On the evening in question Irons was on the bench, Plante was in the stands, and Hall was in the net. Hall, never at ease before a game even at the best of times, was extra nervous on this evening because he was wearing a mask for the first time in an NHL game.

Things started poorly for Hall, then quickly moved from bad to worse. He gave up a 60-foot goal to Vic Hadfield at the 76-second mark, and the Rangers were pressing for another when defenseman Noel Picard froze the puck near the end boards to relieve the pressure. However, referee Vern

RULE 74

(a) The puck must at all times be kept in motion.

Hockey Hall of Fame

Robbie Irons has the distinction of having the shortest NHL career of any goaltender to play in the League. Irons, who played 12 seasons in the IHL, faced no shots and allowed no goals in his three-minute stay in the NHL spotlight.

RULE 75

(a) Should a scramble take place or a player accidentally fall on the puck and the puck be out of sight of the Referee, he shall immediately blow his whistle and stop the play. . . .

(b) If at any time while play is in progress, a puck other than the one legally in play shall appear on the playing surface, the play shall not be stopped but shall continue with the legal puck until the play then in progress is completed by change of possession.

Buffey penalized Picard for not keeping the puck in motion, giving the Rangers a powerplay. Hall couldn't believe the call, and let the referee know his feelings. Ten seconds after Picard went to the box, Hall erupted and flicked his glove at Buffey, connecting with the referee's shoulder. That contact earned Hall a game misconduct, the only time in his career he was tossed from a game.

Hall's banishment meant that Irons had to come into the game to replace him and Plante had to come out of the stands to serve as the back-up goaltender (see Rule 15d). For some reason, Bowman was less than confident that Irons could handle the job, so he told the rookie to feign an equipment problem after taking his warm-up so Plante could enter the game. After taking a dozen or so practice shots, the straps on Irons's pads "mysteriously" came loose and he went to the bench for repairs.

Referee Buffey warned the Blues to get the game going or face a delay-of-game penalty. Bowman had no choice but to use Irons. By the 5:01 mark of the first period Plante was dressed and ready, and he was called to replace Irons. So, after 3 minutes of action (no shots, no saves, and no goals), Robbie Irons's NHL career was over. After his brief fling at fame, Irons returned to the IHL and played with Fort Wayne until the early 1980s. He never got another chance to return to the "big time."

PUCK OUT OF SIGHT AND ILLEGAL PUCK

Enforcement of this rule has caused some angry moments. The referee is obliged to blow the whistle if he has lost sight of the puck. Often a referee has blown a play dead only to have the puck suddenly appear in the back of the net, causing all sorts of trouble for the on-ice officials. This has happened on hundreds of occasions, but here are a couple of the more interesting scenarios.

In 1961–62 the New York Rangers made the playoffs for the first time in five seasons and met the Toronto Maple Leafs in the semifinals. The Broadway Blues weren't given much of a chance to defeat the first-place Leafs, but they proved to be worthy adversaries, bouncing back from a 2-game deficit to tie the series at 2 games apiece. In game five on April 5, 1962, the Leafs jumped into an early 2–0 lead, but once again the Rangers battled back, tying the match and forcing the game into overtime.

After neither team could settle matters in the first extra period, the Leafs turned on the pressure. Gump Worsley had already faced 52 shots and was continuing to stone the Leafs when, early in the second extra frame, there was a scramble near the Rangers' goal. Worsley stopped a point-blank drive by Leaf Frank Mahovlich and ended up sprawled on his back with the puck tucked under his head. Worsley waited a moment or two, then began to get up, thinking that play had been whistled dead. Just as he lifted his head, Leaf Red Kelly poked the puck into the net. Immediately the Rangers stormed around referee Eddie Powers, who warded off all arguments by explaining that he had kept the puck in sight the entire time. Since it was visible, it was playable.

Worsley explained, "I figured I was down there long enough and nothing was happening, so I lifted my head and that's where the puck was. When I lifted my head . . . Olé."

Kelly's goal stood, giving the Leafs a 3–2 victory and the lead in the series. The Rangers never recovered from Kelly's "heads-up" play and dropped the decisive sixth game 7–1.

On the other side of the coin comes this bizarre turn of events, one in which the puck was visible but the referee and goaltender both lost sight of it. In game three of the 1953 semifinals between the Montreal Canadiens and Chicago Black Hawks, Hawk winger Vic Lynn unleashed a shot that glanced off Canadien Rocket Richard's stick and spiraled into the air. Referee Sammy Babcock lost sight of the flying disk and blew his whistle just as the puck bounced off Canadien goaltender Gerry McNeil's shoulder and dropped into the net.

The Black Hawks poured onto the ice to congratulate Lynn, but Babcock waved off the goal, saying he had blown the play dead when he lost sight of the puck. The Hawks were livid and Chicago general manager Bill Tobin threatened to protest the game. That turned out not to be necessary since the Hawks held on for a 2–1 victory. NHL president Clarence Campbell agreed that the whistle was "kind of fast, but it was just a mistake by the referee."

At times it's hard enough to follow the flight path of a single skittering puck, so you can imagine the confusion caused when five pucks suddenly appeared on the ice during a game between the Montreal Canadiens and New York Rangers on February 5, 1955. A fan had crawled into the rafters high above the rink at the Montreal Forum and dropped four extra pucks onto the ice. The referee alertly whistled the play dead before the quintet of pucks caused any more consternation. Moments later the local constabulary apprehended the fleeing rafter-dweller. You might say that he was caught rubber-handed.

 RULE 76

Play shall not be stopped if the puck touches an official anywhere on the rink, regardless of whether a team is shorthanded or not. . . .

(Note 1) If a goal is scored as a result of being deflected directly into the net off an official the goal shall not be allowed.

PUCK STRIKING OFFICIAL

Until the 1940–41 season, if the puck struck an official, play was immediately halted and a faceoff was conducted in the area where play had been stopped. In 1940 the League passed a rule that allowed play to continue if the puck hit an official in the center-ice zone. That area of contact was expanded in 1942 to include the center-ice zone forward to the minor-penalty-shot line. Finally, in 1945, the NHL passed the current rule that allows play to continue regardless of where the referee or linesman has been hit. One aspect of the old rules remains: No goal can be allowed if the puck enters the net after deflecting off a referee or linesman.

This rule was finally called into effect late in the 1995–96 season during a game between the Philadelphia Flyers and the Boston Bruins. Philly had already secured a berth in the post-season parade but the Bruins were still fighting for their playoff lives. With the teams tied 2-2 in the second period, there was a scrum near the center ice red line. A Flyers defender dug the puck out of the mass of skates and fired it along the boards into the Bruins zone. Boston goaltender Bill Ranford started to leave the net so he could cut the puck off as it caromed around the corner of the rink. Unfortunately for Ranford, the puck deflected off the skate of linesman Ron Asseltine and ricocheted directly into the vacated Boston net. Before the Flyers could celebrate their sudden turn of good fortune, Referee Bill McCreary quickly pointed out the details of Rule 76 and the goal was disallowed. The Bruins scored twice in the third period and went on to win the match 4-2. The win allowed the Bruins to reach the playoffs for a record 29th consecutive season.

REFUSING TO START PLAY

There have only been two instances of game forfeiture in the history of the NHL. The most famous occurred on March 17, 1955, when the Montreal Canadiens and Detroit Red Wings were battling for first place in the standings. On March 16 Canadien star Maurice "Rocket" Richard was suspended by NHL president Clarence Campbell for the rest of the season (four games) and the entire playoffs for punching linesman Cliff Thompson during a game against the Boston Bruins on March 13. During the St. Patrick's game, with Campbell in attendance, the Montreal fans expressed their displeasure at Richard's sentence by attacking Campbell and unleashing a canister of smoke and tear gas during the first intermission. The fire marshal ordered the Montreal Forum cleared and the game was suspended. Detroit was leading 4–1 at the time, so Campbell ordered the game forfeited in Detroit's favor.

Hockey Hall of Fame

RULE 77

(a) If when both teams are on the ice, one team for any reason shall refuse to play when ordered to do so by the Referee, he shall warn the Captain and allow the team so refusing fifteen seconds within which to begin the play or resume play. If at the end of that time, the team shall still refuse to play, the Referee shall impose a two-minute penalty on a player of the offending team to be designated by the Manager or Coach of that team through the playing Captain. Should there be a repetition of the same incident, the Referee shall notify the Manager or Coach that he has been fined the sum of two hundred dollars ($200). Should the offending team still refuse to play, the Referee shall have no alternative but to declare that the game be forfeited to the non-offending club and the case shall be reported to the Commissioner for further action.

NHL president Clarence Campbell is attacked by an angry Montreal Canadien fan seconds before the tear-gas bomb explosion in the Montreal Forum on March 17, 1955.

Jack Adams —
The game has been
forfeited to Detroit
You are entitled to
take your team on
your way any time
now
Mr Selke agrees to
this decision as the Fire
Department has ordered the
building closed
Lo

This was the official notice that
NHL president Clarence
Campbell delivered to Detroit
general manager Jack Adams
informing him the Canadiens
had forfeited the game to the
Red Wings.

The first forfeiture in NHL history took place on January 26, 1921, when the Ottawa Senators, unhappy with a referee's ruling, left the ice during a game against the Montreal Canadiens. The Habs were leading 5–3 at the time, and that score was posted as the final result. Another forfeiture in NHL history took place on March 13, 1933. At this time the League had no rules in place to cover a team's refusal to finish a game. The Chicago Black Hawks, languishing in last place in the American Division, were in Boston for a tilt with the Bruins. The Hawks carried a 2–1 lead into the dying minutes of the game only to see Bruin Eddie Shore tie the score at 2–2.

Early in overtime Boston's Marty Barry scored to give the Beantowners a 3–2 lead. Chicago's Art Coulter felt that the puck had not entered the net and tried to make that point with goal judge Louis Leycroft. Leycroft refused to change his mind, so Coulter tried to change it for him by jabbing him through the screen with his stick. Referee Bill Stewart gave Coulter a game misconduct and ordered him from the ice. Black Hawk coach Tommy Gorman called Stewart over to the bench, then reached out and pulled the referee's sweater over his head and punched him. Stewart broke free and banished Gorman from the game. When Gorman refused to budge, the referee had the local constabulary remove him from the bench. Coach Gorman insisted the players follow him to the dressing room, and after some consultation, captain Charlie Gardiner and the rest of the Hawks left the ice and refused to return.

Stewart gave the Hawks a "1-minute" warning to return, then rang his referee's bell and called the Bruins to center ice. Stewart dropped the puck between defenseman Eddie Shore and center Art Chapman, who calmly took the puck and shot it into the Hawks' empty net. With that, Stewart declared the game over and left the ice. But no one knew what the score was. Was it 1–0, 3–2, or 4–2? The NHL decided the game would go into the books as a 3–2 Bruin victory.

The following season, a rule was introduced that ensured there would be no further confusion. Any team that refused to continue a game in regular time or overtime would be given a 2-minute warning to return to the ice. After that time the game was to be awarded to the nonoffending team, and all goals were to count.

SLASHING

A slashing penalty was introduced as part of the hooking penalty in 1940–41, and the infraction remains one of the most dangerous mentioned in the *NHL Rule Book*. Numerous suspensions have been issued for slashing, mostly for wild swings of the stick at an opposing player. It's ironic that the referee's signal for slashing is a chopping motion on the wrist, because that's where most of the damage from slashing occurs.

At no time was slashing more in the news than during the 1991–92 season. The first incident was the "slash heard 'round the world," while the second was the "slash not seen by anyone in the world." And both played key roles in the annual passion play known as the Stanley Cup playoffs.

All through the playoffs media attention had been focused on players taking "dives" or faking injuries to ensure that penalties would be called. So many players had taken dives that it became difficult to distinguish between the actors and the aggrieved.

The first and more serious incident occurred during game two of the New York Rangers–Pittsburgh Penguins Patrick Division finals on May 5, 1992. Mario Lemieux, the NHL's dominant player at the time, had already almost singlehandedly rescued the Penguins from a three-games-to-one deficit against the Washington Capitals, collecting 17 points in the seven-game set. As it turned out, the term "singlehandedly" proved to be more than a turn of phrase.

Early in the first period, with the Penguins on the powerplay and already up 1–0 thanks to a goal by Kevin Stevens, Lemieux broke free from his Ranger shadow and was streaking through the neutral zone when Adam Graves laid a two-hander across Lemieux's wrist, just above the top of the glove. Lemieux fell to the ice in pain and referee Dan Marouelli assessed a 2-minute minor for slashing against Graves. Lemieux went to the dressing room and never returned to action as the Rangers scored 3 goals in the third period to record a series-tying 4–2 victory.

When it was determined that Lemieux had broken a small bone in his wrist, the Penguins sent a tape of the incident to the NHL office and demanded that Graves be disciplined. The tapes were reviewed by NHL vice president

🏒 RULE 78

(a) A minor or major penalty, at the discretion of the Referee, shall be imposed on any player who impedes or seeks to impede the progress of an opponent by "slashing" with his stick.

Slashing: A chopping motion with the edge of one hand across the opposite forearm.

Brian O'Neill, who decided to hold a disciplinary hearing on May 8. This allowed Graves to dress for game three on May 7, and he went on to score a timely marker in the Rangers' 6–5 overtime win.

The following day O'Neill suspended Graves for four games, removing one of the Rangers' top snipers from the series. The Pittsburgh Penguins rallied to win the next three contests and move into the Wales Conference finals against the Boston Bruins. Lemieux was back for game three of that set and went on to win the Conn Smythe Trophy as playoff MVP. The Penguins became back-to-back Stanley Cup champions.

Another star of the 1991–92 playoff season whose effectiveness was hampered by a slash to the wrist was Chicago Black Hawk center Jeremy Roenick. However, unlike the source of Lemieux's injury, the party guilty of tapping Roenick went virtually unnoticed. Roenick and the Chicago Black Hawks were at the time enjoying the franchise's finest postseason performance since 1973, winning an NHL-record eleven consecutive playoff games to reach the Stanley Cup finals. Roenick was Chicago's main offensive weapon, collecting 20 points in fourteen games.

However, in the finals against the Pittsburgh Penguins, Roenick was largely ineffective. Prior to game three, Roenick showed up wearing a cast, disclosing that a pair of slashes by Penguins Kevin Stevens and Rick Tocchet in game two of the series had sprained and nearly broken his thumb. Neither player was penalized, leading Hawk coach Mike Keenan to suggest that while Roenick could have taken a "dive" to make sure a penalty was called, "Jeremy's not the type of player who will go down."

The Penguins went on to eliminate the Hawks in four straight games, with Roenick only registering 2 points in the sweep. The following season the NHL introduced rules to crack down on "diving" while promising to introduce new penalties under which the punishment would better fit the crime.

RULE 79

(a) A major penalty and a game misconduct penalty shall be imposed on a player who spears or butt-ends an opponent.

SPEARING AND BUTT-ENDING

Spearing is one of the most severe infractions on the books in the National Hockey League. Because the infraction is often considered to be an intentional foul and can cause serious injury, a spearing penalty is almost always followed by a fine and/or suspension.

Today, a spearing foul is penalized by a 5-minute major and a game misconduct. However, in the 1960s, a spearing call was only a 5-minute major, meaning that the guilty party could return to the ice. A game between the Toronto Maple Leafs and Chicago Black Hawks on December 6, 1963, went a long way in convincing the NHL that a rule change was needed.

Throughout much of the evening, Eddie Shack of the Maple Leafs and Black Hawk tough guy Reggie Fleming had been sparring with each other. In the third period, Shack was given a high-sticking penalty for combing Fleming's hair with his stick. Moments after he returned to the ice, Fleming speared Shack in the groin and he was assessed a major penalty by referee Frank Udvari. As Shack groaned on the ice and Fleming stewed in the penalty box, Maple Leaf defenseman Bobby Baun came over to the penalty box to express his opinion of Fleming's actions. However, his progress was interrupted by Black Hawk center Stan Mikita. Soon, Fleming, Baun, and Mikita were engaged in fisticuffs.

Originally, referee Udvari sent all three players to the penalty box, but on reflection, he decided to issue game misconduct penalties to the trio. However, Baun, Fleming, and Mikita had to exit the box to leave the ice, and as they were crossing to their respective dressing rooms, the benches emptied and a huge brawl broke out. During the commotion, Black Hawk forward Murray Balfour and Maple Leaf rear guard Carl Brewer became involved in a shoving match near the Leaf's bench. Suddenly, Balfour emerged from the melee with a deep cut over his eye, and he immediately complained to the on-ice officials that either Leaf coach Punch Imlach or Leaf trainer Bob Haggert had slugged him. Upon investigation, it was determined that a fan had snuck up to the Leaf bench and actually thrown a punch at Balfour.

This incensed Howie Young, a fiery Chicago defenseman who was constantly embroiled in hot water both on and off the ice. Young steamed over to the Leafs' bench and challenged the fan to a tussle. While the fan may have been hesitant to tackle Young, Dick Shatto, an All Star running back with the Toronto Argonauts football club who was sitting in the crowd,

(b) In addition to the major penalty imposed under this rule, an automatic fine of one hundred dollars ($100) will also be imposed.

Spearing: A jabbing motion with both hands thrust out in front of the body.

was not. Shatto removed his suit jacket and was preparing to engage Mr. Young when Toronto's finest appeared on the scene and escorted both the fan and Mr. Shatto to safety.

When the smoke finally cleared, seven players were ejected and both coaches were brought up on the carpet by Clarence Campbell, who issued severe fines to all parties. When asked if there was to be any investigation of the Murray Balfour incident, Mr. Campbell replied, "Balfour left the bench on his own accord and if he got punched, that's his business. He was the author of his own misfortune."

START OF GAME AND PERIODS

These rules were completely overhauled following an embarrassing communication breakdown during game six of the Montreal Canadiens–Quebec Nordiques division finals on April 20, 1984. The two teams have long been intraprovincial rivals, so much so that any series between them is known as the "Battle of Quebec." In this particular game, which ironically was played on Good Friday, the tempers were short and the battles were long.

Quebec came into Montreal trailing in the series three games to two, but opened up an early 1–0 lead on a goal by Peter Stastny. The Nordiques nursed that advantage through the first 40 minutes of play. As the teams were heading to the dressing room at the end of the second period, Nordique Dale Hunter elbowed Canadien Guy Carbonneau. This started a commotion that eventually escalated into a complete free-for-all involving all the players on both sides. During the scuffle Louis Sleiger of the Nordiques "sucker-punched" former teammate Jean Hamel, knocking Hamel from the game. When the officials finally got the teams off the ice and into their dressing rooms, the long procedure of solving the penalty mess began.

Referee Bruce Hood prolonged the intermission for an extra 10 minutes but the scene remained one of confusion. Hood decided to eject four players—Sleiger, Peter Stastny, Chris Nilan, and Mario Tremblay—and informed the off-ice officials which players were getting turfed. When Hood and his linesmen went back on the ice for the third frame, they were shocked to see that none of the banned players had left

🏒 RULE 80

(c) During the pre-game warm-up (which shall not exceed twenty minutes in duration) and before the commencement of play in any period, each team shall confine its activity to its own end of the rink. . . .
(d) Twenty minutes before the time scheduled for the start of the game, both teams shall vacate the ice and proceed to their dressing rooms while the ice is being flooded. Both teams shall be signalled by the Game Timekeeper to return to the ice together in time for the scheduled start of the game.
(f) At the end of each period, the home team players must proceed directly to their dressing room while the visiting team players must wait for a signal from the Referee to proceed only if they have to go on the ice to reach their dressing room. Failure to comply with this regulation will result in a two-minute bench minor for delay of game.

the game. In the midst of the mayhem, there had been a breakdown in communication and the expelled players were never informed of their punishment. The officials were still in shock moments later when the whole feud started up again, a battle that grew so intense that two brothers, Mark Hunter of the Canadiens and Dale Hunter of the Nordiques, squared off with each other.

When the on-ice officials finally separated the two teams, eleven players were given game misconducts. Quebec added another goal early in the third period, but Montreal stormed back with 5 goals in 8 minutes to win the game and the series.

After the series the League passed new rules concerning the pregame warm-up period and procedures for leaving the ice at the conclusion of the game and period.

THROWING STICK

This version of the throwing-the-stick rule was first introduced into the rule book on January 17, 1916. Throwing the stick had always been a offense, the penalty being banishment from the game. But League officials soon realized that a player would gladly sacrifice himself to prevent the other team from scoring the winning goal. So to combat the repeated tossing of sticks, the new rule awarded an automatic goal against the offending team.

Today the net has to be empty for an "automatic" goal to be awarded, but until the mid-1930s, when the penalty-shot rule was first written, any time a player threw his stick in an attempt to stop an opponent from scoring, a goal was awarded. At the time the rule stated, "When a player deliberately throws his stick to prevent a score, the referee shall immediately award a goal to the side offended against and the puck shall be faced and the game re-started as though a goal had actually been scored."

This drastic measure wasn't used often but it did come into play in a game between the Montreal Canadiens and Chicago Black Hawks on February 10, 1938. The Hawks and Habs were entangled in a close-checking 1–1 tie when speedy Canadien center Paul Haynes broke free from his Black Hawk shadow six minutes into the second period.

RULE 81

(a) When any player of the defending side or Manager, Coach or Trainer, deliberately throws or shoots a stick or any part thereof or any other object at the puck in his defending zone, the Referee shall allow the play to be completed and if a goal is not scored, a penalty shot shall be awarded to the non-offending side, which shot shall be taken by the player designated by the Referee as the player fouled.

If however, the goal being unattended and the attacking player having no defending player to pass and having a chance to score on an "open net", a stick or any part thereof or any other object be thrown or shot by a member of the defending team, including the Manager, Coach or Trainer, thereby preventing a shot on the "open net", a goal shall be awarded to the attacking side.

Haynes was just about to unleash a drive at goalkeeper Mike Karakas when Black Hawk left winger Lou Trudell threw his stick across the ice, knocking the puck off Haynes's stick. However, instead of signaling a penalty shot against the Hawks, referee Mickey Ion awarded a goal to Haynes and the Canadiens, giving the Flying Frenchmen a 2–1 victory over the Hawks.

It was the first case of an "awarded" goal in the NHL since March 12, 1927, when Reg Noble of the Montreal Maroons threw his stick at Ace Bailey of the newly named Toronto Maple Leafs. Bailey had stripped Noble of the puck at the Maroons blueline and broken in all alone on Maroon goalie Clint Benedict. Just as Bailey was about to shoot, Noble's stick came flying across the ice. Referee Bobby Hewitson whistled the play dead and awarded a goal to Bailey. It would prove to be the only marker of the contest, as the Leafs hung on for the 1–0 victory.

Throwing a stick into the stands will always get a player into trouble. In the case of goaltender Warren Skorodenski, that trouble consisted of a twenty-game suspension.

The 1983–84 season started poorly for Skorodenski and quickly got worse. First he was sent to the minors by the Chicago Black Hawks. Then, because of a "disagreement" Skorodenski had with Springfield Indian coach Doug Sauter, the Hawks loaned his services to the Sherbrooke Jets of the American Hockey League.

All seemed back on track for Skorodenski until a game against the New Haven Nighthawks on November 20, 1983. The Jets fell behind early and quickly found themselves on the short end of a 6–2 score. However, Sherbrooke battled back to tie the game 6–6, forcing the match into overtime. Early in the extra session referee Dave Lynch penalized Skorodenski for tripping, setting up a rare overtime powerplay for New Haven. Only 5 seconds after the penalty was called, Daryl Evans scored for the Nighthawks, giving them a 7–6 victory.

The combination of the wasted comeback and the overtime penalty call prompted Skorodenski to go on a rampage. He threw his goalie stick into the crowd and stormed over to Lynch, bumping the referee in the chest and knocking him back into the boards.

AHL president Jack Butterfield suspended Skorodenski for twenty games, stating that the tempestuous goalie had not only made physical contact with an on-ice official but had also aggravated the situation by tossing his stick into the crowd. Skorodenski obviously learned his lesson. He played pro hockey until 1989 and never ran afoul of League authorities again.

TIME OF MATCH

When hockey became a real game with rules and officials, the match itself was played in two 30-minute halves, with a short intermission. When the National Hockey Association was formed in 1910, League officials were concerned that 30-minute halves often tired out the players and slowed the pace of the game, especially since substitutions were not allowed. They suggested that the game be divided into three 20-minute periods, with an intermission between each. This way the players could rest, the pace of the game would pick up, and the enjoyment of the fans would increase. It was also noted that two intermissions would help concession sales of popcorn and peanuts. Only one small alteration has been made in this rule in the last sixty-five years. Prior to the start of the 1966–67 season, the NHL increased the length of the intermissions from 10 to 15 minutes.

In 1992–93 the League announced that all games would start 10 minutes after the hour or half hour, and that there would be a series of "TV time-outs" during each period, even if the game in question was not being televised. The inclusion of breaks and uniform start times provided for a consistent game length leaguewide.

Over the years, various rule changes have helped speed up games. The "touch-up" delayed-offside rule cut 2 to 3 minutes of time off games. When the NHL increased the height of the protective glass behind the net to 12 feet in 1986–87, and also increased the height of the corner glass, it cut as much as 8 minutes; pucks going over the glass meant fewer faceoffs.

Prior to the start of the 1974–75 season, the NHL experimented with a series of new rules designed to eliminate some of the delays that had hampered the game in 1973–74. Game six of the 1974 finals, a 1–0 victory by the Philadelphia Flyers

RULE 82

(a) The time allowed for a game shall be three twenty-minute periods of actual play with a rest intermission between periods.

Play shall be resumed promptly following each intermission upon the expiry of fifteen minutes from the completion of play in the preceding period. . . .

over the Boston Bruins, had taken well over 3 hours to play, prompting the League to make a series of changes. New procedures included an end to warm-ups for replacement goaltenders; minor penalties for refusing to go directly to the penalty box; and quick drops on faceoffs. Two of the more revolutionary rules that were tried during the preseason but eventually dropped were the "change-on-the-fly" rule and the "free-shot" rule.

The change-on-the-fly rule substantially cut back on the time allowed for player changes during stoppages in the action, encouraging line changes while the play was ongoing. Although this rule was greatly successful during the exhibition season—some games were played in less than 2 hours—the Board of Governors rejected endorsing it for regular-season play. The American Hockey League did implement the rule for the 1974–75 season, but it was less than successful at the minor-league level and was quickly dropped.

The "free-shot" rule was an extension of the "free-face-off" rule that was first tried during the 1970–71 exhibition season. Under the terms of the free-faceoff rule, if the defensive team froze the puck instead of moving it, a "free faceoff" was called. A player from the attacking team would move into the faceoff circle, and the linesman would drop the puck. The attacking player had two choices: He could stay in the circle and pass the puck, or he could move out of the faceoff circle with the puck and shoot at the net.

This rule really stirred the emotions of the goaltending fraternity. Jacques Plante, then with the Maple Leafs, told one reporter that if a free faceoff was called against Toronto, he would step aside and let the opposing player shoot at the empty net rather than be a "target in a shooting gallery." The rule was used through the exhibition season, but it was rarely called, and it resulted in only one goal.

In an attempt to speed the flow of the game and reduce the number of stoppages in the defensive zone, the League reworked the free-faceoff rule, coming up with a "free-shot" rule that gave the attacking team a free shot from the left or right faceoff circle if the defending team was guilty of freezing the puck. Any player on the ice at the time could take the shot, but it had to be taken from the side of the ice where the infraction had occurred.

On September 19, 1974, the free-shot rule received its first workout. In a game between the Pittsburgh Penguins and New York Islanders, Penguin rookie Kelly Pratt was awarded a free shot and fired the puck past goaltender Billy Smith to give Pittsburgh a 4–2 victory. Interestingly, this was the only goal Pratt would score in his NHL career. After appearing in twenty-two games during the 1974–75 season without a goal, he was reassigned to the AHL's Hershey Bears and never played in the NHL again. At the conclusion of the exhibition season the Board of Governors voted against making the free-shot rule a permanent part of the *NHL Rule Book.*

One of the most important—but underrated—rule changes in hockey concerned resurfacing the ice. Until the 1940–41 season the ice surface was only flooded or resurfaced at the beginning of a game. Between periods rink attendants would scrape excess snow off the ice, but no attempt was made to completely clean and flood the ice.

(c) In the interval between periods, the ice surface shall be flooded unless mutually agreed to the contrary.

Hockey Hall of Fame

Although the ice was only flooded once a night in the early years of the game, the surface was scrapped by uniformed attendants in between periods.

In 1940 the NHL decided that the ice should be properly cleaned between periods. This helped increase the tempo of the game and eliminated many of the delays previously necessary to repair cracked or rutted portions of the ice during stoppages in play. A proper job required a crew of eight to ten men with large metal shovels or scrapers to remove the surface snow, and another group to wheel around large barrels that spread a coat of hot water over the ice so its surface could refreeze clean and smooth. At the time, there was no quicker way to do a proper job.

In the mid-1940s a California rink attendant at Paramount Studios named Frank Zamboni came up with an idea for a motorized ice-resurfacing vehicle that could be driven and operated by one man. Zamboni's idea caught the attention of figure skating queen and Olympic gold medalist Sonja Henie, whose ice revue shows and motion pictures were world famous. When Henie threw her support behind the project, Zamboni was able to design a prototype and create the first automatic ice-cleaning machine. Dubbed the "mechanical monster," it was built on the chassis of an old war surplus Jeep and equipped with special tires to prevent it from skidding or slipping on the ice. A combination sweeper, snow scraper, flooder, and ice conditioner, the "Zamboni" was an instant success.

The first NHL rink to use the new invention was the Montreal Forum, which employed its first Zamboni on March 10, 1955. By the early 1960s every NHL rink had one

The first Zamboni was a rather crude-looking machine, but within seven years, Frank Zamboni had perfected his motorized ice-cleaning vehicle to the point where every NHL arena had ordered one.

Hockey Hall of Fame

of the machines, and soon the Zamboni was as much a part of the atmosphere of the hockey arena as the organist, score clock, and popcorn vendor.

In 1994–95 the NHL passed a new bylaw that required every NHL arena to use two resurfacers to clear the ice between periods, creating better ice conditions and allowing more time for on-ice promotions and displays.

TIED GAME

Overtime was a feature of the NHL from the moment the League was formed. From 1917–18 to 1920–21, regular-season games were played until a winner was decided regardless of how long that took. In 1921–22 the League decided that if a game remained tied after 20 minutes of extra time, it would end a tie. On February 11, 1922, the Toronto St. Pats and Ottawa Senators played to a 4–4 draw, the first "sister-kisser" in NHL history.

In 1928–29 the League dropped the concept of "sudden death" overtime and initiated a 10-minute overtime period if a game was tied after 60 minutes. All goals scored during this extra period would count, and if the game remained dead-locked it would go into the books as a tie.

This created some interesting games for historians to mull over. The most goals scored in a single overtime was 4, which occurred twice. On March 11, 1934, the Montreal Maroons scored 4 overtime goals to defeat the New York Americans 7–3, and on November 27, 1942, the Boston Bruins erupted for a quartet of goals against the Americans for a 6–2 win over the New Yorkers.

The individual record for goals in an overtime period belongs to Toronto Maple Leaf forward Ken Doraty. Doraty, who scored only 15 goals in his career, fired the only hat-trick of his career in overtime on January 16, 1934, to give the Leafs a 7–4 win over the Ottawa Senators.

On November 21, 1942, with war raging in Europe, NHL president Frank Calder announced that he was sus-pending all overtime. It was common practice for the railroads to delay their trains to allow the players time to get from the rink to the station, but with the war on, it was important to maintain strict train schedules. The last regular-season overtime game was played on November 10, 1942, with the New York Rangers posting a 5–3 win over the Chicago Black Hawks.

Forty-one years later, the NHL once again put overtime back into the game. If any regular-season game ended in a tie after 60 minutes, a 5-minute sudden death overtime period would be played. On October 8, 1983, Bob Bourne scored in overtime to give the New York Islanders an 8–7 win over the

RULE 83

(a) During League games, if at the end of the three regular twenty-minute periods the score shall be tied, the teams will play an additional period of not more than five (5) minutes with the team scoring first being declared the winner. . . .

Washington Capitals in the first regular-season overtime game since 1942.

There have been twenty tied games in the Stanley Cup playoffs, sixteen of them occurring between 1927 and 1936 when the opening rounds were two-game, total-goal series and ties were a common result. The other four tied games were due to a combination of the rule book and circumstances beyond the control of the League. The best-of-five Stanley Cup finals between the Boston Bruins and Ottawa Senators in 1927 featured a pair of tie games. Game one was halted after 20 minutes of overtime because—according to newspaper reports—the "ice was so lumpy the players were unable to pilot the puck." Although the two sides were willing to continue, NHL president Frank Calder and the officials deemed the ice surface unsafe. After the match, Calder decided that "no game shall extend beyond 20 minutes of overtime." Calder's edict came into play two games later as game three was also declared a tie after both teams struggled to a 1–1 draw after one overtime period. In the 1951 semi-finals between the Toronto Maple Leafs and Boston Bruins, game two went into the books as a 1–1 tie after one overtime period because Toronto's Sunday curfew law prohibited a new period from starting after midnight on Saturday.

The most recent playoff game to end without a winner was game four of the 1988 Stanley Cup finals between the Edmonton Oilers and Boston Bruins. At the 16:37 mark of the second period, just as Oiler Craig Simpson scored to tie the game at 3–3, there was a massive power failure in Boston Garden. When power could not be restored, the game was declared a draw that would be replayed if necessary at the end of the series. The Oilers made certain this eventuality did not come about by downing the Bruins 6–3 in game five to win the best-of-seven set in a four-game sweep.

TRIPPING, CLIPPING AND KNEEING

Tripping has always been a violation of the rules, and has been in the *NHL Rule Book* since the formation of the League. In the first two decades of NHL play, the tripping infraction was divided into two categories. If a player was tripped when he

 RULE 84

(a) A minor or major penalty, at the discretion of the Referee, shall be imposed on any player who shall place his stick, knee, was not in scoring position, a minor penalty was called. When the penalty-shot rules were put into place in the early 1930s, a trip or any other form of interference on a player in a scoring position resulted in a penalty shot.

New York Ranger center Alexei Kovalev can tell you all you need to know about tripping. He's one of the few players to be suspended for what is usually a minor offense. It happened in a game between the Rangers and Washington Capitals on November 30, 1993. Kovalev and Capital forward Dale Hunter were fighting for possession of the puck behind the Washington net when Kovalev upended the Capital captain. No penalty was called, but the play was whistled dead when the referee noticed that Hunter appeared to be in a great deal of pain. It was determined that he had suffered a sprained knee and would be out of action for an indefinite period.

After the game, a 3–1 win for the Rangers, the Capitals requested that the League review the video of the incident, feeling that Kovalev had purposely tripped Hunter in an attempt to injure him. Even though Wally Harris, the NHL's assistant director of officiating, felt that Kovalev's action was accidental, he forwarded the tape to Brian Burke, the League's senior vice president and director of hockey operations. Burke agreed with the Capitals and sat Kovalev down for five games, the stiffest suspension ever levied for a tripping call.

Hall of Fame referee Frank Udvari was of the opinion that of all the penalty calls in the rule book, referees are the most accurate on tripping calls. "I would say that we referees catch almost one hundred percent of tripping offenses, because we follow the puck. It's the illegal interference behind our backs or down at the far end of the ice that we miss."

As Frank "King" Clancy admitted when he was a referee, "What happens behind my back, stays behind my back. I cannot call what I cannot see."

Tripping is one of the most common penalty calls possibly because, as Udvari said, it rarely goes undetected. In fact, the tripping infraction played a major role in one of the most important Stanley Cup playoff games ever. In the 1961 postseason the five-time defending champion Canadiens were attempting to reach the finals for the eleventh consecutive season. Standing in their way were the Chicago Black Hawks, a

foot, arm, hand or elbow in such a manner that it shall cause his opponent to trip or fall.

Tripping: Strike right leg with right hand below the knee keeping both skates on the ice.

Kneeing: Slapping the knee with palm of hand while keeping both skates on the ice.

Roughing: A thrusting motion with arm extending from side.

team the Habs had neatly dispatched in four straight contests one year earlier. The teams split the first two games in the Montreal Forum, then returned to the now-departed "Madhouse on Madison," Chicago Stadium, for the next two encounters.

Game three was closely played with both teams hesitant to open up. Murray Balfour scored for Chicago late in the second period and the Hawks carried that slim 1–0 advantage into the final moments of the game.

However, with less than 90 seconds remaining on the clock, referee Dalton McArthur fingered Chicago's Billy "Red" Hay for tripping, sending the Canadiens to the powerplay. With only 36 ticks left on the clock, Henri Richard scored for Montreal to tie the game at 1–1 and force overtime.

The teams battled back and forth for 52 minutes of overtime without a winner being decided, although each club had numerous opportunities. McArthur called five penalties in the extra sessions, four of them tripping infractions. Midway through the third overtime, McArthur nabbed Canadien Dickie Moore for tripping, giving the Black Hawks another powerplay opportunity. At the 12:12 mark of the third extra period, Murray Balfour connected to give the Hawks a 2–1 win and the lead in the series. The Montreal bench was incensed at McArthur's penalty call, and after the game was over Montreal coach Toe Blake went on the ice and took a wild swing at McArthur, a move that cost the Habs' bench boss a $2,000 fine, the largest in NHL history. Newspaper headlines read: "Toe gets $2,000 Sock."

Montreal never recovered from the loss and scored only 5 more goals in the entire series. The Habs lost to the Hawks in six games, ending the NHL's most glorious championship streak.

RULE 86

Each team shall be permitted to take one thirty-second time-out during the course of any game, regular-season or playoffs. . . .

TIME-OUTS

Given the number of interruptions in the flow of an average NHL game, many fans were puzzled when the League introduced a time-out rule in 1983. It was designed to be used in close games, when a coach was planning to pull his goaltender or set up a strategic faceoff play. In practice it has become an important piece of game strategy. A properly called time-out allows a coach to keep his number one line on the ice for a double shift in the final minutes of a game, and it allows penalty-killers to catch their breath and stay on the ice for the duration of a penalty. It also allows both coaches to set their defenses for that all-important draw in the dying seconds of the game.

VIDEO GOAL JUDGE

The video-replay rule was introduced prior to the 1991–92 season and, unlike a similar rule in the National Football League, which encountered troubles, it has proved to be a great asset to the NHL.

One aspect of the video-replay rule has created some interesting moments. In the case of a disputed goal where the puck has entered, then exited, the net, play must continue until there is another stoppage. On April 28, 1992, the Detroit Red Wings entered game six of their divisional semi-final game against the Minnesota North Stars on the brink of elimination. The teams battled through 60 minutes of regulation time without a goal being scored. In the closing minutes of the first overtime, Wing Sergei Fedorov skated around Star Chris Dahlquist and blasted a shot that seemed to strike the bar behind Star netminder Jon Casey and come out the other side.

Play continued until an offside call stopped the clock. At that time referee Rob Shick approached the off-ice officials and asked to confer with video-replay supervisor Wally Harris. After a minute or two of consultation it was decided that Fedorov had scored at the 16:13 mark of the first overtime, and that the Wings had won the game 1–0 to stay alive in the series. Since all the players had returned to their benches, it marked the quietest celebration of a playoff overtime goal in NHL history.

The first "unofficial" use of the instant replay occurred during an Edmonton Oilers–Vancouver Canucks tilt on January 27, 1987. The game was a seesaw battle in which the Canucks managed a last-second score to tie the game 4–4 and force overtime. At 4:08 of the extra frame, Oiler Glenn Anderson tipped a shot by defenseman Craig Muni past Canuck netminder Richard Brodeur. Although the puck appeared to deflect off the crossbar and the red light didn't go

RULE 87

The following situations are subject to review by the Video Goal Judge:

(a) Puck crossing the goal line.

(b) Puck in the net prior to the goal frame being dislodged.

(c) Puck in the net prior to, or after expiration of time at the end of the period.

(d) Puck directed into the net by a hand or foot.

(e) Puck deflected into the net off an official.

(f) Puck struck with a high-stick, above the height of the crossbar, by an attacking player prior to entering the goal.

(g) To establish the correct time on the official game clock, provided the game time is visible on the Video Goal Judge's monitors.

on, the Oilers began celebrating anyway, even leaving the ice and returning to the dressing room.

Referee Ron Hoggarth, who still had not officially signaled a goal, went to the penalty time keeper's area where there was a phone link to goal judge George Blore. While he was at the bench, one of the off-ice officials mentioned to Hoggarth that the video replay clearly showed the puck hitting the crossbar. Hoggarth spoke with Blore, who was adamant that the puck had not entered the net. Hoggarth ruled "no goal" and called the Oilers back onto the ice for the final 52 seconds. After the game NHL officials denied that Hoggarth had let the video evidence influence his decision, but the information was there, and it was correct. Four years later, the video replay became an integral part of the game.

Resetting the time clock was added to the video goal judge's responsibilities for the 1994–95 season, and the value of being able to do so accurately was demonstrated on several occasions in the 1995 playoffs. Late in a close game, crowd noise often makes a whistle difficult to hear, occasionally allowing precious fractions of seconds to slip away. The video-replay official can restore this lost time, ensuring that fans and players aren't denied the opportunity to see every second of game action.

Shortly after the conclusion of the 1995–1996 season, the NHL passed a new rule allowing for a video replay to confirm if a player was in the crease prior to the puck entering the net.

APPENDIX

NATIONAL HOCKEY LEAGUE OFFICIAL RULES

RULES GOVERNING
THE GAME
OF ICE HOCKEY

SECTION ONE—THE RINK

RULE 1. RINK

The game of "Ice Hockey" shall be played on an ice surface known as the "RINK".

(NOTE) There shall be no markings on the ice except as provided under these rules without the express written permission of the League.

RULE 2. DIMENSIONS OF RINK

(a) The official size of the rink shall be two hundred feet (200′) long and eighty-five feet (85′) wide. The corners shall be rounded in the arc of a circle with a radius of twenty-eight feet (28′).

The rink shall be surrounded by a wooden or fibreglass wall or fence known as the "boards" which shall extend not less than forty inches (40″) and not more than forty-eight inches (48″) above the level of the ice surface. The ideal height of the boards above the ice surface shall be forty-two inches (42″). Except for the official markings provided for in these rules, the entire playing surface and the boards shall be white in color except the kick plate at the bottom of the board which shall be light yellow in colour.

Any variations from any of the foregoing dimensions shall require official authorization by the League.

(b) The boards shall be constructed in such manner that the surface facing the ice shall be smooth and free of any obstruction or any object that could cause injury to players.

All doors giving access to the playing surface must swing away from the ice surface.

All glass or other types of protective screens and gear to hold them in position shall be properly padded or protected. Protective glass shall be required in front of the penalty benches to provide for the safety of the players on and off the ice. All equipment used to hold the glass or screens in position shall be mounted on the boards on the side away from the playing surface.

RULE 3. GOAL POSTS AND NETS

(a) Eleven feet (11′) from each end of the rink and in the center of a red line two inches (2″) wide drawn completely across the width of the ice and continued vertically up the side of the boards, regulation goal posts and nets shall be set in such manner as to remain stationary during the progress of a game. The goal posts shall be kept in position by means of flexible pegs affixed in the ice or floor. The flexible pegs shall be eight inches (8″) in length.

Where the length of the playing surface exceeds two hundred feet (200′), the goal line and goal posts may be placed not more than fifteen feet (15′) from the end of the rink.

(b) The goal posts shall be of approved design and material, extending vertically four feet (4′) above the surface of the ice and set six feet (6′) apart measured from the inside of the posts. A cross bar of the same material as the goal posts shall extend from the top of one post to the top of the other.

(c) There shall be attached to each goal frame a net of approved design made of white nylon cord which shall be draped in such manner as to prevent the puck coming to rest on the outside of it, yet strung in manner that will keep the puck in the net.

A skirt of heavy white nylon fabric or heavyweight white canvas shall be laced around the base plate of the goal frame in such a way as to protect the net from being cut or broken. This skirt shall not project more than one inch (1″) above the base plate.

(NOTE) The frame of the goal shall be draped with a nylon mesh net so as to completely enclose the back of the frame. The net shall be made of three-ply twisted twine (0.130 inch diameter) or equivalent braided twine of multifilament white nylon with an appropriate tensile strength of 700 pounds. The size of the mesh shall be two and one-half inches (2H″) (inside measurement) from each knot to each diagonal knot when fully stretched. Knotting shall be made as to ensure no sliding of the twine. The net shall be laced to the frame with medium white nylon cord no smaller in size than No. 21.

(d) The goal posts and cross bar shall be painted in red and all other exterior surfaces shall be painted in white.

(e) The red line, two inches (2″) wide, between the goal posts on the ice and extended completely across the rink, shall be known as the "GOAL LINE".

RULE 4. GOAL CREASE

(a) In front of each goal, a "GOAL CREASE" area shall be marked by a red line two inches (2″) in width.

(b) The goal crease shall be laid out as follows: A semi-circle six feet (6′) in radius and two inches (2″) in width shall be drawn using the center of the goal line as the center point. In addition, an 'L'-shaped marking of five inches (5″) in length (both lines) at each front corner will be painted on the ice.

The location of the 'L'-shaped marking is measured by drawing an imaginary four foot (4′) line from the goal line to the edge of the semi-circle. At that point, the 'L' may be drawn.

(c) The goal crease area shall include all the space outlined by the crease lines and extending vertically four feet (4′) to the level of the top of the goal frame. (Note: use paint code PMS 298.)

(d) The complete goal area, which includes all the space outlined by the crease line and the goal line, shall be painted light blue color. (Paint code PMS 298.) The area inside the goal frame to the goal line shall be painted a gloss white color.

(NOTE) On-ice logos must not interfere with any official game markings.

RULE 5. DIVISION OF ICE SURFACE

(a) The ice area between the two goals shall be divided into three parts by lines, twelve inches (12″) in width, and blue in colour, drawn sixty feet (60′) out from the goal lines, and extended completely across the rink, parallel with the goal lines, and continued vertically up the side of the boards.

(b) That portion of the ice surface in which the goal is situated shall be called the "DEFENDING ZONE" of the team defending that goal; the central portion shall be known as the "NEUTRAL ZONE", and the portion farthest from the defended goal as the "ATTACKING ZONE".

(c) There shall also be a line, twelve inches (12″) in width and red in colour, drawn completely across the rink in center ice, parallel with the goal lines and continued vertically up the side of the boards, known as the "CENTER LINE". This line shall contain regular interval markings of a uniform distinctive design, which will readily distinguish it from the two blue lines the outer edges of which must be continuous.

RULE 6. CENTER ICE SPOT AND CIRCLE

A circular blue spot, twelve inches (12″) in diameter, shall be marked exactly in the center of the rink; and with this spot as a center, a circle of fifteen feet (15′) radius shall be marked with a blue line two inches (2″) in width.

RULE 7. FACE-OFF SPOTS IN NEUTRAL ZONE

Two red spots two feet (2′) in diameter shall be marked on the ice in the neutral zone five feet (5′) from each blue line. The spots shall be forty-four feet (44′) apart and each shall be a uniform distance from the adjacent boards.

RULE 8. END ZONE FACE-OFF SPOTS AND CIRCLES

(a) In both end zones and on both sides of each goal, red face-off spots and circles shall be marked on the ice. The face-off spots shall be two feet (2′) in diameter. Within the face-off spot, draw two parallel lines three inches (3″) from the top and bottom of the spot. The area within the two lines shall be painted red, the remainder shall be painted white.

The circles shall be two inches (2″) wide with a radius of fifteen feet (15′) from the center of the face-off spots. At the outer edge of both sides of each face-off circle and parallel to the goal line shall be marked two red lines, two inches (2″) wide and two feet (2′) in length and three feet (3′) apart.

(b) The location of the face-off spots shall be fixed in the following manner:

Along a line twenty feet (20′) from each goal line and parallel to it, mark two points twenty-two feet (22′) on both sides of the straight line joining the center of the two goals. Each such point shall be the center of a face-off spot and circle.

RULE 9. PLAYERS' BENCHES

(a) Each rink shall be provided with seats or benches for the use of players of both teams and the accommodations provided including benches and doors shall be uniform for both teams. Such seats or benches shall have accommodation for at least fourteen persons of each team, and shall be placed immediately alongside the ice, in the neutral zone, as near to the center of the rink as possible with doors opening in the neutral zone and convenient to the dressing rooms.

Each players' bench should be twenty-four feet (24′) in length and when situated in the spectator area, they shall be separated from the spectators by a protective glass of sufficient height so as to afford the necessary protection for the players. The players' benches shall be on the same side of the playing surface opposite the penalty bench and should be separated by a substantial distance, if possible.

(NOTE) Where physically possible, each players' bench shall have two doors opening in the neutral zone and all doors opening to the playing surface shall be constructed so that they swing inward.

(b) No one but players in uniform, the Manager, Coach and Trainer shall be permitted to occupy the benches so provided.

(NOTE) One non-uniformed player shall be permitted on the players' bench in a coaching capacity. He must be indicated on the Roster Sheet submitted by the Coach to the Referee or Official Scorer prior to the start of the game in accordance with Rule 15—Players in Uniform.

RULE 10. PENALTY BENCH

(a) Each rink must be provided with benches or seats to be known as the "PENALTY BENCH". These benches or seats must be capable of accommodating a total of ten persons including the Penalty Time-keepers. Separate penalty benches shall be provided for each team and they shall be situated on opposite sides of the Timekeeper's area, directly across the ice from the players' benches. The penalty bench(es) must be situated in the neutral zone.

(b) On the ice immediately in front of the Penalty Timekeeper's seat there shall be marked in red on the ice a semi-circle of ten feet (10′) radius and two inches (2″) in width which shall be known as the "REFEREE'S CREASE".

(c) Each Penalty Bench shall be protected from the spectator area by means of a glass partition which shall not be less than five feet (5′) above the height of the boards.

RULE 11. SIGNAL AND TIMING DEVICES

(a) Each rink must be provided with a siren, or other suitable sound device, for the use of Timekeepers.

(b) Each rink shall be provided with some form of electrical clock for the purpose of keeping the spectators, players and game officials accurately informed as to all time elements at all stages of the game including the time remaining to be played in any period and the time remaining to be served by at least five penalized players on each team.

Time recording for both game time and penalty time shall show time remaining to be played or served.

The game time clock shall measure the time remaining in tenths of a second during the last minutes of each period.

(c) Behind each goal, electrical lights shall be set up for the use of the Goal Judges. A red light will signify the scoring of a goal and a green light will signify the end of a period or a game.

(NOTE) A goal cannot be scored when a green light is showing.

RULE 12. POLICE PROTECTION

All clubs shall provide adequate police or other protection for all players and officials at all times.

The Referee shall report to the Commissioner any failure of this protection observed by him or reported to him with particulars of such failure.

SECTION TWO—TEAMS

RULE 13. COMPOSITION OF TEAM

(a) A team shall be composed of six players on the ice who shall be under contract to the Club they represent.

(b) Each player and each goalkeeper listed in the line-up of each team shall wear an individual identifying number at least ten inches (10″) high on the back of his sweater and, in addition, each player and goalkeeper shall wear his surname in full, in block letters three inches (3″) high, across the back of his sweater at shoulder height.

All players of each team shall be dressed uniformly with approved design and colour of their helmets, sweaters, short pants, stockings and skates.

Altered uniforms of any kind, i.e. velcro inserts, over-sized jerseys, etc. will not be permitted. Any player or goalkeeper not complying with this rule shall not be permitted to participate in the game.

Each Member Club shall design and wear distinctive and contrasting uniforms for their home and road games, no parts of which shall be interchangeable except the pants.

RULE 14. CAPTAIN OF TEAM

(a) One Captain shall be appointed by each team, and he alone shall have the privilege of discussing with the Referee any questions relating to interpretation of rules which may arise during the progress of a game. He shall wear the letter "C", approximately three inches (3″) in height and in contrasting colour, in a conspicuous position on the front of his sweater.

In addition, if the permanent Captain is not on the ice, Alternate Captains (not more than two) shall be accorded the privileges of the Captain. Alternate Captains shall wear the letter "A" approximately three inches (3″) in height and in contrasting colour, in a conspicuous position on the front of their sweaters.

(NOTE) Only when the captain is not in uniform, the Coach shall have the right to designate three Alternate Captains. This must be done prior to the start of the game.

(b) The Referee and official Scorer shall be advised prior to the start of each game, the name of the Captain and the Alternate Captains of both teams.

(c) Only the Captain, when invited to do so by the Referee, shall have the privilege of discussing any point relating to the interpretation of rules. Any Captain or player who comes off the bench and makes any protest or intervention with the officials for any purpose must be assessed a misconduct penalty in addition to a minor penalty under Rule 42(b)—Abuse of Officials.

A complaint about a penalty is NOT a matter "relating to the interpretation of the rules" and a minor penalty shall be imposed against any Captain or other player making such a complaint.

(d) No playing Coach or playing Manager or goalkeeper shall be permitted to act as Captain or Alternate Captain.

RULE 15. PLAYERS IN UNIFORM

(a) At the beginning of each game, the Manager or Coach of each team shall list the players and goalkeepers who shall be eligible to play in the game. Not more than eighteen players, exclusive of goalkeepers, shall be permitted.

(b) A list of names and numbers of all eligible players and goalkeepers must be handed to the Referee or Official Scorer before the game, and no change be permitted in the list or addition thereto shall be permitted after the commencement of the game.

    i)   If a goal is scored when an ineligible player is on the ice, the goal will be disallowed.

    ii) The ineligible player will be removed from the game and the club shall not be able to substitute another player on its roster.

(c) Each team shall be allowed one goalkeeper on the ice at one time. The goalkeeper may be removed and another player substituted. Such substitute shall not be permitted the privileges of the goalkeeper.

(d) Each team shall have on its bench, or on a chair immediately beside the bench, a substitute goalkeeper who shall, at all times, be fully dressed and equipped ready to play.

The substitute goalkeeper may enter the game at any time following a stoppage of play, but no warm-up shall be permitted.

(e) Except when both goalkeepers are incapacitated, no player in the playing roster in that game shall be permitted to wear the equipment of the goalkeeper.

(f) In regular League and Playoff games, if both listed goalkeepers are incapacitated, that team shall be entitled to dress and play any available goalkeeper who is eligible. No delay shall be permitted in taking his position in the goal, and he shall be permitted a two-minute warm-up. However, the warm-up is not permitted in the event a goalkeeper is substituted for a penalty shot.

(g) The Referee shall report to the Commissioner for disciplinary action any delay in making a substitution of goalkeepers.

RULE 16. STARTING LINE-UP

(a) Prior to the start of the game, at the request of the Referee, the Manager or Coach of the visiting team is required to name the starting line-up to the Referee or Official Scorer. At any time in the game, at the request of the Referee made to the Captain, the visiting team must place a playing line-up on the ice and promptly commence play.

(b) Prior to the start of the game, the Manager or Coach of the home team, having been advised by the Official Scorer or the Referee the names of the starting line-up of the visiting team, shall name the starting line-up of the home team which information shall be conveyed by the Official Scorer or the Referee to the Coach of the visiting team.

(c) No change in the starting line-up of either team as given to the Referee or Official Scorer, or in the playing line-up on the ice, shall be made until the game is actually in progress. For an infraction of this rule, a bench minor penalty shall be imposed upon the offending team, provided such infraction is called to the attention of the Referee before the second face-off in the first period takes place.

RULE 17. EQUALIZING OF TEAMS

Deleted

RULE 18. CHANGE OF PLAYERS

(a) Players may be changed at any time from the players' bench provided that the player or players leaving the ice shall be within five feet (5′) of his players' bench and out of the play before the change is made.

A goalkeeper may be changed for another player at any time under conditions set out in this section.

(NOTE 1) When a goalkeeper leaves his goal area and proceeds to his players' bench for the purpose of substituting another player, the rear Linesman shall be responsible to see that the substitution made is not illegal by reason of the premature departure of the substitute from the bench (before the goalkeeper is within five feet (5′) of the bench). If the substitution is made prematurely, the Linesman shall stop the play immediately by blowing his whistle unless the non-offending team has possession of the puck in which event the stoppage will be delayed until the puck changes hands. There shall be no time penalty to the team making the premature substitution but the resulting face-off will take place on the center "face-off spot".

(NOTE 2) The Referee shall request that the public address announcer make the following announcement: "Play has been stopped due to premature entry of a player from the players' bench." If in the course of making a substitution, the player entering the game plays the puck with his stick, skates or hands or who checks or makes any physical contact with an opposing player while the retiring player is actually on the ice, then the infraction of "too many men on the ice" will be called.

If in the course of a substitution either the player entering the play or the player retiring is struck by the puck accidentally, the play will not be stopped and no penalty will be called.

(b) If by reason of insufficient playing time remaining, or by reason of penalties already imposed, a bench minor penalty is imposed for deliberate illegal substitution (too many men on the ice) which cannot be served in its entirety within the legal playing time, or at any time in overtime, a penalty shot shall be awarded against the offending team.

(c) A player serving a penalty on the penalty bench, who is to be changed after the penalty has been served, must proceed at once by way of the ice and be at his own players' bench before any change can be made.

For any violation of this rule, a bench minor penalty shall be imposed.

(d) Following the stoppage of play, the visiting team shall promptly place a line-up on the ice ready for play and no substitution shall be made from that time until play has been resumed. The home team may then make any desired substitution which does not result in the delay of the game.

If there is any undue delay by either team in changing lines, the Referee shall order the offending team or teams to take their positions immediately and not permit a line change.

(NOTE) When a substitution has been made under the above rule, no additional substitution may be made until play commences.

(e) The Referee shall give the visiting team a reasonable amount of time to make their change after which he shall put up his hand to indicate that no further change shall be made by the visiting club. At this point, the home team may change immediately. Any attempt by the visiting team to make a change after the Referee's signal shall result in the assessment of a bench minor penalty for delay of game.

RULE 19. INJURED PLAYERS

(a) When a player other than a goalkeeper is injured or compelled to leave the ice during a game, he may retire from the game and be replaced by a substitute, but play must continue without the teams leaving the ice.

(b) If a goalkeeper sustains an injury or becomes ill, he must be ready to resume play immediately or be replaced by a substitute goalkeeper and NO additional time shall be allowed by the Referee for the purpose of enabling the injured or ill goalkeeper to resume his position. The substitute goalkeeper shall be allowed a two-minute warm-up during all pre-season games. No warm-up shall be permitted for a substitute goaltender in all regular League or Playoff games. (See also Section (d).)

(c) The Referee shall report to the Commissioner for disciplinary action any delay in making a goalkeeper substitution.

The substitute goalkeeper shall be subject to the regular rules governing goalkeepers and shall be entitled to the same privileges.

(d) When a substitution for the regular goalkeeper has been made, such regular goalkeeper shall not resume his position until the first stoppage of play thereafter.

(e) If a penalized player has been injured, he may proceed to the dressing room without the necessity of taking a seat on the penalty bench. If the injured player receives a minor penalty, the penalized team shall immediately put a substitute player on the penalty bench, who shall serve the penalty without change. If the injured player receives a major penalty, the penalized team shall place a substitute player on the penalty bench before the penalty expires and no other replacement for the penalized player shall be permitted to enter the game except from the penalty bench. For violation of this rule, a bench minor penalty shall be imposed.

The penalized player who has been injured and been replaced on the penalty bench shall not be eligible to play until his penalty has expired.

(f) When a player is injured so that he cannot continue play or go to his bench, the play shall not be stopped until the injured player's team has secured possession of the puck; if the player's team is in possession of the puck at the time of injury, play shall be stopped immediately unless his team is in a scoring position.

(NOTE) In the case where it is obvious that a player has sustained a serious injury, the Referee and/or Linesman may stop the play immediately.

(g) When play has been stopped by the Referee or Linesman due to an injured player, such player must be substituted for immediately (except goalkeeper).

If when the attacking team has control of the puck in its attacking zone, play is stopped by reason of any injury to a player of the defending team, the face-off shall take place in the defending team's end zone face-off spot.

SECTION THREE—EQUIPMENT

(NOTE) A request for a measurement of any equipment covered by this section shall be limited to one request per team during the course of any stoppage in play.

RULE 20. STICKS

(a) The sticks shall be made of wood or other material approved by the Rules Committee, and must not have any projections. Adhesive tape of any colour may be wrapped around the stick at any place for the purpose of reinforcement or to improve control of the puck. In the case of a goalkeeper's stick, there shall be a knob of white tape or some other protective material approved by the League. This knob must not be less than one-half inch (½") thick at the top of the shaft.

Failure to comply with this provision of the Rule, the goalkeeper's stick is deemed unfit for play and must be changed without the application of a minor penalty.

(b) No stick shall exceed sixty inches (60") in length from the heel to the end of the shaft nor more than twelve and one-half inches (12½") from the heel to the end of the blade.

The blade of the stick shall not be more than three inches (3") in width at any point nor less than two inches (2"). All edges of the blade shall be beveled. The curvature of the blade of the stick shall be restricted in such a way that the distance of a perpendicular line measured from a straight line drawn from any point at the heel to the end of the blade to the point of maximum curvature shall not exceed one-half inch (½").

(c) The blade of the goalkeeper's stick shall not exceed three and one-half

inches (3½") in width at any point except at the heel where it must not exceed four and one-half inches (4½") in width; nor shall the goalkeeper's stick exceed fifteen and one-half inches (15½") in length from the heel to the end of the blade.

There is to be no measurement of the curvature of the blade on the goalkeeper's stick. All other elements of the stick are subject to a measurement and the appropriate applicable penalty.

The widened portion of the goalkeeper's stick extending up the shaft from the blade shall not extend more than twenty-six inches (26") from the heel and shall not exceed three and one-half inches (3½") in width.

(d) A minor penalty plus a fine of two hundred dollars ($200) shall be imposed on any player or goalkeeper who uses a stick not conforming to the provisions of this rule.

(NOTE 1) When a formal complaint is made by the Captain or Alternate Captain of a team, against the dimensions of any stick, the Referee shall take the stick to the Timekeeper's bench where the necessary measurement shall be made immediately. The result shall be reported to the Penalty Timekeeper who shall record it on the back of the penalty record.

If the complaint is not sustained, a bench minor penalty shall be imposed against the complaining club in addition to a fine of one hundred dollars ($100).

(NOTE 2) A player who participates in the play while taking a replacement stick to his goalkeeper shall incur a minor penalty under this rule but the automatic fine of two hundred dollars ($200) shall not be imposed. If his participation causes a foul resulting in a penalty, the Referee shall report the incident to the Commissioner for disciplinary action.

(NOTE 3) A request for a stick measurement in regular playing time or overtime of any game is permitted, provided that such a request is not made following the scoring of a goal. (NOTE: This applies to the goal scorer's stick only.)

(e) In the event that a player scores on a penalty shot while using an illegal stick, the goal shall be disallowed and no further penalty imposed. However, if no goal is scored, the player taking the penalty shot shall receive a minor penalty.

(f) A minor penalty plus a ten-minute misconduct penalty shall be imposed on any player who refuses to surrender his stick for measurement when requested to do so by the Referee. In addition, this player shall be subject to a two hundred dollar ($200) fine.

RULE 21. SKATES

(a) All hockey skates shall be of a design approved by the Rules Committee. All skates worn by players (but not goalkeepers) and by the Referee and Linesmen shall be equipped with an approved safety heel.

When the Referee becomes aware that any person is wearing a skate that does not have the approved safety heel, he shall direct its replacement at the next intermission. If such replacement is not carried out, the Referee shall report the incident to the Commissioner for disciplinary action.

(b) The use of speed skates or fancy skates or any skate so designed that it may cause injury is prohibited.

RULE 22. GOALKEEPER'S EQUIPMENT

(a) With the exception of skates and stick, all the equipment worn by the goalkeeper must be constructed solely for the purpose of protecting the head or body, and he must not wear any garment or use any contrivance which would give him undue assistance in keeping goal.

(NOTE) Cages on gloves and abdominal aprons extending down the front of the thighs on the outside of the pants are prohibited. "Cage" shall mean any lacing or webbing or other material in the goalkeeper's glove joining the thumb and index finger which is in excess of the minimum necessary to fill the gap when the goalkeeper's thumb and forefinger in the glove are fully extended and spread and includes any pocket or pouch effect produced by excess lacing or webbing or other material between the thumb and forefinger when fully extended or spread.

Protective padding attached to the back or forming part of goal-keeper's gloves shall not exceed eight inches (8″) in width nor more than sixteen inches (16″) in length at any point.

(b) The leg guards worn by goalkeepers shall not exceed twelve inches (12″) in extreme width when on the leg of the player.

(NOTE) At the commencement of each season or at random during the season and prior to Playoffs, goalkeepers' leg guards and gloves shall be checked by League staff and any violation of this rule shall be reported to the club involved and to the Commissioner of the League.

(c) Protective masks of a design approved by the Rules Committee may be worn by goalkeepers.

RULE 23. PROTECTIVE EQUIPMENT

(a) All protective equipment, except gloves, headgear and goalkeepers' leg guards must be worn under the uniform. For violation of this rule, after warning by the Referee, a minor penalty shall be imposed.

(NOTE) Players including the goalkeeper violating this rule shall not be permitted to participate in the game until such equipment has been corrected or removed.

(b) All players of both teams shall wear a helmet of design, material and construction approved by the Rules Committee at all times while participating in a game, either on the playing surface or the players' or penalty benches.

Players may elect for exemption from the operation of this sub-section (b) by execution of an approved Request and Release form and filing it with the League Office.

(c) A glove from which all or part of the palm has been removed or cut to permit the use of the bare hand shall be considered illegal equipment and if any player wears such a glove in play, a minor penalty shall be imposed on him.

When a complaint is made under this rule, and such complaint is not sustained, a bench minor penalty shall be imposed against the complaining club.

RULE 24. DANGEROUS EQUIPMENT

(a) The use of pads or protectors made of metal, or of any other material likely to cause injury to a player, is prohibited.

(NOTE) All elbow pads which do not have a soft protective outer covering of sponge rubber or similar material at least one-half inch (H″) thick shall be considered dangerous equipment.

(b) A mask or protector of a design approved by the Rules Committee may be worn by a player who has sustained a facial injury.

In the first instance, the injured player shall be entitled to wear any protective device prescribed by the club doctor. If any opposing club objects to the device, it may record its objection with the Commissioner.

(NOTE) The Officiating Department is specifically authorized to make a check of each team's equipment to ensure the compliance with this rule. It shall report its findings to the Commissioner for his disciplinary action.

RULE 25. PUCK

(a) The puck shall be made of vulcanized rubber, or other approved material, one inch (1″) thick and three inches (3″) in diameter and shall weigh between five and one-half ounces (5½ oz.) and six ounces (6 oz.). All pucks used in competition must be approved by the Rules Committee.

(b) The home team shall be responsible for providing an adequate supply of official pucks which shall be kept in a frozen condition. This supply of pucks shall be kept at the penalty bench under the control of one of the regular Off-ice Officials or a special attendant.

SECTION FOUR—PENALTIES

RULE 26. PENALTIES

Penalties shall be actual playing time and shall be divided in the following classes:

(1) Minor penalties
(2) Bench minor penalties
(3) Major penalties
(4) Misconduct penalties
(5) Match penalties
(6) Penalty shot

When coincident penalties are imposed on players of both teams, the penalized players of the visiting team shall take their positions on the penalty bench first in the place designated for visiting players.

(NOTE) When play is not actually in progress and an offense is committed by any player, the same penalty shall apply as though play was actually in progress.

RULE 27. MINOR PENALTIES

(a) For a "MINOR PENALTY", any player, other than a goalkeeper, shall be ruled off the ice for two minutes during which time no substitute shall be permitted.

(b) A "BENCH MINOR" penalty involves the removal from the ice of one player of the team against which the penalty is assessed for a period of two minutes. Any player except a goalkeeper of the team may be designated to serve the penalty by the Manager or Coach through the playing Captain and such player shall take his place on the penalty bench promptly and serve the penalty as if it was a minor penalty imposed upon him.

(c) If while a team is "short-handed" by one or more minor or bench minor penalties, the opposing team scores a goal, the first of such penalties shall automatically terminate.

(NOTE) "Short-handed" means that the team must be below the numerical strength of its opponents on the ice at the time the goal is scored. The minor or bench minor penalty which terminates automatically is the one which causes the team scored against to be "short-handed". Thus coincident minor penalties to both teams do NOT cause either side to be "short-handed".

This rule shall also apply when a goal is scored on a penalty shot, or when an awarded goal is given.

When the minor penalties of two players of the same team terminate at the same time, the Captain of that team shall designate to the Referee which of such players will return to the ice first and the Referee will instruct the Penalty Timekeeper accordingly.

When a player receives a major penalty and a minor penalty at the same time, the major penalty shall be served first by the penalized player, except under Rule 28(c) in which case the minor penalty will be recorded and served first.

(NOTE) This applies to the case where BOTH penalties are imposed on the SAME player. See also Note to Rule 33.

(d) When ONE minor penalty is assessed to ONE player of EACH team at the same stoppage in play, these penalties will be served without substitution provided there are no other penalties in effect and visible on the penalty clocks.

Unless paragraph one of this Rule is applicable, when coincident minor penalties or coincident minor penalties of equal duration are imposed against players of both teams, the penalized players shall all take their places on the penalty benches and such penalized players shall not leave the penalty bench until the first stoppage of play following the expiry of their respective penalties. Immediate substitution shall be made for an equal number of minor penalties OR coincident minor penalties of equal duration to each team so penalized and the penalties of the players for which substitutions have been made shall not be taken into account for the purpose of the Delayed Penalty Rule (Rule 33).

RULE 28. MAJOR PENALTIES

(a) For the first "MAJOR PENALTY" in any one game, the offender, except the goalkeeper, shall be ruled off the ice for five minutes during which time no substitute shall be permitted.

An automatic fine of one hundred dollars ($100) shall also be added when a major penalty is imposed for any foul causing injury to the face or head of an opponent by means of a stick.

(b) For the third major penalty in the same game to the same player, or for a major for butt-ending, checking from behind, clipping, cross-checking, high-sticking, slashing or spearing, he shall be ruled off the ice for the balance of the game, but a substitute shall be permitted to replace the player so suspended after five minutes have elapsed. (Major penalty plus game misconduct with automatic fine of two hundred dollars ($200).)

(NOTE) In accordance with Rule 58(c) a goalkeeper shall not be assessed a game misconduct penalty when he is being assessed a major penalty for highsticking.

(c) When coincident major penalties or coincident penalties of equal duration, including a major penalty, are imposed against players of both teams, the penalized players shall all take their places on the penalty benches and such penalized players shall not leave the penalty benches until the first stoppage of play following the expiry of their respective penalties. Immediate substitutions shall be made for an equal number of major penalties, or coincident penalties of equal duration including a major penalty to each team so penalized, and the penalties of the players for which substitutions have been made shall not be taken into account for the purpose of the Delayed Penalty Rule, (Rule 33).

Where it is required to determine which of the penalized players shall be designated to serve the delayed penalty under Rule 33—Delayed Penalties, the penalized team shall have the right to make such designation not in conflict with Rule 27—Minor Penalties.

RULE 29. MISCONDUCT PENALTIES

(a) In the event of "MISCONDUCT" penalties to any players except the goalkeeper, the players shall be ruled off the ice for a period of ten minutes each. A substitute player is permitted to immediately replace a player serving a misconduct penalty. A player whose misconduct penalty has expired shall remain in the penalty box until the next stoppage of play.

When a player receives a minor penalty and a misconduct penalty at the same time, the penalized team shall immediately put a substitute player on the penalty bench and he shall serve the minor penalty without change.

When a player receives a major penalty and a misconduct penalty at the same time, the penalized team shall place a substitute player on the penalty bench before the major penalty expires and no replacement for the penalized player shall be permitted to enter the game except from the penalty bench. Any violation of this provision shall be treated as an illegal substitution under Rule 18 calling for a bench minor penalty.

(b) A misconduct penalty imposed on any player at any time shall be accompanied with an automatic fine of one hundred dollars ($100).

(c) A "GAME MISCONDUCT" penalty involves the suspension of a player for the balance of the game but a substitute is permitted to replace immediately the player so removed. A player incurring a game misconduct penalty shall incur an automatic fine of two hundred dollars ($200) and the case shall be reported to the Commissioner who shall have full power to impose such further penalties by way of suspension or fine on the penalized player or any other player involved in the altercation.

(d) The Referee may impose a "GROSS MISCONDUCT" penalty on any player, Manager, Coach or Trainer who is guilty of gross misconduct of any kind. Any person incurring a "gross misconduct" penalty shall be suspended for the balance of the game and shall incur an automatic fine of two hundred dollars ($200) and the case shall be referred to the Commissioner of the League for further disciplinary action.

(NOTE) For all game misconduct and gross misconduct penalties regardless of when imposed, a total of ten minutes shall be charged in the records against the offending player.

(e) In regular League games, any player who incurs a total of three game misconduct penalties shall be suspended automatically for the next League game of his team. For each subsequent game misconduct penalty, the automatic suspension shall be increased by one game. For each suspension of a player, his club shall be fined one thousand dollars ($1000).

In Playoff games, any player who incurs a total of two game misconduct penalties shall be suspended automatically for the next Playoff game of his team. For each subsequent game misconduct penalty during the Playoffs, the automatic suspension shall be increased by one game. For each suspension of a player during Playoffs, his club shall be fined one thousand dollars ($1000).

(f) In regular League games, any player who incurs a total of two game misconduct penalties for stick related infractions penalized under Rule 28(b) shall be suspended automatically for the next League game of his team. For each subsequent game misconduct penalty, the automatic suspension shall be increased by one game.

In Playoff games any player who incurs a total of two game misconduct penalties for stick related infractions penalized under Rule 28(b) shall be suspended automatically for the next Playoff game of his team. For each subsequent game misconduct penalty during the Playoffs the automatic suspension shall be increased by one game.

Prior to the commencement of each Stanley Cup Finals, a player will have his current stick-related, boarding and checking from behind misconducts removed from his current playoff record. They will remain part of his historical record.

(NOTE 1) Any game misconduct penalty for which a player has been assessed an automatic suspension or supplementary discipline in the form of game suspension(s) by the Commissioner shall NOT be taken into account when calculating the total number of offenses under this subsection.

(NOTE 2) When a player has played in 41 consecutive regular league games without being assessed a stick-related major and a game misconduct according to Rule 28(b)—Major Penalties or Rule 29 (f)—Misconduct Penalties, he will have the previous game misconduct penalties removed from his current record. They will remain part of his historical record.

(NOTE 3) When a player has played in 41 consecutive regular league games without being assessed a boarding and/or a checking from behind major and a game misconduct according to Rule 45(c)(d)(e)—Board Checking and Checking from Behind, he will have the previous game misconduct penalties removed from his current record. They will remain part of his historical record.

(NOTE 4) A player's total games played will cover a two year time period from the date of the first game misconduct penalty for each category of foul.

(NOTE 5) The automatic suspensions incurred under this subsection in respect to League games shall have no effect with respect to violations during Playoff games.

RULE 30. MATCH PENALTIES

A "MATCH" penalty involves the suspension of a player for the balance of the game and the offender shall be ordered to the dressing room immediately. A substitute player is permitted to replace the penalized player after five minutes playing time has elapsed when the penalty is imposed under Rule 44—Attempt to Injure or Rule 49—Deliberate Injury of Opponents.

(NOTE 1) Regulations regarding additional penalties and substitutes are specifically covered in individual Rules 44, 49 and 64. Any additional penalty shall be served by a player to be designated by the Manager or Coach of the offending team through the playing Captain, such player to take his place in the penalty box immediately.

For all match penalties, regardless of when imposed, or prescribed additional penalties, a total of ten minutes shall be charged in the records against the offending player.

(NOTE 2) When coincident match penalties have been imposed under Rule 44, Rule 49 or Rule 64 to a player on both teams, Rule 28(c) covering coincident major penalties will be applicable with respect to player substitution.

(NOTE 3) The Referee is required to report all match penalties and the surrounding circumstances to the Commissioner of the League immediately following the game in which they occur.

RULE 31. PENALTY SHOT

(a) Any infraction of the rules which calls for a "PENALTY SHOT" shall be taken as follows:

The Referee shall ask to announce over the public address system the name of the player designated by him or selected by the team entitled to take the shot (as appropriate) and shall then place the puck on the center face-off spot and the player taking the shot will, on the instruction of the Referee, play the puck from there and shall attempt to score on the goalkeeper. The player taking the shot may carry the puck in any part of the neutral zone or his own defending zone but once the puck has crossed the attacking blue line it must be kept in motion towards the opponent's goal line and once it is shot, the play shall be considered complete. No goal can be scored on a rebound of any kind (an exception being the puck off the goal post, then the goalkeeper and then directly into the goal), and any time the puck crosses the goal line, the shot shall be considered complete.

Only a player designated as a goalkeeper or alternate goalkeeper may defend against the penalty shot.

(b) The goalkeeper must remain in his crease until the player taking the penalty shot has touched the puck and in the event of violation of this rule or any foul committed by a goalkeeper, the Referee shall allow the shot to be taken and if the shot fails, he shall permit the penalty shot to be taken over again.

The goalkeeper may attempt to stop the shot in any manner except by throwing his stick or any object, in which case a goal shall be awarded. (NOTE) See Rule 81.

(c) In cases where a penalty shot has been awarded under Rule 50(c), deliberately displacing goal post during course of a breakaway; under Rule 62(d), interference; under Rule 66(m), illegal entry into the game; under Rule 81(a) for throwing a stick; and under Rule 84(b), fouling from behind, the Referee shall designate the player who has been fouled as the player who shall take the penalty shot.

In cases where a penalty shot has been awarded under Rule 18(b), deliberate illegal substitution with insufficient playing time remaining; under Rule 50(d), deliberately displacing goal post; under Rule 53(c), falling on the puck in the crease; under Rule 57(d), picking up the puck from the crease area, the penalty shot shall be taken by a player selected by the Captain of the non-offending team from the players on the ice at the time when the foul was committed. Such selection shall be reported to the Referee and cannot be changed.

If by reason of injury, the player designated by the Referee to take the penalty shot is unable to do so within a reasonable time, the shot

may be taken by a player selected by the Captain of the non-offending team from the players on the ice when the foul was committed. Such selection shall be reported to the Referee and cannot be changed.

(d) Should the player in respect to whom a penalty shot has been awarded himself commit a foul in connection with the same play or circumstances, either before or after the penalty shot has been awarded, be designated to take the shot, he shall first be permitted to do so before being sent to the penalty bench to serve the penalty except when such penalty is for a game misconduct, gross misconduct or match penalty in which case the penalty shot shall be taken by a player selected by the Captain of the non-offending team from the players on the ice at the time when the foul was committed.

If at the time a penalty shot is awarded, the goalkeeper of the penalized team has been removed from the ice to substitute another player, the goalkeeper shall be permitted to return to the ice before the penalty shot is taken.

(e) While the penalty shot is being taken, players of both sides shall withdraw to the sides of the rink and in front of their own player's bench.

(f) If, while the penalty shot is being taken, any player of the opposing team shall have by some action interfered with or distracted the player taking the shot and, because of such action, the shot should have failed, a second attempt shall be permitted and the Referee shall impose a misconduct penalty on the player so interfering or distracting.

(g) If a goal is scored from a penalty shot, the puck shall be faced-off at center ice. If a goal is not scored, the puck shall be faced-off at either of the end face-off spots in the zone in which the penalty shot was tried.

(h) Should a goal be scored from a penalty shot, a further penalty to the offending player shall not be applied unless the offense for which the penalty shot was awarded was such as to incur a major or match penalty or misconduct penalty, in which case the penalty prescribed for the particular offense shall be imposed.

If the offense for which the penalty shot was awarded was such as would normally incur a minor penalty, then regardless of whether the penalty shot results in a goal or not, no further minor penalty shall be served.

(i) If the foul upon which the penalty shot is based occurs during actual playing time, the penalty shot shall be awarded and taken immediately in the usual manner notwithstanding any delay occasioned by a slow whistle by the Referee to permit the play to be completed, which delay results in the expiry of the regular playing time in any period.

The time required for the taking of a penalty shot shall not be included in the regular playing time or overtime.

RULE 32. GOALKEEPER'S PENALTIES

(a) A goalkeeper shall not be sent to the penalty bench for an offense which incurs a minor penalty, but instead, the minor penalty shall be served by another member of his team who was on the ice when the offense was committed, said player to be designated by the Manager or Coach of the offending team through the playing Captain and such substitute shall not be changed.

(NOTE) A penalized player may not serve a goalkeeper's penalty.

(b) A goalkeeper shall not be sent to the penalty bench for an offense which incurs a major penalty, but instead, the major penalty shall be served by another member of his team who was on the ice when the offense was committed, said player to be designated by the Manager or Coach of the offending team through the playing Captain and such substitute shall not be changed.

(c) Should a goalkeeper incur three major penalties in one game penalized under Rule 28(b)—Major Penalties, he shall be ruled off the ice for the balance of the playing time and his place shall be taken by a member of his own club, or by a regular substitute goalkeeper who is available. Such player will be allowed the goalkeeper's equipment. (Major penalty plus game misconduct penalty and automatic fine of two hundred dollars ($200).)

(d) Should a goalkeeper on the ice incur a misconduct penalty, this penalty shall be served by another member of his team who was on the ice when the offense was committed, said player to be designated by the Manager or Coach of the offending team through the Captain and, in addition, the goalkeeper shall be fined one hundred dollars ($100).

(e) Should a goalkeeper incur a game misconduct penalty, his place will then be taken by a member of his own club, or by a regular substitute goalkeeper who is available, and such player will be allowed the goalkeeper's full equipment. In addition, the goalkeeper shall be fined two hundred dollars ($200).

(f) Should a goalkeeper incur a match penalty, his place will then be taken by a member of his own club, or by a substitute goalkeeper who is available, and such player will be allowed the goalkeeper's full equipment. However, any additional penalties as specifically called for by the individual rules covering match penalties will apply, and the offending team shall be penalized accordingly, such additional penalties to be served by other members of the team on the ice when the offenses were committed, said players to be designated by the Manager or Coach of the offending team through the Captain. (See Rules 44, 49 and 64.)

(g) Should a goalkeeper incur a match penalty, the case shall be investigated promptly by the Commissioner who shall have full power to fine or suspend the penalized goalkeeper or any other players in the altercation.

(h) A minor penalty shall be imposed on a goalkeeper who leaves the immediate vicinity of his crease during an altercation. In addition, he shall be subject to a fine of two hundred dollars ($200) and this incident shall be reported to the Commissioner for such further disciplinary action as may be required.

(NOTE) All penalties imposed on a goalkeeper, regardless of who serves the penalty or any substitution, shall be charged in the records against the goalkeeper.

(i) If a goalkeeper participates in the play in any manner when he is beyond the center red line, a minor penalty shall be imposed upon him.

RULE 33. DELAYED PENALTIES

(a) If a third player of any team shall be penalized while two players of the same team are serving penalties, the penalty time of the third player shall not commence until the penalty time of one of the two players already penalized has elapsed. Nevertheless, the third player penalized must at once proceed to the penalty bench but may be replaced by a substitute until such time as the penalty time of the penalized player shall commence.

(b) When any team shall have three players serving penalties at the same time and because of the delayed penalty rule, a substitute for the third offender is on the ice, none of the three penalized players on the penalty bench may return to the ice until play has stopped. When play has been stopped, the player whose full penalty has expired may return to the play.

Provided however that the Penalty Timekeeper shall permit the return to the ice in the order of expiry of their penalties, of a player or players when, by reason of the expiration of their penalties, the penalized team is entitled to have more than four players on the ice.

(c) In the case of delayed penalties, the Referee shall instruct the Penalty Timekeeper that penalized players whose penalties have expired shall only be allowed to return to the ice when there is a stoppage of play.

When the penalties of two players of the same team will expire at the same time, the Captain of that team will designate to the Referee which of such players will return to the ice first and the Referee will instruct the Penalty Timekeeper accordingly.

When a major and a minor penalty are imposed at the same time on players of the same team, the Penalty Timekeeper shall record the minor as being the first of such penalties.

(NOTE) This applies to the case where the two penalties are imposed on DIFFERENT players of the same team. See also Note to Rule 27—Minor Penalties.

RULE 34. CALLING OF PENALTIES

(a) Should an infraction of the rules which would call for a minor, major, misconduct, game misconduct or match penalty be committed by a player of the side in possession of the puck, the Referee shall immediately blow his whistle and penalize the offending player.

The resulting face-off shall be made at the place where the play was stopped unless the stoppage occurs in the attacking zone of the player penalized in which case the face-off shall be made at the nearest face-off spot in the neutral zone.

(b) Should an infraction of the rules which would call for a minor, major, misconduct, game misconduct or match penalty be committed by a player of the team not in possession of the puck, the Referee will blow his whistle and impose the penalty on the offending player upon completion of the play by the team in possession of the puck.

(NOTE) There shall be no signal given by the Referee for a misconduct or game misconduct penalty under this section.

The resulting face-off shall be made at the place where the play was stopped, unless during the period of a delayed whistle due to a foul by a player of the side NOT in possession, the side in possession ices the puck, shoots the puck so that it goes out of bounds or is unplayable, then the face-off following the stoppage shall take place in the neutral zone near the defending blue line of the team shooting the puck.

If the penalty to be imposed is a minor penalty and a goal is scored on the play by the non-offending side, the minor penalty shall not be imposed but major and match penalties shall be imposed in the normal manner regardless of whether or not a goal is scored.

When the penalty to be imposed is applicable under Rule 58(c)(1)—High Sticks or Rule 79 (c)—Spearing and Butt-Ending, and a goal is scored, two minutes of the appropriate penalty will be assessed to the offending player. (This will be announced as a double minor for the appropriate foul and the player will serve two minutes only.)

(NOTE 1) "Completion of the play by the team in possession" in this rule means that the puck must have come into the possession and control of an opposing player or has been "frozen". This does not mean a rebound off the goalkeeper, the goal or the boards, or any accidental contact with the body or equipment of an opposing player.

(NOTE 2) If after the Referee has signalled a penalty but before the whistle has been blown, the puck shall enter the goal of the non-offending team as the direct result of a player of that team, the goal shall be allowed and the penalty signalled shall be imposed in the normal manner.

(NOTE 3) If when a team is "short-handed" by reason of one or more minor or bench minor penalties, the Referee signals a further minor penalty or penalties against the "short-handed" team and a goal is scored by the non-offending side before the whistle is blown, then the goal shall be allowed. The penalty or penalties signalled shall be assessed and the first of the minor penalties already being served shall automatically terminate under Rule 27(c)—Minor Penalties.

(c) Should the same offending player commit other fouls on the same play, either before or after the Referee has blown his whistle, the offending player shall serve such penalties consecutively.

RULE 34A. SUPPLEMENTARY DISCIPLINE

In addition to the automatic fines and suspensions imposed under these rules, the Commissioner may, at his discretion, investigate any incident that occurs in connection with any pre-season, exhibition, League or Playoff game and may assess additional fines and/or suspensions for any offense committed during the course of a game or any aftermath thereof by a player, Trainer, Manager, Coach or club executive, whether or not such offense has been penalized by the Referee.

(NOTE) If an investigation is requested by a club or by the League on its own initiative, it must be initiated within seventy-two (72) hours following the completion of the game in which the incident occurred.

RULE 34B. SUSPENSIONS ARISING FROM PRE-SEASON AND EXHIBITION GAMES

Whenever suspensions are imposed as a result of infractions occurring during pre-season and exhibition games, the Commissioner shall exercise his discretion in scheduling the suspensions to ensure that no team shall be short more players in any regular League game than it would have been had the infractions occurred in regular League games.

SECTION FIVE—OFFICIALS

RULE 35. APPOINTMENT OF OFFICIALS

(a) The Commissioner shall appoint a Referee, two Linesmen, Game Timekeeper, Penalty Timekeeper, Official Scorer and two Goal Judges for each game.

(b) The Commissioner shall forward to all clubs a list of Referees, Linesmen, and Off-ice Officials, all of whom must be treated with proper respect at all times during the season by all players and officials of clubs.

RULE 36. REFEREE

(a) The REFEREE shall have general supervision of the game and shall have full control of all game officials and players during the game, including stoppages; and in case of any dispute, his decision shall be final. The Referee shall remain on the ice at the conclusion of each period until all players have proceeded to their dressing rooms.

(b) All Referees and Linesmen shall be dressed in black trousers and official sweaters.

They shall be equipped with approved whistles and metal tape measures with minimum length of six feet.

(c) The Referee shall order the teams on the ice at the appointed time for the beginning of a game and at the commencement of each period. If for any reason, there is more than fifteen minutes' delay in the commencement of the game or any undue delay in resuming play after the fifteen-minute intervals between periods, the Referee shall state in his report to the Commissioner the cause of the delay and the club or clubs which were at fault.

(d) It shall be his duty to see to it that all players are properly dressed, and that the approved regulation equipment (including the approved on-ice branded exposure program) is in use at all times during the game.

(e) The Referee shall, before starting the game, see that the appointed Game Timekeeper, Penalty Timekeeper, Official Scorer and Goal Judges are in their respective places and satisfy himself that the timing and signalling equipment are in order.

(f) It shall be his duty to impose such penalties as are prescribed by the rules for infractions thereof and he shall give the final decision in matters of disputed goals. The Referee may consult with the Linesmen, Goal Judge or Video Goal Judge before making his decision.

(g) The Referee shall announce to the Official Scorer or Penalty Timekeeper all goals legally scored as well as penalties, and for what infractions such penalties are imposed.

The Referee shall cause to be announced over the public address system the reason for not allowing a goal every time the goal signal light is turned on in the course of play. This shall be done at the first stoppage of play regardless of any standard signal given by the Referee when the goal signal light was put on in error.

The Referee shall report to the Official Scorer the name or number of the goal scorer but he shall not give any information or advice with respect to assist.

(NOTE) The name of the scorer and any player entitled to an assist will be announced on the public address system. In the event that the Referee disallows a goal for any violation of the rules, he shall report the reason for disallowance to the Official Scorer who shall announce the Referee's decision correctly over the public address system.

The infraction of the rules for which each penalty has been imposed will be announced correctly, as reported by the Referee, over the public address system. Where players of both teams are penalized on the same play, the penalty to the visiting player will be announced first.

Where a penalty is imposed by the Referee which calls for a mandatory or automatic fine, only the time portion of the penalty will be reported by the Referee to the Official Scorer and announced on the public address system, and the fine will be collected through the League office.

(h) The Referee shall see to it that players of opposing teams are separated on the penalty bench to prevent feuding.

(i) He shall not halt the game for any infractions of the rules concerning off-side play at the blue line or center line, or any violation of Rule 61, icing the puck. Determining infractions of these rules is the duty of the Linesmen unless, by virtue of some accident, the Linesman is prevented from doing so in which case the duties of the Linesman shall be assumed by the Referee until play is stopped.

(j) Should a Referee accidentally leave the ice or receive an injury which incapacitates him from discharging his duties while play is in progress, the game shall be automatically stopped.

(k) If, through misadventure or sickness, the Referee and Linesmen appointed are prevented from appearing, the Managers or Coaches of the two clubs shall agree on a Referee and Linesman. If they are unable to agree, they shall appoint a player from each side who shall act as Referee and Linesman; the player of the home club acting as Referee and the player of the visiting club as Linesman.

(l) If the regularly appointed officials appear during the progress of the game, they shall at once replace the temporary officials.

(m) Should a Linesman appointed be unable to act at the last minute or through sickness or accident be unable to finish the game, the Referee shall have the power to appoint another in his stead, if he deems it necessary, or if required to do so by the Manager or Coach of either of the competing teams.

(n) If, owing to illness or accident, the Referee is unable to continue to officiate, one of the Linesmen shall perform the duties of the Referee during the balance of the game, the Linesman to be selected by the Referee. In the event that an NHL Supervisor is in attendance at a game where a spare official is present, he shall have the authority to substitute the injured Referee with the spare official.

(o) The Referee shall check club rosters and all players in uniform before signing reports of the game.

(p) The Referee shall report to Commissioner promptly and in detail the circumstances of any of the following incidents:

i) When a stick or part thereof is thrown outside the playing area— Rule 81(c)—Throwing Stick;

ii) Every obscene gesture made by any person involved in the playing or conduct of the game whether as a participant or as an official of either team or of the League, which gesture he has personally observed or which has been brought to his attention by any game official—Rule 68(a)—Obscene or Profane Language or Gestures;

iii) When any player, Trainer, Coach or club executive becomes involved in an altercation with a spectator—Rule 63(b)—Interference by/with Spectators;

iv) Every infraction under Rule 28(b)—Major Penalties, major and game misconducts.

(q) In the event of failure by a club to comply with a provision of the League constitution, by-laws, resolutions, rules or regulations affecting the playing of a game, the Referee shall, if so directed by the Commissioner or his designee, refuse to permit the game to proceed until the offending club comes into compliance with such provision.

Should the offending club persist in its refusal to come into compliance, the Referee shall, with the prior approval of the Commissioner or his designee, declare the game forfeited and the non-offending club the winner. Should the Referee declare the game forfeited because both clubs have refused to comply with such a provision, the visiting club shall be declared the winner.

If the game is declared forfeited prior to its having commenced, the score shall be recorded as 1–0 and no player shall be credited with any personal statistics.

If the game was in progress at the time it is declared forfeited, the score shall be recorded as zero for the loser and 1, or such greater number of goals that had been scored by it, for the winner; however, the players on both clubs shall be credited with all personal statistics earned up to the time the forfeit was declared.

RULE 37. LINESMAN

(a) The duty of the LINESMAN is to determine any infractions of the rules concerning off-side play at the blue line or center line, or any violation of Rule 61—Icing the Puck.

He shall stop the play when the puck goes outside the playing area, when it is interfered with by any ineligible person, when it is struck above the height of the shoulder and when the goal post has been displaced from its normal position. He shall stop the play for off-sides occurring on face-offs and for premature entry into face-off circles. He shall stop the play when he has observed that a goal has been scored which has not been observed by the Referee. He shall stop the play when there has been a premature substitution for a goalkeeper under Rule 18(a)—Change of Players; for injured players under Rule 19(f)—Injured Players; the calling of a double-minor for Cross-checking under Rule 48(a)—Cross-checking; for a player deliberately batting the puck to a teammate under Rule 57(e)—Handling Puck with Hands; the calling of a double-minor penalty for accidental high sticks, under Rule 58(c)—High Sticks; interference by spectators under Rule 63(a)—Interference by/with Spectators; the calling of a double-minor penalty to a player who attempts to poke, jab, spear or butt-end an opponent, under Rule 79(c)—Spearing and Butt-ending; and the calling of a penalty under Rule 81(a)—Throwing Stick; for deliberately throwing a stick in the defensive zone.

(b) He shall face-off the puck at all times, except at the start of the game, at the beginning of each period and after a goal has been scored.

(c) He shall, when requested to do so by the Referee, give his version of any incident that may have taken place during the playing of the game.

(d) He shall not stop the play to impose any penalty except when a major penalty is warranted to a player on the ice when a serious incident has been observed by him but not by the Referee and/or when he observes any violation of Rules 18(a) and (c), change of players (too many men on the ice); Rule 42(k), articles thrown on the ice from vicinity of players' or penalty bench; Rule 42(l), interference with game officials by player, Coach, Trainer or club executive; Rule 46(c), stick thrown on ice from players' bench and Rule 50(c), delaying the game by deliberately displacing the post from its normal position. He shall report such violation to the Referee who shall impose a bench minor penalty against the offending team.

In addition, when assessing a major penalty to a player, he may, at his discretion, assess a minor penalty to a player of the opposing team that he deems instigated the incident for which the major penalty was assessed.

He shall report immediately to the Referee his version of the circumstances with regard to interference on a goaltender when a goal is scored.

He shall report immediately to the Referee his version of any infraction of the rules constituting a major or match foul or game misconduct or any conduct calling for a bench minor penalty or misconduct penalty under these rules.

RULE 38. GOAL JUDGE

(a) There shall be one GOAL JUDGE at each goal. They shall not be members of either club engaged in a game, nor shall they be replaced during its progress, unless after the commencement of the game it becomes apparent that either Goal Judge, on account of partisanship or any other cause, is guilty of giving unjust decisions, when the Referee may appoint another Goal Judge to act in his stead.

(b) Goal Judges shall be stationed behind the goals during the progress of play, in properly protected areas, if possible, so that there can be no interference with their activities. They shall not change goals during the game.

(c) In the event of a goal being claimed, the Goal Judge of that goal shall decide whether or not the puck has passed between the goal posts and entirely over the goal line.

RULE 39. PENALTY TIMEKEEPER

(a) The PENALTY TIMEKEEPER shall keep, on the official forms provided, a correct record of all penalties imposed by the officials including the names of the players penalized, the infractions penalized, the duration of each penalty and the time at which each penalty was imposed. He shall report in the Penalty Record each penalty shot awarded, the name of the player taking the shot and the result of the shot.

(b) The Penalty Timekeeper shall check and ensure that the time served by all penalized players is correct. He shall be responsible for the correct posting of penalties on the scoreboard at all times and shall promptly call to the attention of the Referee any discrepancy between the time recorded on the clock and the official correct time and he shall be responsible for making any adjustments ordered by the Referee.

He shall upon request, give a penalized player correct information as to the unexpired time of his penalty.

(NOTE 1) The infraction of the rules for which each penalty has been imposed will be announced twice over the public address system as reported by the Referee. Where players of both teams are penalized on the same play, the penalty to the visiting player will be announced first.

(NOTE 2) Misconduct penalties and coincident major penalties should not be recorded on the timing device but such penalized players should be alerted and released at the first stoppage of play following the expiration of their penalties.

(c) Upon the completion of each game, the Penalty Timekeeper shall complete and sign four copies of the Penalty Record to be distributed as quickly as possible to the following persons:

(1) One copy to the Official Scorer for transmission to the League Commissioner;

(2) One copy to the visiting Coach or Manager;

(3) One copy to the home Coach or Manager;

(4) One copy to the home team Public Relations Department.

(d) The Officiating Department shall be entitled to inspect, collect and forward to League headquarters the actual work sheets used by the Penalty Timekeeper in any game.

RULE 40. OFFICIAL SCORER

(a) Before the start of the game, the Official Scorer shall obtain from the Manager or Coach of both teams a list of all eligible players and the starting line-up of each team which information shall be made known to the opposing Manager or Coach before the start of play, either personally or through the Referee.

The Official Scorer shall secure the names of the Captain and Alternate Captains from the Manager or Coach at the time the line-ups are collected and will indicate those nominated by placing the letter "C" or "A" opposite their names on the Referee's Report of Match. All this information shall be presented to the Referee for his signature at the completion of the game.

(b) The Official Scorer shall keep a record of the goals scored, the scorers, and players to whom assists have been credited and shall indicate those players on the lists who have actually taken part in the game. He shall also record the time of entry into the game of any substitute goalkeeper. He shall record on the Official Score Sheet a notation where a goal is scored when the goalkeeper has been removed from the ice.

(c) The Official Scorer shall award the points for goals and assists and his decision shall be final. The awards of points for goals and assists shall be announced twice over the public address system and all changes in such awards shall also be announced in the same manner.

No requests for changes in any award of points shall be considered unless they are made at or before the conclusion of actual play in the game by the team Captain.

(d) At the conclusion of the game, the Official Scorer shall complete and sign four copies of the Official Score Sheet for distribution as quickly as possible to the following persons:
   (1) One copy to the Official Scorer to be transmitted to the League Commissioner;
   (2) One copy to the visiting Coach or Manager;
   (3) One copy to the home Coach or Manager;
   (4) One copy to the home team Public Relations Department.

(e) The Official Scorer shall also prepare the Official Report of Match for signature by the Referee and forward it to the League Commissioner together with the Official Score Sheet and the Penalty Record.

(f) The Official Scorer should be in an elevated position, well away from the players' benches, with house telephone communication to the public address announcer.

RULE 41. GAME TIMEKEEPER

(a) The Game Timekeeper shall record the time of starting and finishing of each period in the game. During the game the game timekeeper will start the clock with the drop of the puck and stop the clock upon hearing the Official's whistle or the scoring of a goal.

(b) The Game Timekeeper shall signal the Referee and the competing teams for the start of the game and each succeeding period and the Referee shall start the play promptly in accordance with Rule 82—Time of Match.

For the purpose of keeping the spectators informed as to the time remaining during intermissions, the Game Timekeeper will use the electric clock to record the length of intermissions. The clock will not start for the intermission until all players and officials have left the ice.

To assist in assuring the prompt return to the ice of the teams and the officials, the Game Timekeeper shall give preliminary warnings five and two minutes prior to the resumption of play in each period.

(c) If the rink is not equipped with an automatic signalling device or, if such device fails to function, the Game Timekeeper shall signal the end of each period by blowing a whistle.

(d) He shall cause to be announced on the public address system at the nineteenth minute in each period that there is one minute remaining to be played in the period.

(e) In the event of any dispute regarding time, the matter shall be referred to the Referee for adjustment and his decision shall be final.

(f) The Game Timekeeper is required to synchronize his timing device with the Television Producer of the originating broadcast.

RULE 41A. STATISTICIAN

(a) There shall be appointed for duty at every game played in the League a Statistician and such assistants or alternates as may be deemed necessary.

(b) The duty of the Statistician(s) is to correctly record on official League forms all of the required data concerning the performances of the individual players and teams.

(c) These records shall be compiled and recorded in strict conformity with the instructions printed on the forms supplied and shall be completed as to totals where required and with such accuracy as to ensure that the data supplied is "in balance".

(d) At the conclusion of each game, the Statistician shall sign and distribute four copies of the final and correct Statistician's Report to each of the following persons:
   (1) One copy to the Official Scorer for transmission to the League Commissioner;
   (2) One copy to the visiting Coach or Manager;
   (3) One copy to the home Coach or Manager;
   (4) One copy to the home team Public Relations Department.

SECTION SIX—PLAYING RULES

RULE 42. ABUSE OF OFFICIALS AND OTHER MISCONDUCT

(NOTE) In the enforcement of this rule, the Referee has, in many instances, the option of imposing a misconduct penalty or a bench minor penalty. In principle, the Referee is directed to impose a bench minor penalty in respect to the violations which occur on or in the immediate vicinity of the players' bench but off the playing surface and in all cases affecting non-playing personnel or players. A misconduct penalty should be imposed for violations which occur on the playing surface or in the penalty bench area and where the penalized player is readily identifiable.

(a) A misconduct penalty shall be imposed on any player who uses obscene, profane or abusive language to any person or who intentionally knocks or shoots the puck out of the reach of an official who is retrieving it or who deliberately throws any equipment out of the playing area.

(b) A minor penalty shall be assessed to any player who challenges or disputes the rulings of any official during a game. If the player persists in such challenge or dispute, he shall be assessed a misconduct penalty and any further dispute will result in a game misconduct penalty being assessed to the offending player.

In the event that a teammate of a penalized player challenges or disputes the ruling of the official in assessing the penalty, a misconduct penalty shall be imposed.

(NOTE:) Any player who, having entered the penalty bench, leaves the penalty bench prior to the expiration of his penalty, shall be assessed the appropriate penalties. He shall also be automatically suspended for the next three regular League and/or Playoff games of his club. This rule does not replace any other more severe penalty that may be imposed for leaving the penalty bench. See also Rule 66—Leaving Players' or Penalty Bench.

(c) A misconduct penalty shall be imposed on any player or players who bang the boards with their sticks or other objects at any time, showing disrespect for an Official's decision.

In the event that the Coach, Trainer, Manager or club executive commits an infraction under this rule, a bench minor penalty shall be imposed.

(d) Where coincident penalties are imposed on players of both teams, the penalized players of the visiting team shall take their positions on the penalty bench first in the place designated for visiting players.

(e) Any player who, following a fight or other altercation in which he has been involved is broken up and for which he is penalized, fails to proceed directly and immediately to the penalty bench, or who causes any delay by retrieving his equipment (gloves, sticks, etc. shall be delivered to him at the penalty bench by teammates), shall incur an automatic fine of one hundred dollars ($100) in addition to all other penalties or fines incurred.

(f) Any player who persists in continuing or attempting to continue a fight or altercation after he has been ordered by the Referee to stop, or who resists a Linesman in the discharge of his duties shall, at the discretion of the Referee, incur a misconduct or game misconduct penalty in addition to any penalties imposed.

(g) A misconduct penalty shall be imposed on any player who, after warning by the Referee, persists in any course of conduct (including threatening or abusive language or gestures or similar actions) designed to incite an opponent into incurring a penalty.

If, after the assessment of a misconduct penalty, a player persists in any course of conduct for which he was previously assessed a misconduct penalty, he shall be assessed a game misconduct penalty.

(h) A bench minor penalty shall be imposed against the offending team if any player, club executive, Manager, Coach or Trainer uses obscene, profane or abusive language or gesture to any person or uses the name of any official coupled with any vociferous remarks.

(i) In the case of any club executive, Manager, Coach or Trainer being guilty of such misconduct, he is to be removed from the bench by order of the Referee and his case reported to the Commissioner for further action. (Refer to Rule 68(c)—Obscene or Profane Language or Gestures.)

(j) If any club executive, Manager, Coach or Trainer is removed from the bench by order of the Referee, he must not sit near the bench of his club nor in any way direct or attempt to direct the play of his club.

When a Coach has been removed from the bench, he shall be assessed a Game Misconduct penalty.

(k) A bench minor penalty shall be imposed against the offending team if any player, Trainer, Coach, Manager or club executive in the vicinity of the players' bench or penalty bench throws anything on the ice during the progress of the game or during stoppage of play.

(NOTE) The penalty provided under this rule is in addition to any penalty imposed under Rule 46(c)—Broken Stick.

(l) A bench minor penalty shall be imposed against the offending team if any player, Trainer, Coach, Manager or club executive interferes in any manner with any game official including Referee, Linesmen, Timekeepers or Goal Judges in the performance of their duties.

The Referee may assess further penalties under Rule 67 (Abuse of Officials) if he deems them to be warranted.

(m) A misconduct penalty shall be imposed on any player or players who, except for the purpose of taking their positions on the penalty bench, enter or remain in the Referee's crease while he is reporting to or consulting with any game official including Linesmen, Timekeeper, Penalty Timekeeper, Official Scorer or Announcer.

(n) A minor penalty shall be imposed on any player who is guilty of unsportsmanlike conduct including, but not limited to hair-pulling, biting, grabbing hold of face mask, etc.

(NOTE) If warranted the Referee may apply Rule 29(d)—Gross Misconduct.

(o) A minor penalty shall be imposed on a player who attempts to draw a penalty by his actions ("diving").

RULE 43. ADJUSTMENT TO CLOTHING OR EQUIPMENT

(a) Play shall not be stopped nor the game delayed by reasons of adjustments to clothing, equipment, skates or sticks.

For an infringement of this rule, a minor penalty shall be given.

(b) The onus of maintaining clothing and equipment in proper condition shall be upon the player. If adjustments are required, the player shall leave the ice and play shall continue with a substitute.

(c) No delay shall be permitted for the repair or adjustment of goalkeeper's equipment. If adjustments are required, the goalkeeper shall leave the ice and his place shall be taken by the substitute goalkeeper immediately.

(d) For an infraction of this rule by a goalkeeper, a minor penalty shall be imposed.

RULE 44. ATTEMPT TO INJURE

(a) A match penalty shall be imposed on any player who deliberately attempts to injure an opponent and the circumstances shall be reported to the Commissioner for further action. A substitute for the penalized player shall be permitted at the end of the fifth minute.

(b) A game misconduct penalty shall be imposed on any player who deliberately attempts to injure an Official, Manager, Coach or Trainer in any manner and the circumstances shall be reported to the Commissioner for further action. (See also Rule 67—Physical Abuse of Officials.)

(NOTE) The Commissioner, upon preliminary investigation indicating the probable imposition of supplementary disciplinary action, may order the immediate suspension of a player who has incurred a match penalty under this rule, pending the final determination of such supplementary disciplinary action.

RULE 45. BOARD CHECKING AND CHECKING FROM BEHIND

(a) A minor or major penalty, at the discretion of the Referee based upon the degree of violence of the impact with the boards, shall be imposed on any player who bodychecks, cross-checks, elbows, charges or trips an opponent in such a manner that causes the opponent to be thrown violently into the boards.

(NOTE) Any unnecessary contact with a player playing the puck on an obvious "icing" or "off-side" play which results in that player being knocked into the boards is "boarding" and must be penalized as such. In other instances where there is no contact with the boards, it should be treated as "charging".

"Rolling" an opponent (if he is the puck carrier) along the boards where he is endeavoring to go through too small an opening is not boarding. However, if the opponent is not the puck carrier, then such action should be penalized as boarding, charging, interference or, if the arms or stick are employed, it should be called holding or hooking.

(b) When a major penalty is imposed under this rule, an automatic fine of one hundred dollars ($100) shall be imposed.

(c) When a major penalty is imposed under this rule for a foul resulting in an injury to the face or head of an opponent, an automatic game misconduct shall be imposed.

(d) Any player who cross-checks, pushes or charges from behind an opponent who is unable to defend himself, shall be assessed a major and a game misconduct. This penalty applies anywhere on the playing surface.

(e) In regular season games any player who incurs a total of two game misconduct penalties for board-checking under Rule 45(c) and (d) shall be suspended automatically for the next League game of his team. For each subsequent game misconduct penalty the automatic suspension shall be increased by one game.

In playoff games, any player who incurs a total of two game misconduct penalties for board-checking under Rule 45(c) and (d) shall be suspended automatically for the next playoff game of his team. For each subsequent game misconduct penalty during the playoffs the automatic suspension shall be increased by one game.

RULE 46. BROKEN STICK

(a) A player without a stick may participate in the game. A player whose stick is broken may participate in the game provided he drops the broken portion. A minor penalty shall be imposed for an infraction of this rule.

(NOTE) A broken stick is one which, in the opinion of the Referee, is unfit for normal play.

(b) A goalkeeper may continue to play with a broken stick until stoppage of play or until he has been legally provided with a stick.

(c) A player who has lost or broken his stick may only receive a stick at his own players' bench or be handed one from a teammate on the ice, and may not receive a stick thrown on the ice from any part of the rink. A minor penalty shall be imposed for an infraction of this rule.

(NOTE) A player tendered a stick thrown on the ice from the players' or penalty bench who does not pick up the stick, will not receive a penalty. The person responsible for throwing the stick will receive the penalty, as covered in Rule 62—Interference.

(d) A goalkeeper whose stick is broken or illegal may not go to the players' bench for a replacement but must receive his stick from a teammate.

For an infraction of this rule, a minor penalty shall be imposed on the goalkeeper.

RULE 47. CHARGING

(a) A minor or major penalty shall be imposed on a player who runs or jumps into or charges an opponent.

(b) When a major penalty is imposed under this rule for a foul resulting in injury to the face or head of an opponent, an automatic fine of one hundred dollars ($100) shall be imposed.

(c) A minor or major penalty shall be imposed on a player who charges a goalkeeper while the goalkeeper is within his goal crease.

(NOTE) If more than two steps or strides are taken, it shall be considered a charge.

A goalkeeper is NOT "fair game" just because he is outside the goal crease area. A penalty for interference or charging (minor or major) should be called in every case where an opposing player makes unnecessary contact with a goalkeeper.

Likewise, Referees should be alert to penalize goalkeepers for tripping, slashing or spearing in the vicinity of the goal.

RULE 48. CROSS-CHECKING

(a) A minor, double minor or major penalty, at the discretion of the Referee, shall be imposed on a player who "cross-checks" an opponent.

(NOTE 1) Cross-check shall mean a check delivered with both hands on the stick and no part of the stick on the ice.

(NOTE 2) A double minor penalty must be assessed for cross-checks delivered to the neck or head area, unless a major or match penalty (Rule 44—Attempt to Injure or Rule 49—Deliberate Injury) is assessed.

(NOTE 3) When a major penalty is assessed for cross-checking, an automatic game misconduct penalty shall be imposed on the offending player.

(b) When a major penalty is imposed under this rule, an automatic fine of one hundred dollars ($100) shall also be imposed.

RULE 49. DELIBERATE INJURY OF OPPONENTS

(a) A match penalty shall be imposed on a player who deliberately injures an opponent in any manner.

(NOTE) Any player wearing tape or any other material on his hands (below the wrist) who cuts or injures an opponent during an altercation shall receive a match penalty under this rule.

(b) In addition to the match penalty, the player shall be automatically suspended from further competition until the Commissioner has ruled on the issue.

(c) No substitute shall be permitted to take the place of the penalized player until five minutes of actual playing time have elapsed from the time the penalty was imposed.

(d) A game misconduct penalty shall be imposed on any player who deliberately injures an official, Manager, Coach or Trainer in any manner and the circumstances shall be reported to the Commissioner for further action.

RULE 50. DELAYING THE GAME

(a) A minor penalty shall be imposed on any player or goalkeeper who delays the game by deliberately shooting or batting the puck with his stick outside the playing area.

(NOTE 1) When the goalkeeper shoots the puck directly (non-deflected) out of the playing surface, except where there is no glass, a penalty shall be assessed for delaying the game.

(NOTE 2) This penalty shall also apply when a player or goalkeeper deliberately bats or shoots the puck with his stick outside the playing area after a stoppage of play.

(b) A minor penalty shall be imposed on any player or goalkeeper who throws or deliberately bats the puck with his hand or stick outside the playing area.

(c) A minor penalty shall be imposed on any player (including the goalkeeper) who delays the game by deliberately displacing a goal post from its normal position. The Referee or Linesmen shall stop play immediately when a goal post has been displaced.

If the goal post is deliberately displaced by a goalkeeper or player during the course of a "breakaway", a penalty shot will be awarded to the non-offending team, which shot shall be taken by the player last in possession of the puck.

(NOTE) A player with a "breakaway" is defined as a player in control of the puck with no opposition between him and the opposing goal and with a reasonable scoring opportunity.

In the event that a goalpost is deliberately displaced by a defending player or goalkeeper, prior to the puck crossing the goal line between the normal position of the goalposts, the Referee, at his discretion, may assess a minor penalty under Rule 50(c) (paragraph 1), a penalty shot under Rule 50(d), or award a goal.

(d) If by reason of insufficient time in the regular playing time or by reason of penalties already imposed, the minor penalty assessed to a player for deliberately displacing his own goal post cannot be served in its entirety within the regular playing time of the game or at any time in overtime, a penalty shot shall be awarded against the offending team.

(e) A bench minor penalty shall be imposed upon any team which, after warning by the Referee to its Captain or Alternate Captain to place the correct number of players on the ice and commence play, fails to comply with the Referee's direction and thereby causes any delay by making additional substitutions, by persisting in having its players off-side, or in any other manner.

RULE 51. ELBOWING AND HEAD-BUTTING

(a) A minor or major penalty, at the discretion of the Referee, shall be imposed on any player who uses his elbow to, in any way, foul an opponent.

(b) When a major penalty is imposed under this rule for a foul resulting in an injury to an opponent, an automatic fine of one hundred dollars ($100) shall also be imposed.

(c) A match penalty shall be imposed on any player who deliberately "head-butts" or attempts to "head-butt" an opponent during an altercation and the circumstances shall be reported to the Commissioner for further action. A substitute player is permitted to replace the penalized player after five minutes playing time has elapsed when the penalty is imposed under Rule 44—Attempt to Injure or Rule 49—Deliberate Injury of Opponents.

RULE 52. FACE-OFFS

(a) The puck shall be "faced-off" by the Referee or the Linesman dropping the puck on the ice between the sticks of the players "facing-off". Players facing-off will stand squarely facing their opponent's end of the rink approximately one stick length apart with the blade of their sticks on the ice.

When the face-off takes place in any of the end face-off circles, the players taking part shall take their position so that they will stand squarely facing their opponent's end of the rink. The sticks of both players facing-off shall have the blade on the ice within the designated white area. The visiting player shall place his stick within the designated white area first.

No other player shall be allowed to enter the face-off circle or come within fifteen feet of the players facing-off the puck and must stand on side on all face-offs.

If a violation of this sub-section of this rule occurs, the Referee or Linesman shall re-face the puck.

(b) If after warning by the Referee or Linesman, either of the players fails to take his proper position for the face-off promptly, the official shall be entitled to face-off the puck notwithstanding such default.

(c) In the conduct of any face-off anywhere on the playing surface, no player facing-off shall make any physical contact with his opponent's body by means of his own body or by his stick except in the course of playing the puck after the face-off has been completed.

For violation of this rule, the Referee shall impose a minor penalty or penalties on the player(s) whose action(s) caused the physical contact.

(NOTE) "Conduct of any face-off" commences when the Referee designates the place of the face-off and he (or the Linesman) takes up his position to drop the puck.

(d) If a player facing-off fails to take his proper position immediately when directed by the official, the official may order him replaced for that face-off by any teammate then on the ice.

No substitution of players shall be permitted until the face-off has been completed and play has resumed except when a penalty is imposed which affects the on-ice strength of either team.

(e) A second violation of any of the provisions of sub-section (a) hereof by the same team during the same face-off shall be penalized with a minor penalty to the player who commits the second violation of the rule. The official must drop the puck twice in order to have a second face-off violation.

During end zone face-offs, all other players on the ice must position their bodies and sticks on their own side of the restraining lines marked on the outer edge of the face-off circles.

If a player other than the player taking the face-off moves into the face-off circle prior to the dropping of the puck, then the offending team's player taking the face-off shall be ejected from the face-off circle.

If a violation of this rule occurs, the Referee or Linesman shall order another face-off, unless the non-offending team wins the draw.

(f) When an infringement of a rule has been committed or a stoppage of play has been caused by any player of the attacking side in the attacking zone, the ensuing face-off shall be made in the neutral zone on the nearest face-off spot.

(NOTE) This includes stoppage of play caused by a player of the attacking side shooting the puck on the back of the defending team's net without any intervening action by the defending team.

(g) When an infringement of a rule has been committed by players of both sides in the play resulting in the stoppage, the ensuing face-off will be made at the place of such infringement or at the place where play is stopped.

(h) When stoppage occurs between the end face-off spots and near end of the rink, the puck shall be faced-off at the end face-off spot on the side where the stoppage occurs unless otherwise expressly provided by these rules.

(i) No face-off shall be made within fifteen feet of the goal or sideboards.

(j) When a goal is illegally scored as a result of a puck being deflected directly off an Official anywhere in the defending zone, the resulting face-off shall be made at the end face-off spot in the defending zone.

(k) When the game is stopped for any reason not specifically covered in the official rules, the puck must be faced-off where it was last played.

(l) The whistle will not be blown by the official to start play. Playing time will commence from the instant the puck is faced-off and will stop when the whistle is blown or a goal is scored.

(m) Following a stoppage of play, should one or both defensemen who are the point players or any player coming from the bench of the attacking team, enter into the attacking zone beyond the outer edge of the corner face-off circle, the ensuing face-off shall take place in the neutral zone near the blue line of the defending team.

RULE 53. FALLING ON PUCK

(a) A minor penalty shall be imposed on a player other than the goalkeeper who deliberately falls on or gathers the puck into his body.

(NOTE) Any player who drops to his knees to block a shot should not be penalized if the puck is shot under him or becomes lodged in his clothing or equipment but any use of the hands to make the puck unplayable should be penalized promptly.

(b) A minor penalty shall be imposed on a goalkeeper who, when he is in his own goal crease, deliberately falls on or gathers the puck into his body or who holds or places the puck against any part of the goal in such a manner as to cause a stoppage of play unless he is actually being checked by an opponent.

(NOTE) Refer to Rule 74(b)—Puck Must Be Kept In Motion for the Rule governing freezing of the puck by a goalkeeper outside of his crease area.

(c) No defending player, except the goalkeeper, will be permitted to fall on the puck, hold the puck or gather the puck into the body or hands when the puck is within the goal crease.

For infringement of this rule, play shall immediately be stopped and a penalty shot shall be ordered against the offending team, but no other penalty shall be given.

(NOTE) The rule shall be interpreted so that a penalty shot will be awarded only when the puck is in the crease at the instant the offense occurs. However, in cases where the puck is outside the crease, Rule 53(a) may still apply and a minor penalty may be imposed, even though no penalty shot is awarded.

RULE 54. FISTICUFFS

(NOTE) An altercation is a situation involving two players, with at least one to be penalized.

(a) A major penalty shall be imposed on any player who engages in fisticuffs. In addition, a minor or a major and/or a game misconduct penalty, at the discretion of the Referee, shall be imposed on any player involved in fisticuffs. A player deemed to be the instigator of fisticuffs shall be assessed a game misconduct. This is in addition to the applicable minor (for instigation) or major penalty deemed worthy by the Referee. If such player is wearing a face shield, he shall be assessed an additional minor penalty. These penalties are in addition to any other penalty incurred in the same incident.

A player who deliberately removes his sweater prior to participating in an altercation shall be assessed a minor penalty for instigation and a game misconduct. This is in addition to other penalties to be assessed to the participants of an altercation.

(b) A minor penalty shall be imposed on a player who, having been struck, shall retaliate with a blow or attempted blow. However, at the discretion of the Referee, a major or a double-minor penalty or a game misconduct penalty may be imposed if such player continues the altercation.

(NOTE 1) It is the intent and purpose of this rule that the Referee shall impose the "major and game misconduct" penalty in all cases where the instigator or retaliator of the fight is the aggressor and is plainly doing so for the purpose of intimidation or punishment.

(NOTE 2) The Referee is provided very wide latitude in the penalties which he may impose under this rule. This is done intentionally to enable him to differentiate between the obvious degrees of responsibility of the participants either for starting the fighting or persisting in continuing the fighting. The discretion provided should be exercised realistically.

(NOTE 3) Referees are directed to employ every means provided by these rules to stop "brawling" and should use this rule and Rules 42(e) and (f)—Abuse of Officials and other Misconduct.

(NOTE 4) Any player wearing tape or any other material on his hands (below the wrist) who cuts or injures an opponent during an altercation will receive a match penalty under Rule 49—Deliberate Injury of Opponents.

(c) A misconduct or game misconduct penalty shall be imposed on any player involved in fisticuffs off the playing surface or with another player who is off the playing surface. These penalties are in addition to any other time penalties assessed.

(d) A game misconduct penalty, at the discretion of the Referee, shall be imposed on any player or goalkeeper who is the first to intervene in an altercation already in progress except when a match penalty is being imposed in the original altercation. This penalty is in addition to any other penalty incurred in the same incident.

(e) When a fight occurs, all players not engaged shall go immediately to the area of their players' bench and in the event the altercation takes place at a players' bench, the players on the ice from that team shall go to their defensive zone.

Failure to comply with the Rule shall, in addition to the other penalties that may be assessed, result in a fine to the team of $1,000 and the Coach of said team in the amount of $1,000.

(f) A game misconduct penalty shall be imposed on any player who is assessed a major penalty for fighting after the original altercation.

Notwithstanding this rule, at the discretion of the Referee, the automatic game misconduct penalty may be waived for a player in the altercation if the opposing player was clearly the instigator of the altercation.

(g) Any teams whose players become involved in an altercation, other than during the periods of the game, shall be fined automatically twenty-five thousand dollars ($25,000) in addition to any other appropriate penalties that may be imposed upon the participating players by supplementary discipline or otherwise.

Any player who would be deemed to be an instigator pursuant to Rule 54(a) at a time other than during the periods of the game shall be suspended automatically for ten (10) games. Such determination may be made by the Referee at the time of the incident or subsequently by the Commissioner or his designee based upon such reports and other information as he deems sufficient, including but not limited to television tapes.

(NOTE) In the case of altercations taking place after the period or game the fine under this rule shall be assessed only in the event that an altercation is commenced after the period or game has terminated.

RULE 55. GOALS AND ASSISTS

(NOTE) It is the responsibility of the Official Scorer to award goals and assists, and his decision in this respect is final notwithstanding the report of the Referee or any other game official. Such awards shall be made or withheld strictly in accordance with the provisions of this rule. Therefore, it is essential that the Official Scorer be thoroughly familiar with every aspect of this rule, be alert to observe all actions which could affect the making of an award and, above all, the awards must be made or withheld with absolute impartiality.

In case of an obvious error in awarding a goal or an assist which has been announced, it should be corrected promptly but changes should not be made in the official scoring summary after the Referee has signed the Game Report.

(a) A goal shall be scored when the puck shall have been put between the goal posts by the stick of a player of the attacking side, from in front and below the cross bar, and entirely across a red line, the width of the diameter of the goal posts drawn on the ice from one goal post to the other with the goal frame in its proper position.

(b) A goal shall be scored if the puck is put into the goal in any way by a player of the defending side. The player of the attacking side who last played the puck shall be credited with the goal but no assist shall be awarded.

(c) A goal cannot be scored by an attacking player who bats or kicks the puck directly into the net. A goal cannot be scored where an attacking player bats or kicks the puck and it is deflected off any player or goalkeeper into the net.

(d) If an attacking, stationary player deflects the puck with his skate or foot into the net, the goal shall be allowed. The player who deflected the puck shall be credited with the goal. The goal shall not be allowed if the puck has been intentionally kicked/deflected with his skate or foot into the net In addition, the goal shall not be allowed if the puck has been thrown or otherwise deliberately directed into the goal by any means other than a stick.

(e) If a goal is scored as a result of being deflected directly into the net off an official, the goal shall not be allowed. Refer to Rule 76—Puck Striking Official.

(f) Should a player legally propel a puck into the goal crease of the opponent club and the puck should become loose and available to another player of the attacking side, a goal scored on the play shall be legal.

(g) Any goal scored, other than as covered by the official rules, shall not be allowed.

(h) A "goal" shall be credited in the scoring records to a player who shall have propelled the puck into the opponent's goal. Each "goal" shall count one point in the player's record.

(i) When a player scores a goal, an "assist" shall be credited to the player or players taking part in the play immediately preceding the goal, but no more than two assists can be given on any goal. Each "assist" shall count one point in the player's record.

(j) Only one point can be credited to any one player on a goal.

RULE 56. GROSS MISCONDUCT:

Refer to Rule 29—Misconduct Penalty

RULE 57. HANDLING PUCK WITH HANDS

(a) If a player, except a goalkeeper, closes his hand on the puck, the play shall be stopped and a minor penalty shall be imposed on him. A goalkeeper who holds the puck with his hands for longer than three seconds shall be given a minor penalty unless he is actually being checked by an opponent.

(b) A goalkeeper must not deliberately hold the puck in any manner which, in the opinion of the Referee, causes a stoppage of play, nor throw the puck forward towards the opponent's net, nor deliberately drop the puck into his pads or onto the goal net, nor deliberately pile up snow or obstacles at or near his net, that in the opinion of the Referee, would tend to prevent the scoring of a goal.

(NOTE) The object of this entire rule is to keep the puck in play continuously and any action taken by the goalkeeper which causes an unnecessary stoppage must be penalized without warning.

(c) The penalty for infringement of this rule by the goalkeeper shall be a minor penalty.

(NOTE) In the case of the puck thrown forward by the goalkeeper being taken by an opponent, the Referee shall allow the resulting play to be completed, and if goal is scored by the non-offending team, it shall be allowed and no penalty given; but if a goal is not scored, play shall be stopped and a minor penalty shall be imposed against the goalkeeper.

(d) A minor penalty shall be imposed on a player, except the goalkeeper, who, while play is in progress, picks up the puck off the ice with his hand.

If a player, except a goalkeeper, while play is in progress, picks up the puck with his hand from the ice in the goal crease area, the play shall be stopped immediately and a penalty shot shall be awarded to the non-offending team.

(e) A player shall be permitted to stop or "bat" a puck in the air with his open hand, or push it along the ice with his hand, and the play shall not be stopped unless, in the opinion of the Referee, he has deliberately directed the puck to a teammate in any zone other than the defensive zone, in which case the play shall be stopped and the puck faced-off at the spot where the offense occurred. Play will not be stopped for any hand pass by players in their own defensive zone.

(NOTE) The object of this rule is to ensure continuous action and the Referee should NOT stop play unless he is satisfied that the directing of the puck to a teammate was, in fact, DELIBERATE.

A goal cannot be scored by an attacking player who bats the puck with his hand directly into the net. A goal cannot be scored by an attacking player who bats the puck and it is deflected into the net off any player or goalkeeper.

RULE 58. HIGH STICKS

(a) The carrying of sticks above the normal height of the WAIST of the opponent is prohibited and a minor, double-minor or major penalty may be imposed on a player violating this rule, at the discretion of the Referee.

(b) A goal scored by an attacking player who strikes the puck with his stick which is carried above the height of the crossbar of the goal frame shall not be allowed.

A goal scored by a defending player who strikes the puck with his stick which is carried above the height of the crossbar of the goal frame shall be allowed.

(c) When a player carries or holds any part of his stick above the normal height of the WAIST of the opponent so that injury results the Referee shall:

(1) assess a double-minor penalty when it is deemed to be accidental in nature by the officials;

(2) assess a major and game-misconduct when the high stick is deemed to be careless by the officials. Refer to Rule 29(f) and 28(b). When a major penalty is imposed under this rule for a foul resulting in injury to an opponent, an automatic fine of one hundred dollars ($100) shall also be imposed. Also, when a major penalty is imposed under this rule, the player, excluding goalkeepers, shall receive automatically a game misconduct penalty.

(d) Batting the puck above the normal height of the shoulders with a stick is prohibited. When a puck is struck with a high stick and subsequently comes into the possession of a teammate, there shall be a whistle. If a territorial advantage is gained by the offending team, the ensuing face-off will be where the high-stick occurred. If a territorial disadvantage occurs to the offending team, the ensuing face-off will be where the puck is touched. Play continues following a high-sticked puck if:

(1) the puck has been batted to an opponent in which case the play shall continue.

(2) a player of the defending side shall bat the puck into his own goal in which case the goal shall be allowed.

(NOTE) When a player bats the puck to an opponent under sub-section 1, the Referee shall give the "washout" signal immediately. Otherwise, he will stop the play.

(e) When either team is below the numerical strength of its opponent and a player of the team of greater numerical strength causes a stoppage of play by striking the puck with his stick above the height of his shoulder, the resulting face-off shall be made at one of the end face-off spots adjacent to the goal of the team causing the stoppage.

RULE 59. HOLDING AN OPPONENT

(a) A minor penalty shall be imposed on a player who holds an opponent with hands or stick or in any other way.

(b) A minor penalty shall be assessed to a player who uses his hand to hold an opponent's stick.

RULE 60. HOOKING

(a) A minor penalty shall be imposed on a player who impedes or seeks to impede the progress of an opponent by "hooking" with his stick.

(b) A major penalty shall be imposed on any player who injures an opponent by "hooking". When a major penalty is imposed under this rule for a foul resulting in injury to the face or head of an opponent, an automatic fine of one hundred dollars ($100) shall also be imposed.

(NOTE) When a player is checking another in such a way that there is only stick-to-stick contact, such action is neither hooking nor holding.

RULE 61. ICING THE PUCK

(a) For the purpose of this rule, the center red line will divide the ice into halves. Should any player of a team, equal or superior in numerical strength to the opposing team, shoot, bat or deflect the puck from his own half of the ice beyond the goal line of the opposing team, play shall be stopped and the puck faced-off at the end face-off spot of the offending team, unless on the play, the puck shall have entered the net of the opposing team, in which case the goal shall be allowed.

For the purpose of this rule, the point of last contact with the puck by the team in possession shall be used to determine whether icing has occurred or not.

(NOTE 1) If during the period of a delayed whistle due to a foul by a player of the side NOT in possession, the side in possession "ices" the puck, then the face-off following the stoppage of play shall take place in the neutral zone near the defending blue line of the team icing the puck.

(NOTE 2) When a team is "short-handed" as the result of a penalty and the penalty is about to expire, the decision as to whether there has been an "icing" shall be determined at the instant the penalty expires. The action of the penalized player remaining in the penalty box will not alter the ruling.

(NOTE 3) For the purpose of interpretation of the rule, "icing the puck" is completed the instant the puck is touched first by a defending player (other than the goalkeeper) after it has crossed the goal line and if in the action of so touching the puck, it is knocked or deflected into the net, it is NO goal.

(NOTE 4) When the puck is shot and rebounds from the body or stick of an opponent in his own half of the ice so as to cross the goal line of the player shooting, it shall not be considered as "icing".

(NOTE 5) Notwithstanding the provisions of the section concerning "batting" the puck in respect to the "icing the puck" rule, the provisions of the final paragraph of Rule 57(e) apply and NO goal can be scored by batting the puck with the hand into the opponent's goal whether intended or not.

(NOTE 6) If while the Linesman has signalled a slow whistle for a clean interception under Rule 71(c), the player intercepting shoots or bats the puck beyond the opponent's goal line in such a manner as to constitute "icing the puck", the Linesman's "slow whistle" shall be considered exhausted the instant the puck crosses the blue line and "icing" shall be called in the usual manner.

(b) If a player of the side shooting the puck down the ice who is on-side and eligible to play the puck does so before it is touched by an opposing player, the play shall continue and it shall not be considered a violation of this rule.

(c) If the puck was so shot by a player of a side below the numerical strength of the opposing team, play shall continue and the face-off shall not take place.

(NOTE) If the team returns to full strength following a shot by one of its players, play shall continue and the face-off shall not take place.

(d) If, however, the puck shall go beyond the goal line in the opposite half of the ice directly from either of the players while facing-off, it shall not be considered a violation of this rule.

(e) If, in the opinion of the Linesman, a player of the opposing team except the goalkeeper is able to play the puck before it passes his goal line, but has not done so, the face-off shall not be allowed and play shall continue. If, in the opinion of the Referee, the defending side intentionally abstains from playing the puck promptly when they are in a position to do so, he shall stop the play and order the resulting face-off on the adjacent corner face-off spot nearest the goal of the team at fault.

(NOTE) The purpose of this section is to enforce continuous action and both Referee and Linesmen should interpret and apply the rule to produce this result.

(f) If the puck touches any part of a player of the opposing side, including his skates or his stick, or if it passes through any part of the goal crease before it reaches the opposing team's goal line, or if it touches any part of the opposing team's goalkeeper, including his skates or his stick, at any time before or after crossing the goal line, it shall not be considered icing.

(NOTE) If a goalkeeper takes any action to dislodge the puck from the back of the net, icing shall be washed out.

(g) If a goalkeeper has been removed from the playing surface for an extra player (teams at equal or superior in numerical strength), the icing rule shall be in effect if the puck passes through or touches any part of the goal crease before it crosses the goal line.

(h) If the Linesman shall have erred in calling an "icing the puck" infraction (regardless of whether either team is short-handed), the puck shall be faced-off on the center ice face-off spot.

RULE 62. INTERFERENCE

(NOTE) A strict standard of interference must be adhered to in all areas of the rink, with emphasis on interference in the Neutral Zone.

(a) A minor penalty shall be imposed on a player who interferes with or impedes the progress of an opponent who is not in possession of the puck.

(b) A minor penalty shall be imposed on a player who restrains an opponent who is attempting to "forecheck".

(c) A minor penalty shall be imposed on an attacking player who deliberately checks a defensive player who is not in possession of the puck.

(d) A minor penalty shall be imposed on a player who shall cause an opponent who is not in possession of the puck to be forced off-side, causing a stoppage in play.

(e) A minor penalty shall be imposed on a player who deliberately knocks a stick out of an opponent's hand, or who prevents a player who has dropped his stick or any other piece of equipment from regaining possession of it.

(f) A minor penalty shall be imposed on a player who knocks or shoots any abandoned or broken stick or illegal puck or other debris towards an opposing puck carrier in a manner that could cause him to be distracted. (See also Rule 81 (a) – Throwing Stick.)

(g) A minor penalty shall be imposed on any player on the players' bench or penalty bench who, by means of his stick or his body, interferes with the movements of the puck or any opponent on the ice during the progress of the play.

(h) If when the goalkeeper has been removed from the ice, any member of his team (including the goalkeeper) not legally on the ice, including the Manager, Coach or Trainer, interferes by means of his body, stick or any other object with the movements of the puck or an opposing player, the Referee shall immediately award a goal to the non-offending team.

(i) When a player in control of the puck on his opponent's side of the center red line and having no other opponent to pass than the goalkeeper is interfered with by a stick or any part thereof or any other object thrown or shot by any member of the defending team including the Manager, Coach or Trainer, a penalty shot shall be awarded to the non-offending team.

NOTE 1 Body Position: Body position shall be determined as the player skating in front of or beside his opponent, traveling in the same direction. A player who is behind an opponent, who does not have the puck, may not use his stick or body in order to restrain his opponent, but must skate in order to gain or reestablish his proper position in order to make a check.

A player is allowed the ice he is standing on (body position) and is not required to move in order to let an opponent proceed. A player may "block" the path of an opponent provided he is doing so by skating in the same direction. Moving laterally and without establishing body position, then making contact with the non-puck carrier is not permitted and will be penalized as interference. A player is always entitled to use his body position to lengthen an opponent's path to the puck, provided his stick is not utilized; his free hand is not used and he does not take advantage of his body position to deliver an otherwise illegal check.

NOTE 2 Possession of the Puck: The last player to touch the puck, other than the goalkeeper, shall be considered the player in possession. The player deemed in possession of the puck may be checked legally, provided the check is rendered immediately following his loss of possession.

NOTE 3 Restrain: The actions of a player who does not have body position, but instead uses illegal means (e.g. hook with stick; hold with hands) to impede an opponent who is not in possession of the puck. Illegal means are acts which allow a player to establish, maintain or restore body position, other than by skating.

NOTE 4 Pick: A "pick" is the action of a player who checks an opponent who is not in possession of the puck and is unaware of the impending check/hit. A player who is aware of an impending hit, not deemed to be a legal "battle for the puck", may not be interfered with by a player delivering a "pick". A player delivering a "pick" is one who moves into an opponent's path without initially having body position, thereby taking him out of the play.

NOTE 5 Free Hand: A free hand is the one that is not evident holding the player's own stick. Free hand use is permitted to "fend off" an opponent or his stick, but may not be used to hold an opponent's stick or body.

NOTE 6 Stick: Any reference made to the use of the stick implies any portion of the stick. It is generally accepted that the blade or end of the shaft are used in stick restraining tactics.

RULE 63. INTERFERENCE BY/WITH SPECTATORS

(a) In the event of a player being held or interfered with by a spectator, the Referee or Linesman shall blow the whistle and play shall be stopped unless the team of the player interfered with is in possession of the puck at this time when the play shall be allowed to be completed before blowing the whistle and the puck shall be faced-off at the spot where last played at time of stoppage.

(b) Any player who physically interferes with the spectators shall automatically incur a gross misconduct penalty and the Referee shall report all such infractions to the Commissioner who shall have full power to impose such further penalty as he shall deem appropriate.

(c) In the event that objects are thrown on the ice which interfere with the progress of the game, the Referee shall blow the whistle and stop the play and the puck shall be faced-off at the spot play is stopped.

(NOTE) The Referee shall report to the Commissioner for disciplinary action all cases in which a player becomes involved in an altercation with a spectator.

RULE 64. KICKING A PLAYER

A match penalty shall be imposed on any player who kicks or attempts to kick another player.

Whether or not an injury occurs, the Referee will impose a five minute time penalty under this rule. Refer to Rule 44—Attempt to Injure or Rule 49—Deliberate Injury of an Opponent.

RULE 65. KICKING THE PUCK

Kicking the puck shall be permitted in all zones. A goal cannot be scored by an attacking player who kicks the puck directly into the net, whether intended or not. A goal cannot be scored by an attacking player who kicks the puck and it is deflected into the net off any player, goalkeeper or Official.

A goal cannot be scored by an attacking player who kicks any equipment (stick, glove, helmet, etc.) at the the puck, and it subsequently crosses the goal line.

(b) For violation of this rule, a game misconduct penalty shall be imposed on the player who was the first or second player to leave the players' or penalty bench from either or both teams.

(c) The first player to leave the players' or penalty bench from either or both teams shall be suspended automatically without pay for the next ten (10) regular League and/or playoff games of his team.

(d) The second player to leave the bench from either or both teams shall be suspended automatically without pay for the next five (5) regular League and/or playoff games.

(NOTE) The determination as to the players penalized under (c) and (d) of this rule shall be made by the Referee in consultation with the Linesmen and off-ice officials. In the event that he is unable to identify the offending players, the matter will be referred to the Commissioner or his designee and such determinations may be made subsequently based on reports and other information including but not limited to television tapes.

(e) Any team that has a player penalized under (a) shall be fined ten thousand dollars ($10,000) for the first instance. This fine shall be increased by five thousand dollars ($5000) for each subsequent occurrence over the next following three-year period.

(f) All players including the first and second players who leave the bench during an altercation shall be subject to an automatic fine in the amount equal to the maximum permitted under the collective bargaining agreement.

(g) Any player who leaves the penalty bench during an altercation and is not the first player, shall be suspended automatically without pay for the next five (5) regular League and/or playoff games.

(h) Except at the end of each period or on expiration of his penalty, no player may, at any time, leave the penalty bench.

(i) A penalized player who leaves the penalty bench before his penalty has expired, whether play is in progress or not, shall incur an additional minor penalty, after serving his unexpired penalty.

(j) Any penalized player leaving the penalty bench during stoppage of play and during an altercation shall incur a minor penalty plus a game misconduct penalty after serving his unexpired time.

(k) If a player leaves the penalty bench before his penalty is fully served, the Penalty Timekeeper shall note the time and signal the Officials who will stop play when the offending player's team obtains possession of the puck.

(l) In the case of a player returning to the ice before his time has expired through an error of the Penalty Timekeeper, he is not to serve an additional penalty, but must serve his unexpired time.

(m) If a player of the attacking side in possession of the puck shall be in such a position as to have no opposition between him and the opposing goalkeeper, and while in such position he shall be interfered with by a player of the opposing side who shall have illegally entered the game, the Referee shall impose a penalty shot against the side to which the offending player belongs.

(n) If the opposing goalkeeper has been removed and an attacking player in possession of the puck shall have no player of the defending team to pass and a stick or a part thereof or any other object is thrown or shot by an opposing player, or the player is fouled from behind thereby being prevented from having a clear shot on an open goal, a goal shall be awarded against the offending team.

If when the opposing goalkeeper has been removed from the ice, a player of the side attacking the unattended goal is interfered with by a player who shall have entered the game illegally, the Referee shall immediately award a goal to the non-offending team.

(o) If a Coach or Manager gets on the ice after the start of a period and before that period is ended, the Referee shall impose a bench minor penalty against the team and report the incident to the Commissioner for disciplinary action.

(p) Any club executive or Manager committing the same offense will be automatically fined two hundred dollars ($200).

(q) If a penalized player returns to the ice from the penalty bench before his penalty has expired by his own error or the error of the Penalty Timekeeper, any goal scored by his own team while he is illegally on the ice shall be disallowed but all penalties imposed on either team shall be served as regular penalties.

(r) If a player shall illegally enter the game from his own players' bench or from the penalty bench, any goal scored by his own team while he is illegally on the ice shall be disallowed but all penalties imposed on either team shall be served as regular penalties.

(s) A bench minor penalty shall be imposed on a team whose player(s) leave the players' bench for any purpose other than a change of players and when no altercation is in progress.

(t) Any player who has been ordered to the dressing room by the Referee and returns to his bench or to the ice for any reason before the appropriate time shall be assessed a game misconduct penalty and shall be suspended automatically without pay for the next ten (10) regular League and/or playoff games.

(u) The Coach(es) of the team(s) whose player(s) left the players' bench(es) during an altercation may be suspended, pending a review by the Commissioner. The Coach(es) also may be fined a maximum of ten thousand dollars ($10,000).

(v) For all suspensions imposed on players under this rule, the club of the player shall pay to the League a sum equal to the pro-rata of that player's salary covered by the suspension. For purposes of computing amounts due for a player's suspension, the player's fixed salary shall be divided by the number of days in the regular season and then, said result shall be multiplied by the number of games suspended.

In addition, any club that is deemed by the Commissioner to pay or reimburse to the player the amount of the fine or loss of salary assessed under this rule shall be fined automatically one hundred thousand dollars ($100,000).

(NOTE) In the event that suspensions imposed under this rule cannot be completed in regular League and/or playoff games in any one season, the remainder of the suspension shall be served the following season.

RULE 67. PHYSICAL ABUSE OF OFFICIALS

(a) Any player who deliberately applies physical force in any manner against an official, in any manner attempts to injure an official, deliberately makes contact with an official, physically demeans an official or deliberately applies physical force to an official solely for the purpose of getting free of such an official during or immediately following an altercation shall receive a game misconduct penalty.

In addition, the following disciplinary penalties shall apply:

CATEGORY I

Any player who deliberately strikes an official and causes injury or who deliberately applies physical force in any manner against an official with intent to injure, or who in any manner attempts to injure an official shall be automatically suspended for not less than 20 games. (For the purpose of the rule, "intent to injure" shall mean any physical force which a player knew or should have known could reasonably be expected to cause injury.)

CATEGORY II

Any player who deliberately applies physical force to an official in any manner (excluding actions as set out in Category One), which physical force is applied without intent to injure, shall be automatically suspended for not less than 10 games.

CATEGORY III

Any player who, by his actions, physically demeans an official or who deliberately applies physical force to an official solely for the purpose of getting free of such an official during or immediately following an altercation shall be suspended for not less than 3 games.

Immediately after the game in which such game misconduct penalty is imposed, the Referee shall, in consultation with the Linesmen, decide the category of the offense. He shall make an oral report to the Commissioner and advise of the category and of the offense. In addition, he shall file a written report to the Commissioner in which he may request a review as to the adequacy of the suspension. The player and club involved shall be notified of the decision of the Referee on the morning following the game and the player may request the Commissioner to review, subject to the provisions of this rule, the penalty imposed by the Referee. Such request must be filed with the Commissioner in writing not later than 72 hours following notification of the penalty. No appeal to the Board of Governors pursuant to By-Law 17 shall be available to the player unless a review has been conducted as provided herein.

If a review of the incident is requested by either the player or by the official, a hearing will be conducted by the Commissioner as soon as practical prior to the fourth game of any suspension. The player's suspension shall continue pending the outcome of the hearing by the Commissioner.

After any review as called for hereby, the Commissioner shall issue an order either:

(1) sustaining the minimum suspension, or . . .

(2) increasing the number of games within the category, or . . .

(3) changing to a lower category, or . . .

(4) changing to a lower category and increasing the number of games within the category.

A player shall have the right of appeal from any such order pursuant to By-Law 17.11. Upon such appeal, the Board of Governors' determination shall be one of the four alternatives listed above.

The penalties imposed under this rule shall not be deemed to limit the right of the Commissioner with respect to any action that he might otherwise take under By-Law 17.

In the event that the player has committed more than one offense under this rule, in addition to the penalties imposed under this rule, his case shall be referred to the Commissioner of the League for consideration of supplementary disciplinary action. (In all instances where the Commissioner is referred to in this rule, it shall mean the Commissioner or his designee.)

(b) Any Club Executive, Manager, Coach or Trainer who holds or strikes an Official shall be automatically suspended from the game, ordered to the dressing room and the matter will be reported to the Commissioner for further disciplinary action.

RULE 68. OBSCENE OR PROFANE LANGUAGE OR GESTURES

(a) Players shall not use obscene gestures on the ice or anywhere in the rink before, during or after the game. For a violation of the rule, a game misconduct penalty shall be imposed and the Referee shall report the circumstances to the Commissioner of the League for further disciplinary action.

(b) Players shall not use profane language on the ice or anywhere in the rink before, during or after a game. For violation of this rule, a misconduct penalty shall be imposed except when the violation occurs in the vicinity of the players' bench in which case a bench minor penalty shall be imposed.

(NOTE) It is the responsibility of all game officials and all club officials to send a confidential report to the Commissioner setting out the full details concerning the use of obscene gestures or language by any player, Coach or other official. The Commissioner shall take such further disciplinary action as he shall deem appropriate.

(c) Club Executives, Managers, Coaches and Trainers shall not use obscene or profane language or gestures anywhere in the rink. For violation of this rule, a bench minor penalty shall be imposed.

RULE 69. OFF-SIDES

(a) The position of the player's skates and not that of his stick shall be the determining factor in all instances in deciding an "off-side". A player is off-side when both skates are completely over the outer edge of the determining center line or blue line involved in the play.

(NOTE 1) A player is "on-side" when either of his skates are in contact with or on his own side of the line at the instant the puck completely crosses the outer edge of that line regardless of the position of his stick. However, if while an off-side call is delayed, players of the offending team clear the zone, the Linesman shall drop his arm and the play is no longer off-side.

(NOTE 2) It should be noted that while the position of the player's skates is what determines whether a player is "off-side", nevertheless the question of an "off-side" never arises until the puck has completely crossed the outer edge of the line at which time the decision is to be made.

(b) If in the opinion of the Linesman, an intentional off-side play has been made, the puck shall be faced-off at the end face-off spot in the defending zone of the offending team.

(NOTE 1) An intentional off-side is one which is made for the purpose of securing a stoppage of play regardless of the reason, whether either team is short-handed.

(NOTE 2) If, while an off-side call is delayed, a player of the offending team deliberately touches the puck to create a stoppage of play, the Linesman will signal an intentional off-side.

(c) If a Linesman errs in calling an off-side pass infraction (regardless of whether either team is short-handed), the puck shall be faced-off on the center ice face-off spot.

RULE 70. PASSES

(a) The puck may be passed by any player to a player of the same side within any one of the three zones into which the ice is divided, but it may not be passed forward from a player in one zone to a player of the same side in another zone, except by players of the defending team who may make and take forward passes from their own defending zone to the center line without incurring an off-side penalty. This forward pass from the defending zone must be completed by the pass receiver who is preceded by the puck across the center line, otherwise the play shall be stopped and the face-off shall be at the point from which the pass was made.

(NOTE 1) The position of the puck and not that of the player's skates shall be the determining factor in deciding from which zone the pass was made.

(NOTE 2) Passes may be completed legally at the center red line in exactly the same manner as passes at the attacking blue line.

(NOTE 3) In the event the player has preceded the puck at the center line he may become eligible to play the puck if he makes skate contact with the line prior to playing the puck.

(b) Should the puck having been passed, contact any part of the body, stick or skates of a player of the same side who is legally on-side, the pass shall be considered to have been completed.

(c) The player last touched by the puck shall be deemed to be in possession.

Rebounds off goalkeepers' pads or other equipment shall not be considered as a change of possession or completion of the play by the team when applying Rule 34(b)—Calling of Penalties.

(d) If a player in the neutral zone is preceded in the attacking zone by the puck passed from the neutral zone, he shall be eligible to take possession of the puck anywhere in the attacking zone except when the "Icing the Puck" rule applies.

(e) If a player in the same zone from which a pass is made is preceded by the puck into succeeding zones, he shall be eligible to take possession of the puck in that zone except where the "Icing the Puck" rule applies.

(f) If an attacking player passes the puck backward toward his own goal from the attacking zone, an opponent may play the puck anywhere regardless of whether the opponent was in the same zone at the time the puck was passed. (No "slow whistle".)

RULE 71. PRECEDING PUCK INTO ATTACKING ZONE

(a) Players of the attacking team must not precede the puck into the attacking zone.

(b) For violation of this rule, the play is stopped and the puck shall be faced-off in the neutral zone at the face-off spot nearest the attacking zone of the offending team.

(NOTE) A player actually controlling the puck who shall cross the line ahead of the puck shall not be considered "off-side".

(c) If however, notwithstanding the fact that a member of the attacking team shall have preceded the puck into the attacking zone, the puck is cleanly intercepted by a member of the defending team at or near the blue line and is carried out or passed by them into the neutral zone, the "off-side" shall be ignored and play permitted to continue. (Officials will carry out this rule by means of the "slow whistle".)

(d) If a player legally carries or passes the puck back into his own defending zone while a player of the opposing team is in such defending zone, the "off-side" shall be ignored and play permitted to continue. (No "slow whistle".)

(NOTE) If a puck clearly deflects off a defending player in the neutral zone, back into the defending zone, all attacking players are eligible to play the puck.

RULE 72. PROTECTION OF GOALKEEPER

(a) A minor penalty for interference shall be imposed on a player who, by means of his stick or his body, interferes with or impedes the movements of the goalkeeper by actual physical contact.

(NOTE) A goalkeeper is not "fair game" just because he is outside the goal crease area. A penalty for interference or charging (minor or major) should be called in every case where an opposing player makes unnecessary contact with the goalkeeper.

Likewise, referees should be alert to penalize goalkeepers for tripping, slashing, or spearing in the vicinity of the goal.

(b) Unless the puck is in the goal crease area, a player of the attacking side may not stand in the goal crease. If the puck should enter the net while such conditions prevail the goal shall not be allowed. If an attacking player has physically interfered with the goalkeeper, prior to or during the scoring of the goal, the goal will be disallowed and a penalty for goaltender interference will be assessed. The ensuing face-off shall be taken in the neutral zone at the face-off spot nearest the attacking zone of the offending team.

(c) If a player of the attacking side has been physically interfered with by the action of any defending player so as to cause him to be in the goal crease and the puck should enter the net while the player so interfered with is still in the goal crease, the goal shall be allowed.

(d) A minor penalty shall be assessed to a player of the attacking side who having been interfered with fails to avoid making contact with the goalkeeper. In addition, if a goal is scored the goal shall be disallowed.

(e) A minor penalty for interference shall be imposed on any attacking player, who makes deliberate contact with a goalkeeper whether in or out of the crease. At the discretion of the Referee a major penalty may be imposed under Rule 47(c)—Charging.

(f) A minor and misconduct penalty shall be imposed on an attacking player, not in possession of the puck, who is tripped or caused to fall and fails to attempt to avoid contact with the goalkeeper whether he is in or out of his crease.

(g) In the event that a goalkeeper has been pushed into the net together with the puck after making the stop, the goal will be disallowed. If applicable, the appropriate penalties will be assessed.

RULE 73. PUCK OUT OF BOUNDS OR UNPLAYABLE

(a) When the puck goes outside the playing area at either end or either side of the rink, or strikes any obstacles above the playing surface other than the boards or glass, it shall be faced-off from where it was shot or deflected unless otherwise expressly provided in these rules.

(b) When the puck becomes lodged in the netting on the outside of either goal so as to make it unplayable, or if it is frozen between opposing players intentionally or otherwise, the Referee shall stop the play and face-off the puck at either of the adjacent face-off spots unless in the opinion of the Referee, the stoppage was caused by a player of the attacking team, in which case the resulting face-off shall be conducted in the neutral zone.

(NOTE) This includes a stoppage of play caused by a player of the attacking side shooting the puck onto the back of the defending team's net without any intervening action by the defending team.

The defending team and/or the attacking team may play the puck off the net at any time. However, should the puck remain on the net for more than three seconds, play shall be stopped and the face-off shall take place in the end face-off zone except when the stoppage is caused by the attacking team, then the face-off shall take place on a face-off spot in the neutral zone.

(c) A minor penalty shall be imposed on a goalkeeper who deliberately drops the puck on the goal netting to cause a stoppage of play.

(d) If the puck comes to rest on top of the boards surrounding the playing area, it shall be considered to be in play and may be played legally by hand or stick.

RULE 74. PUCK MUST BE KEPT IN MOTION

(a) The puck must at all times be kept in motion.

(b) A minor penalty shall be imposed on any player, including the goalkeeper, who holds, freezes or plays the puck with his stick, skates or body in such a manner as to deliberately cause a stoppage of play.

(NOTE) With regard to a goalkeeper, this rule applies outside of his goal crease area.

RULE 75. PUCK OUT OF SIGHT AND ILLEGAL PUCK

(a) Should a scramble take place or a player accidentally fall on the puck and the puck be out of sight of the Referee, he shall immediately blow his whistle and stop the play. The puck shall then be faced-off at the point where the play was stopped unless otherwise provided for in the rules.

(b) If at any time while play is in progress, a puck other than the one legally in play shall appear on the playing surface, the play shall not be stopped but shall continue with the legal puck until the play then in progress is completed by change of possession.

RULE 76. PUCK STRIKING OFFICIAL

Play shall not be stopped if the puck touches an official anywhere on the rink, regardless of whether a team is shorthanded or not. A puck that deflects back into the defensive zone, off an official who is in the neutral zone, may be deemed to be off-side as per Rule 69

(NOTE 1) If a goal is scored as a result of being deflected directly into the net off an official the goal shall not be allowed.

RULE 77. REFUSING TO START PLAY

(a) If when both teams are on the ice, one team for any reason shall refuse to play when ordered to do so by the Referee, he shall warn the Captain and allow the team so refusing fifteen seconds within which to begin the play or resume play. If at the end of that time, the team shall still refuse to play, the Referee shall impose a two-minute penalty on a player of the offending team to be designated by the Manager or Coach of that team through the playing Captain. Should there be a repetition of the same incident, the Referee shall notify the Manager or Coach that he has been fined the sum of two hundred dollars ($200). Should the offending team still refuse to play, the Referee shall have no alternative but to declare that the game be forfeited to the non-offending club and the case shall be reported to the Commissioner for further action.

(b) If a team, when ordered to do so by the Referee through its club executive, Manager or Coach, fails to go on the ice and start play within five minutes, the club executive, Manager or Coach shall be fined five hundred dollars ($500), the game shall be forfeited and the case shall be reported to the Commissioner for further action.

(NOTE) The Commissioner of the League shall issue instructions pertaining to records, etc., of a forfeited game.

RULE 78. SLASHING

(a) A minor or major penalty, at the discretion of the Referee, shall be imposed on any player who impedes or seeks to impede the progress of an opponent by "slashing" with his stick.

(b) A major and a game misconduct penalty shall be imposed on any player who injures an opponent by slashing. In addition, a fine of one hundred dollars ($100) shall be imposed for each major penalty assessed under this rule.

(NOTE) Referees should penalize as "slashing" any player who swings his stick at any opposing player (whether in or out of range) without actually striking him or where a player, on the pretext of playing the puck, makes a wild swing at the puck with the object of intimidating an opponent.

(c) Any player who swings his stick at another player in the course of an altercation shall be subject to a fine of not less than two hundred dollars ($200), with or without suspension, to be imposed by the Commissioner.

(NOTE) The Referee shall impose the normal appropriate penalty provided in the other sections of this rule and shall, in addition, report promptly to the Commissioner all infractions under this section.

RULE 79. SPEARING AND BUTT-ENDING

(a) A major penalty and a game misconduct penalty shall be imposed on a player who spears or butt-ends an opponent.

(b) In addition to the major penalty imposed under this rule, an automatic fine of one hundred dollars ($100) will also be imposed.

(NOTE 1) "Spearing" shall mean stabbing an opponent with the point of the stick blade while the stick is being carried with one or both hands.

(NOTE 2) "Butt-ending" shall mean using the end of the shaft of the stick in a jabbing motion.

(NOTE 3) "Spearing" and "Butt-ending" may also be treated as a deliberate attempt to injure under Rule 44.

(c) A double-minor penalty will be imposed by the officials on a player who attempts to spear, poke, jab or butt-end an opponent.

(NOTE) Attempts to spear or butt-end will include all cases where a gesture is made without contact.

RULE 80. START OF GAME AND PERIODS

(a) The game shall be commenced at the time scheduled by a "face-off" in the center of the rink and shall be renewed promptly at the conclusion of each intermission in the same manner.

No delay shall be permitted by reason of any ceremony, exhibition, demonstration or presentation unless consented to reasonably in advance by the visiting team.

(b) Home clubs shall have the choice of goals to defend at the start of the game except where both players' benches are on the same side of the rink, in which case the home club shall start the game defending the goal nearest to its own bench. The teams shall change ends for each period of regulation time and, in the playoffs, for each period of overtime. (See Rule 83(a)—NOTE—Tied Games)

(c) During the pre-game warm-up (which shall not exceed twenty minutes in duration) and before the commencement of play in any period, each team shall confine its activity to its own end of the rink. Refer to Rule 54(g)—Fisticuffs.

(NOTE 1) The Game Timekeeper shall be responsible for signalling the commencement and termination of the pre-game warm-up and any violation of this rule by the players shall be reported to the Commissioner by the supervisor when in attendance at the game.

(NOTE 2) Players shall not be permitted to come on the ice during a stoppage of play or at the end of the first and second periods for the purpose of warming-up. The Referee will report any violation of this rule to the Commissioner for disciplinary action.

(d) Twenty minutes before the time scheduled for the start of the game, both teams shall vacate the ice and proceed to their dressing rooms while the ice is being flooded. Both teams shall be signalled by the Game Timekeeper to return to the ice together in time for the scheduled start of the game.

(e) At the beginning of the game, if a team fails to appear on the ice promptly without proper justification, a fine shall be assessed against the offending team, the amount of the fine to be decided by the Commissioner.

At the beginning of the second and third periods, and overtime periods in playoffs (0:00 on the clock), clubs must be on the ice or be observed to be proceeding to the ice. For failure to comply, a bench minor penalty for delay of game shall be imposed.

(f) At the end of each period, the home team players must proceed directly to their dressing room while the visiting team players must wait for a signal from the Referee to proceed only if they have to go on the ice to reach their dressing room. Failure to comply with this regulation will result in a two-minute bench minor for delay of game.

RULE 81. THROWING STICK

(a) When any player of the defending side or Manager, Coach or Trainer, deliberately throws or shoots a stick or any part thereof or any other object at the puck in his defending zone, the Referee shall allow the play to be completed and if a goal is not scored, a penalty shot shall be awarded to the non-offending side, which shot shall be taken by the player designated by the Referee as the player fouled.

If however, the goal being unattended and the attacking player having no defending player to pass and having a chance to score on an "open net", a stick or any part thereof or any other object be thrown or shot by a member of the defending team, including the Manager, Coach or Trainer, thereby preventing a shot on the "open net", a goal shall be awarded to the attacking side.

(NOTE 1) If the officials are unable to determine the person against whom the offense was made, the offended team, through the Captain, shall designate a player on the ice at the time the offense was committed to take the shot.

(NOTE 2) For the purpose of this rule, an open net is defined as one from which a goalkeeper has been removed for an additional attacking player.

(b) A minor penalty shall be imposed on any player on the ice who throws his stick or any part thereof or any other object in the direction of the puck in any zone, except when such act has been penalized by the assessment of a penalty shot or the award of a goal.

(NOTE) When the player discards the broken portion of a stick by tossing it to the side of the ice (and not over the boards) in such a way as will not interfere with play or opposing player, no penalty will be imposed for so doing.

(c) A misconduct or game misconduct penalty, at the discretion of the Referee, shall be imposed on a player who throws his stick or any part thereof outside the playing area. If the offense is committed in protest of an official's decision, a minor penalty for unsportsmanlike conduct plus a game misconduct penalty shall be assessed to the offending player.

RULE 82. TIME OF MATCH

(a) The time allowed for a game shall be three twenty-minute periods of actual play with a rest intermission between periods.

Play shall be resumed promptly following each intermission upon the expiry of fifteen minutes from the completion of play in the preceding period. A preliminary warning shall be given by the Game Timekeeper to the officials and to both teams five minutes prior to the resumption of play in each period and the final warning shall be given two minutes prior to resumption of play to enable the teams to start play promptly.

(NOTE) For the purpose of keeping the spectators informed as to the time remaining during intermissions, the Game Timekeeper will use the electric clock to record length of intermissions.

(b) The team scoring the greatest number of goals during the three twenty-minute periods shall be the winner and shall be credited with two points in the League standing.

(c) In the interval between periods, the ice surface shall be flooded unless mutually agreed to the contrary.

(d) If any unusual delay occurs within five minutes of the end of the first or second periods, the Referee may order the next regular intermission to be taken immediately and the balance of the period will be completed on the resumption of play with the teams defending the same goals after which, the teams will change ends and resume play of the ensuing period without delay.

(NOTE) If a delay takes place with more than five minutes remaining in the first or second period, the Referee will order the next regular intermission to be taken immediately only when requested to do so by the home club.

RULE 83. TIED GAME

(a) During League games, if at the end of the three regular twenty-minute periods the score shall be tied, the teams will play an additional period of not more than five (5) minutes with the team scoring first being declared the winner. If at the end of the overtime period, the score remains tied, each team shall be credited with one point in the League standing.

(NOTE) The overtime period will be commenced immediately following a two-minute rest period during which the players will remain on the ice. The teams will not change ends for the overtime period.

(b) Special conditions for the duration and number of periods of Playoff games shall be arranged by the Board of Governors.

RULE 84. TRIPPING, CLIPPING AND KNEEING

(a) A minor or major penalty, at the discretion of the Referee, shall be imposed on any player who shall place his stick, knee, foot, arm, hand or elbow in such a manner that it shall cause his opponent to trip or fall.

(NOTE 1) If in the opinion of the Referee, a player is unquestionably hook-checking the puck and obtains possession of it thereby tripping the puck carrier, no penalty shall be imposed.

(NOTE 2) Accidental trips occurring simultaneously with or after a stoppage of play will not be penalized.

(b) When a player, in control of the puck on the opponent's side of the center red line and having no other opponent to pass than the goalkeeper, is tripped or otherwise fouled from behind thus preventing a reasonable scoring opportunity, a penalty shot shall be awarded to the non-offending side. Nevertheless, the Referee shall not stop play until the attacking side has lost possession of the puck to the defending side.

(NOTE) The intention of this rule is to restore a reasonable scoring opportunity which has been lost by reason of a foul from behind when the foul is committed on the opponent's side of the center red line. "Control of the puck" means the act of propelling the puck with the stick. If while it is being propelled, the puck is touched by another player or his equipment, hits the goal or goes free, the player shall no longer be considered to be "in control of the puck".

(c) If, when the opposing goalkeeper has been removed from the ice, a player in control of the puck is tripped or otherwise fouled with no opposition between him and the opposing goal thus preventing a reasonable scoring opportunity, the Referee shall immediately stop the play and award a goal to the attacking team.

(d) A player may not deliver a check in a "clipping" manner, nor lower his own body position to deliver a check on or below an opponent's knees.

A player who commits this foul will be assessed a minor penalty for "clipping." If an injury occurs as a result of this "clipping" check, the player must be assessed a major and a game misconduct. "Clipping" is the act of throwing the body across or below the knee (front or back) of an opponent; charging or falling into the knees of an opponent after approaching him from the behind, front or side. An illegal "low hit" is a check that is delivered by a player who may or may not have both skates on the ice, with his sole intent to check the opponent in the area of his knees. A player may not lower his body position to deliver a check to an opponent's knees.

(e) A minor, major or match penalty shall be imposed on any player who knees an opponent. A match penalty shall be imposed on any player who deliberately knees or attempts to knee an opponent during an altercation and the circumstances shall be reported to the Commissioner for further action. A substitute player is permitted to replace the penalized player after five minutes of playing time has elapsed, when the penalty is imposed under Rule 44—Attempt to Injure or Rule 49—Deliberate Injury of Opponents.

RULE 85. UNNECESSARY ROUGHNESS

At the discretion of the Referee, a minor penalty or a double-minor penalty may be imposed on any player deemed guilty of unnecessary roughness.

RULE 86. TIME-OUTS

Each team shall be permitted to take one thirty-second time-out during the course of any game, regular-season or playoffs. This time-out must be taken during a normal stoppage of play. Any player designated by the Coach will indicate to the Referee that his team is exercising its option and the Referee will report the time-out to the Game Timekeeper who shall be responsible for signalling the termination of the time-out.

(NOTE 1) All players including goalkeepers on the ice at the time of the time-out will be allowed to go to their respective benches. Only one team is allowed a time-out per stoppage and no time-out will be allowed after a reasonable amount of time has elapsed during a normal stoppage of play.

(NOTE 2) For the purposes of this rule, a commercial stoppage in play is deemed to be an "official time-out" and not charged to either team.

RULE 87. VIDEO GOAL JUDGE

The following situations are subject to review by the Video Goal Judge:

(a) Puck crossing the goal line.

(b) Puck in the net prior to the goal frame being dislodged.

(c) Puck in the net prior to, or after expiration of time at the end of the period.

(d) Puck directed into the net by a hand or foot.

(e) Puck deflected into the net off an official.

(f) Puck struck with a high-stick, above the height of the crossbar, by an attacking player prior to entering the goal.

(g) To establish the correct time on the official game clock, provided the game time is visible on the Video Goal Judge's monitors.

INDEX